Copyright 2020 by Jaxon Balfe -All rights reserved.

No part of this publication may be reproduced, distributed, or transmitted in any form or by any means, including photocopying, recording, or other electronic or mechanical methods, without the prior written permission of the publisher, except in the case of brief quotations embodied in reviews and certain other non-commercial uses permitted by copyright law.

This Book is provided with the sole purpose of providing relevant information on a specific topic for which every reasonable effort has been made to ensure that it is both accurate and reasonable. Nevertheless, by purchasing this Book you consent to the fact that the author, as well as the publisher, are in no way experts on the topics contained herein, regardless of any claims as such that may be made within. It is recommended that you always consult a professional prior to undertaking any of the advice or techniques discussed within. This is a legally binding declaration that is considered both valid and fair by both the Committee of Publishers Association and the American Bar Association and should be considered as legally binding within the United States.

CONTENTS

Introduction 20
Chapter 1: Instant Pot - An Instant Path to Health 21
Chapter 2 Breakfast and Brunch Recipe 25
    Apple Cinnamon Oatmeal 25
    Cashew and Mango Oatmeal 25
    Chocolate Oatmeal 25
    Espresso Oatmeal 25
    Strawberry Oatmeal 25
    Peaches Oatmeal 26
    Pumpkin Spice Oatmeal 26
    Blueberry Breakfast Bowl 26
    Cauliflower and Barley Bowls 26
    Cheesy Cauliflower Bowls 26
    Breakfast Banana Bread 27
    Zucchini Toast 27
    Cauliflower Breakfast Hash 27
    Potato and Spinach Hash 27
    Sweet Potato Hash 28
    Banana and Raisin Porridge 28
    Millet and Oats Porridge 28
    Pearl Barley Porridge 28
    Pomegranate Porridge 28
    Squash Porridge with Apples 29
    Eggs and Bacon Breakfast Risotto 29
    French Eggs 29
    Ham and Spinach Frittata 29
    Mini Frittata 29
    Eggs En Cocotte 30
    Cheesy Bacon Quiche 30

Veggie Quiche 30

Western Omelet 30

Breakfast Rice Pudding 31

Bread Pudding 31

Strawberry and Orange Juice Compote 31

Banana Quinoa 31

Creamy Tomatoes and Quinoa 32

Strawberry Quinoa 32

Blackberry Egg Cake 32

Special Pancake 32

Broccoli and Egg Casserole 32

Cheesy Egg and Bacon Muffins 33

Pumpkin and Apple Butter 33

Breakfast Cobbler 33

Tofu and Sweet Potato Mix 33

Brown Rice and Chickpeas Medley 34

Breakfast Arugula Salad 34

Cranberry Beans Salad 34

Swiss Chard Salad 34

Pineapple and Peas Breakfast Curry 34

Garlic Eggplants with Tomato Sauce 35

Celeriac and Bacon Mix 35

Turkey Breast and Avocado Breakfast 35

Breakfast Coconut Yogurt 35

Fruit Yogurt 36

Super Thick Cashew and Almond Milk Yogurt 36

Chapter 3 Desserts Recipe 37

Tapioca Pudding 37

Chocolate Chia Pudding 37

Coconut Pudding 37

Cream and Cinnamon Puddings	37
Lemon and Maple Syrup Pudding	37
Pineapple Pudding	38
Coconut Cream and Cinnamon Pudding	38
Coconut and Avocado Pudding	38
Cocoa and Milk Pudding	38
Cream Cheese Pudding	39
Cinnamon Butter Bites	39
Keto Almond Bread	39
Apple Bread	39
Bulletproof Hot Choco	40
Coconut Boosters	40
Keto Brownies	40
Chocolate Mug Cake	40
Chocolate Cake	41
Dates and Ricotta Cake	41
Simple Banana Cake	41
Simple Pumpkin and Yogurt Cake	41
Ginger Cookies Cheesecake	42
Coconut Pancake	42
Ketogenic Vanilla Jell-O	42
Nut-Free Keto Fudge	42
Easy Sweet Soufflé	42
Tasty Blackberry Pie	43
Easy Lemon Pie	43
Cherry Pie	43
Peanut Butter Cups	43
Simple Cake Bars	44
White Chocolate Mousse	44
Simple Ricotta Mousse	44

Special Cookies 44

Lemon Cookies 44

Delicious Berry Cobbler 45

Baked Custard 45

Rhubarb and Strawberries Mix 45

Winter Cherry Mix 45

Stuffed Strawberries 46

Glazed Fruits 46

Apples and Wine Sauce 46

Poached Pears 46

Flavored Pears 46

Lemon and Orange Jam 47

Easy Plum Jam 47

Ginger and Peach Marmalade 47

Strawberry and Chia Marmalade 47

Peach and Cinnamon Compote 47

Blueberry and Coconut Sweet Bowls 48

Cocoa and Walnuts Sweet Cream 48

Chapter 4 Fish and Seafood Recipe 49

Lemony Salmon 49

Savory Salmon with Dill 49

Salmon with Basil Pesto 49

Salmon Tandoori 49

Simple Steamed Salmon Fillets 49

Instant Pot Curried Salmon 50

Lemon Pepper Salmon 50

Chili-Garlic Salmon 50

Steamed Herbed Red Snapper 50

Steamed Greek Snapper 51

Cod with Orange Sauce 51

Steamed Lemon Mustard Salmon	51
Quick Salmon	51
Lemon Pepper Salmon	52
Flounder with Dill and Capers	52
Italian Salmon with Lemon Juice	52
Thai Fish Curry	52
Coconut Curry Cod	52
Cod Meal	53
Tuna Salad with Lettuce	53
Steamed Chili-Rubbed Tilapia	53
Halibut and Broccoli Casserole	53
Halibut with Pesto	53
Halibut En Papillote	54
Red Curry Halibut	54
Thyme-Sesame Crusted Halibut	54
Steamed Cod with Ginger and Scallions	54
Cheddar Creamy Haddock	55
Yogurt Fish Patties	55
Steamed Tilapia	55
Lemon White Fish	55
Wild Alaskan Cod with Cherry Tomatoes	55
Buttery Smoked Cod with Scallions	56
Easy Mahi Mahi with Enchilada Sauce	56
Sardine and Plum Tomato Curry	56
Lemon-Butter Grouper	56
Sole Fillets with Pickle-Mayo Sauce	57
Orange-Butter Sea Bass	57
Sea Bass Risotto with Leeks	57
Creamy Shrimp Pasta	57
Shrimp Green Curry	58

Chili-Lime Shrimps 58

Szechuan Shrimps 58

Simple Shrimp 58

Shrimps with Mango Basil 59

Simple Curried Shrimps 59

Shrimp Scampi 59

Instant Pot Lemon Shrimps 59

Shrimp Boil 59

Fast Shrimp Scampi 60

Spicy Prawns 60

Delicious and Simple Octopus 60

Teriyaki Scallops 60

Sea Scallops with Champagne Butter Sauce 60

Buttery Steamed Lobster Tails 61

Instant Pot Boiled Mussels 61

Mussels with White Wine and Shallots 61

Tomato Mussels 61

Steamed Crab Legs 62

Boiled Garlic Clams 62

Chapter 5 Poultry Recipe 63

Salsa Chicken 63

Garlicky Greek Chicken 63

Cajun Chicken with Zucchini 63

Chicken Peas Rice 63

Chicken Coconut Curry 63

Classic Lemon Chicken 64

Garlicky Chicken 64

Instant Pot Pesto Chicken 64

Instant Pot Emergency Broccoli Chicken 64

Chicken Cacciatore 65

Whole Roasted Chicken with Lemon and Rosemary	65
Easy Asian Chicken	65
Cashew Chicken with Sautéed Vegetables	65
Chicken Curry	66
Smoky Paprika Chicken	66
Spiced Chicken Drumsticks	66
Chili Lime Chicken	66
Lemony Fennel Chicken	67
Creamy Chicken with Mushrooms	67
Thai Peanut Chicken	67
Chinese Steamed Chicken	67
Chicken Stew with Tomatoes and Spinach	68
Crispy Chicken Wings	68
Basil and Tomatoes Chicken Soup	68
Mexican Shredded Chicken	68
Sesame Chicken	68
Eggplant and Chicken Sauté	69
Cheesy Jalapeño Chicken	69
BBQ Chicken	69
Broccoli Chicken with Parmesan	69
Ginger Chicken Congee	69
Chicken Yogurt Salsa	70
Lemon Garlic Chicken	70
Broccoli Chicken with Black Beans	70
Thyme Chicken with Brussels Sprouts	70
Fennel Chicken	71
Filipino Chicken Adobo	71
Paprika Chicken with Tomatoes	71
Chicken with Artichokes and Bacon	71
Crispy Chicken with Herbs	72

Cheesy Chicken Tenders 72

Chicken Wings and Scallions and Tomato Sauce 72

Simple Lime Turkey Wings 73

Pomegranate-Glazed Turkey with Cranberries 73

Balsamic Turkey and Onions 73

Allspice Turkey Drumsticks with Beer 73

Cilantro Turkey with Pomegranate Glaze 74

Thyme Duck and Chives 74

Cream Turkey Dinner 74

Sautéed Turkey with Cauliflower Purée 74

Turkey Rice Bowl 75

Chapter 6 Vegan and Vegetarian Recipe 76

Corn on Cob 76

Roasted Brussels Sprouts 76

Steamed Lemon Artichokes 76

Chickpea and Lentil Salad 76

Chickpea Avocado Salad 76

Mediterranean Couscous Salad 77

Summer Beet Salad 77

Zucchini Bulgur Meal 77

Broccoli Cream Pasta 78

Cauliflower Pasta 78

Onion Penne Pasta 78

Tangy Spinach Pasta 78

Mushroom Rice Meal 79

Pure Basmati Rice Meal 79

Mushroom Spinach Casserole 79

Coconut Cauliflower Rice 79

Coconut Milk Rice 80

Tomato Onion Rice 80

Chickpea Egg Bowl	80
Asparagus and Mushrooms	80
Broccoli and Mushrooms	81
Instant Pot Mushrooms	81
Instant Pot Steamed Asparagus	81
Steamed Paprika Broccoli	81
Sautéed Brussels Sprouts And Pecans	82
Coconut Cabbage	82
Cauliflower Mushroom Risotto	82
Vegetarian Smothered Cajun Greens	82
Caramelized Onions	82
Zucchini and Tomato Melange	83
Instant Pot Veggie Stew	83
Zucchini and Bell Pepper Stir Fry	83
Eggplant, Zucchini, And Tomatoes	83
Instant Pot Baby Bok Choy	84
Sesame Bok Choy	84
Instant Pot Artichokes	84
Cauliflower Mash	84
Vegetarian Mac and Cheese	84
Couscous with Vegetables	85
Quinoa and Veggies	85
Greek Style Beans	85
Stuffed Peppers	86
Garlic Baby Potatoes	86
Stuffed Sweet Potatoes	86
Italian Vegetable Medley	86
Instant Ratatouille	87
Kale and Sweet Potatoes with Tofu	87
Puréed Chili Carrots	87

Lemon Artichokes 87

Tomato and Tofu Bake 87

Potato Mash 88

Mango Tofu Curry 88

Graceful Vegetarian Recipe 88

Zucchini and Tomato 88

Dump Cake 88

Chapter 7 Beef, Lamb and Pork Recipe 90

Beef and Cauliflower 90

Beef and Corn Chili 90

Beef Meatballs with Tomato 90

Beef Tenderloin with Cauliflower 90

Bell Pepper and Beef 91

Big Papa's Roast 91

Corned Beef 91

Garlic Prime Rib 91

Garlicky Beef 92

Ginger Short Ribs 92

Gingered Beef Tenderloin 92

Herbed Sirloin Tip Roast 92

Instant Pot Rib Roast 93

Lemon Beef Meal 93

Mushroom and Beef Meal 93

Sautéed Beef and Green Beans 93

Super Beef Chili 93

Sweet Apricot Beef 94

Sweet Potato Beef 94

Cheesy Veal Steaks 94

Rosemary Lamb 95

Adobo Pork Chops 95

Asian Lemongrass Pork	95
Asian Striped Pork	95
Balsamic Pulled Pork Casserole	96
Basic Pork Chops	96
Blueberry Pork Yum	96
Coconut Pork	96
Creamy Pork Pasta	97
Easy Chinese Pork	97
Eggplant Lasagna	97
Garlicky Pork Tenderloin	97
Indian Roasted Pork	98
Instant Pot Rib	98
Italian Pork Cutlets	98
Mexican Chili Pork	98
Mexican Pulled Pork	99
Mustard Pork and Mushrooms	99
Paprika Pork Loin Roast	99
Pear and Pork Butt	99
Pine Nut Pork	100
Pork and Sweet Potato	100
Pork Chops and Peas	100
Pork Chops with Onions	100
Pork Coconut Curry	101
Pork Medallions and Mushrooms	101
Pork Potato Lunch	101
Pork Tenderloin with Celery	101
Pork Vindaloo (Curry Pork)	102
Pork with Coconut Meat	102
Pork with Jasmine Rice	102
Pork with Paprika and Mushrooms	102

Pork with Turnip 103

Smokey and Spicy Pork Roast 103

Spicy Pulled Pork 103

Sunday Pork Roast 104

Super Stew 104

Tomato Chili Pork 104

Bacon and Peas 104

Canadian Bacon 105

Fried Rice with Sausage and Egg 105

Sausage and Peppers 105

Chapter 8 Soups and Stews Recipe 106

Asian Egg Drop Soup 106

Asparagus Soup 106

Bacon and Potato Soup 106

Beet Soup 106

Black Bean Soup 107

Broccoli Cheddar Soup 107

Cabbage Soup 107

Carrot and Mushroom Soup 107

Carrot Soup 107

Cheesy Broccoli Soup 108

Chicken and Tomato Soup 108

Chicken Soup 108

Coconut Seafood Soup 108

Creamy Broccoli Chicken Bone Soup 109

Egg Drop Soup with Shredded Chicken 109

Fish Soup 109

Ginger Halibut Soup 109

Greek Veggie Soup 110

Leek and Salmon Soup 110

Leftover Chicken Soup	110
Lemon Chicken Soup	110
Low Carb Chicken Noodle Soup	111
Low Carb Ham and Bean Soup	111
Minestrone	111
Mushroom Chicken Soup	111
Onion Soup with Pork Stock	112
Poached Egg Chicken Bone Soup	112
Potato Soup	112
Pumpkin Soup	112
Salmon Meatballs Soup	113
Swiss Chard and Leek Soup	113
Thai Coconut Shrimp Soup	113
Thai Tom Saap Pork Ribs Soup	113
Turkey with Ginger and Turmeric Soup	113
Turmeric Chicken Soup	114
Salmon Head Soup	114
Simple Chicken and Kale Soup	114
Vegetable and Lentil Soup	114
White Bean and Kale Soup	115
Bean and Tomato Stew	115
Beef Tomato Stew	115
Calamari Stew	115
Chicken and Quinoa Stew	116
Chicken Tomato Stew	116
Kale and Veal Stew	116
Kidney Bean Stew	116
Salmon Stew	117
Slow-Cooked Cabbage and Chuck Roast Stew	117
Veal and Buckwheat Groat Stew	117

Veggie Stew 117

White Bean and Swiss Chard Stew 118

Chili Con Carne (Chili with Meat) 118

Chapter 9 Snacks and Appetizers Recipe 119

Asian Wings 119

Baby Carrots Snack 119

BBQ Chicken Wings 119

BBQ Square Ribs 119

Black Bean Salsa 119

Chunky Warm Salsa 120

Blue Cheese Dip 120

Chicken Dip 120

Cumin Dip 120

Ham and Cheese Dip 120

Pinto Bean Dip 121

Steamed Asparagus with Mustard Dip 121

Brussels Sprouts and Apples Appetizer 121

Creamy Broccoli Appetizer 121

Lemony Endives Appetizer 122

Carrot and Beet Spread 122

Cashew Spread 122

Crab Spread 122

Creamy Avocado Spread 122

Scallion and Mayo Spread 123

Simple Egg Spread 123

Special Ranch Spread 123

Zucchini Spread 123

Cheesy Shrimp and Tomatoes 124

Chicken Meatballs in Barbecue Sauce 124

Chili Endives Platter 124

Fish and Carrot Balls	124
Greek Meatballs	125
Green Olive Pâté	125
Broccoli and Bacon Appetizer Salad	125
Brussels Sprouts and Broccoli Appetizer Salad	125
Cheesy Broccoli Appetizer Salad	126
Grated Carrot Appetizer Salad	126
Creamy Endives Appetizer Salad	126
Green Beans Appetizer Salad	126
Crunchy Brussels Sprouts Salad	126
Kale and Carrots Salad	127
Kale and Wild Rice Appetizer Salad	127
Minty Kale Salad with Pineapple	127
Watercress Appetizer Salad	127
Goat Cheese Mushrooms	127
Hummus	128
Simple Red Pepper Hummus	128
Lettuce Wrapped Tofu	128
Maple Brussels Sprouts with Orange Juice	128
Mexican Corn on the Cob	129
Mushroom Bacon Skewers	129
Prosciutto Wrapped Asparagus	129
Southern Peanuts	129
Chapter 10 Broths and Sauces Recipe	**131**
Béarnaise Sauce	131
Chimichurri Sauce	131
Creamy Cheese Sauce	131
Hollandaise Sauce	131
Satay Sauce	131
Caesar Salad Dressing	132

Spicy Thousand Island Dressing 132

Chicken Bone Broth 132

Chili Aioli 132

Keto Gravy 132

Ranch Dip 133

Chapter 11 Beans, Grains and Legumes Recipe 134

Vegan Rice Pudding 134

Almond Arborio Risotto 134

Butternut Squash Arborio Risotto 134

Quinoa Risotto 134

Parmesan Risotto 134

Green Tea Rice Risotto 135

Mixed Rice Meal 135

Basmati Rice 135

Mexican Rice 135

Multigrain Rice 136

Raisin Butter Rice 136

Basic Tomato Rice 136

Black Olives in Tomato Rice 136

Confetti Basmati Rice 136

Cauliflower and Pineapple Rice 137

Chickpea and Tomato Rice 137

Chipotle-Style Cilantro Rice 137

Copycat Cilantro Lime Rice 137

Khichdi Dal 137

Couscous with Spinach and Tomato 138

Israeli Couscous 138

Creamy Polenta 138

Honey Polenta with Toasted Pine Nuts 138

Wheat Berries 139

Peaches and Steel-Cut Oats 139

Strawberry and Rolled Oats 139

Coconut Quinoa 139

Quinoa Pilaf 139

Quinoa with Cranberry and Almond 140

Quinoa with Vegetables 140

Brothy Heirloom Beans with Cream 140

Refried Pinto Beans 140

Simple Pinto Beans with Spices 141

Simple Italian Flavor Cannellini Beans 141

Black-Eyed Peas with Ham 141

Creamy Corn Kernels with Cottage Cheese 141

Creamy Fig Millet 141

Cheesy Grits with Half-and-Half 142

Ritzy Corn, Lentil, and Brown Rice Stew 142

Chapter 12 Pasta and Side Dishes Recipe 143

Minty Carrots 143

Simple Corn Side Dish 143

Pearl Onions Side Dish 143

Acorn Squash Side Dish 143

Simple Spinach Side Dish 143

Tasty Maple Acorn Squash Dish 144

Kidney Beans and Corn Side Dish 144

Green Beans and Cranberries Side Dish 144

Green Cabbage and Tomatoes Side Dish 144

Brown Rice Salad 145

Radishes Side Salad 145

Tomatoes Side Salad 145

Arborio Rice Side Salad 145

Haricots Verts Side Salad 145

Sweet and Sour Side Salad 146

Brussels Sprouts Side Salad 146

Tomatoes and Corn Side Salad 146

Tasty Carrots and Walnuts Salad 146

Tomatoes and Burrata Side Salad 146

Delicious Green Beans and Blue Cheese 147

Kale Sauté 147

Mixed Veggies 147

Creamy Spinach 147

Garlic Green Beans 148

Tasty Spinach and Salami 148

Braised Collard Greens 148

Chinese Mustard Greens 148

Collard Greens and Peas 148

Chestnut Mushrooms 149

Cauliflower and Grapes 149

Tasty Carrots Mix 149

Sweet Pearl Onion Mix 149

Eggplant and Cashews Mix 150

Red Onions and Apples Mix 150

Delicious Shiitake Mushrooms Mix 150

Flavored Parmesan Mushrooms 150

Tasty Mushrooms and Rosemary 150

Brussels Sprouts and Chestnuts 151

Tasty Vidalia Onions Mix 151

Parmesan Zucchini Fries 151

Simple Buttery Potatoes 151

Green Beans Fries 151

Appendix:Recipes Index 153

Introduction

Many individuals enjoy pressure-cooking. The instant pot is a multi-cooker that performs more than seven functions. The Instant Pot enables one to prepare a wide range of recipes, including meat, fish, eggs, beans, cakes, poultry, yogurt, vegetables, and many more. What makes the Instant Pot exceptional is because you can utilize various cooking programs like a steamer, rice cooker, and sauté pan, thus saving more money, time, and space as compared to purchasing the appliances separately.

This book has been carefully written to meet the needs of everyone who likes cooking and would like to save money, and the time they spend on cooking. The Instant Pot serves as a multi-use programmable piece of equipment that will ensure you prepare delicious meals quickly through multiple selections of cooking settings in a single pot. We give credit of the development to smart Canadian technology specialists aiming at having the appliance as the best device for the kitchen for multiple reasons like pressure-cooking, making cake and stir-frying, among others. It was created to serve as a one-stop-shop to allow home cooks to prepare a flavorful meal with the press of a button. With the help of the appliance, you can make nearly every meal you desire.

In this book, we will explore the variety of easy delicious dishes you can cook with your Instant Pot. We will explore a wide range of dishes, from breakfast to pasta, soups to stews, desserts to appetizers, meat to beef, side dishes to vegetables, and use a healthy ingredient in the process. Most recipes will require a maximum of five components. Each recipe contains the preparation time, nutritional information, cooking instructions, and ingredients that are necessary to prepare the dishes. Once you try these delicious dishes with our cookbook, you and your Instant Pot are sure to become inseparable too.

Read on and learn more!

Chapter 1: Instant Pot - An Instant Path to Health

The Instant Pot is a multifunctional cooker that acts as a slow and rice cooker, steamer, yogurt maker, and a pressure cooker. It is a single kitchen appliance or multi-cooker that performs the tasks of seven different machines ranging from an electric pressure cooker, steamer, yogurt machine, rice cooker, sauté pan to warming pot, etc. It functions with the amalgamation of pressure and steam, which enables your foods to cook at a faster rate and safer as compared to other kitchen devices. It is a programmable countertop multi-cooker, which speeds up cooking by 2~6 times using up to 70% less energy.

The Instant Pot can conveniently and consistently cook nutritious, healthy food, making everything from stews, rice pilaf, lentil, bacon, chicken to steamed veggies. The Instant Pot deserves a spot in your kitchen because you can rely on it more than any other kitchen devices.

The Instant Pot is a useful multi-cooker that can execute the functions of a pressure cooker, slow cooker, rice cooker, steamer, and more. It has many safety features that make it safer to use and comes in different models. It comes with preset programs that are specifically designed to cook your food to perfection, whether it be chicken, dessert, cheesecake, stew, soup, or porridge.

Why Instant Pot

The following is a shortlist of some great reasons to invest in an Instant Pot. No doubt, after you start using one regularly, you will be inventing your list, and the list will only keep growing from there.

- **Easy Way to Prepare Food** - Unlike the earlier pressure cooker incarnations, electric ones have timers that you can set, allowing for maximum cooking convenience. Beyond the standard settings such as high, medium, and low, you do not need to worry about temperature or pressure. Unlike a stove, the pressure cooker does it all for you, and much more safely, too. You will not have to check in on your meal every few seconds constantly. Once you have installed your pressure cooker in its designated spot and discovered how useful it is, you are likely to keep it at the ready for the next quick meal simply because of its convenience.
- **The Faster, the Better** - Let us face it; our lives are busy. No one needs to tell you that (although I just did). Cooking meals in the oven can take hours while using the stove requires a wary eye to keep dishes from overcooking. There is a reduction in cooking time by up to 70%. When it might have taken 24 hours before to make a pot of beans, a pressure cooker makes the task so time-efficient that you will no longer have to worry about watching the stove for hours on end.
- **Delicious Can Also Mean Nutritious** - Remember the days of boiling food (like chicken) for hours on end? Boiling washes away vital nutrients, whereas pressure-cooking locks in all those necessary minerals and vitamins. It leaves you wanting to use your pressure cooker more often because of the additional health benefits that are available by following this style of cooking.
- **Fewer Dishes to Clean** - Throw all your ingredients into the pressure cooker and lock the lid. It is the best version of a one-pot meal you have ever made. When it has finished cooking, the only dishes will be the pot and the plates (which will undoubtedly have been licked clean because of how great the recipes in this book will taste!)

Instant Pot Button Functions

The Instant Pot is a piece of incredible kitchen equipment with a beautiful design. It has several buttons whose aims are to achieve particular tasks to help cook your food better. The sensors are designed intelligently to avoid overcooking or burning of your food.

Some of the excellent cooking and safety features that you need to understand to make cooking with the pot easy for you include the following:

Keep Warm/Cancel

It stops any program that has been previously set, putting the cooker in standby. When the cooker is in this standby mode, pressing this key will set forth the KEEP WARM program, which can last as long as 100 hours. No secrets for this option since it will keep the temperature warm to about 145º F but can be adjusted. The KEEP WARM function automatically activates after the timer goes off. Unless the recipe specifies that you need to turn off the machine immediately after cooking, there is no need to rush back to the cooker. You can return to the kitchen whenever you want.

Soup

This setting aims at coming up with a variety of broths and soups. The default is set at 30 minutes of high pressure although this can be adjusted using the ADJUST or '+' and '-' buttons.

Porridge

It is for making oatmeal or porridge with various types of grains. The default here is high pressure for 20 minutes. Make sure you DO NOT use quick release for this setting, as it will result in a significant mess.

Poultry

The setting is used to make meals with poultry, and the default is at high pressure for 15 minutes.

Meat/Stew

The setting is for making meats or stew, and the default is at high pressure for 35 minutes. You can add time by selecting MORE if you want that bone stripping effect on your meat.

Bean/Chili

The setting is specifically for making chili or cooking beans. The default is high pressure for 30 minutes. But if you want well-done beans, then select MORE.

Rice

It is the setting that turns your Instant Pot into a rice cooker. It is a fantastic program for cooking either parboiled or regular rice. For excellent results, use the provided water measurements inside the pot and the rice-measuring cup. The default for this setting is automatic and cooks rice at low pressure.

For instance, the manual indicates that the cooking duration for the rice changes automatically depending on the food content. Cooking 2 cups of rice will take approximately 12 minutes, and more cups will take more time accordingly.

When one attains the working pressure, the pressure keeping time will be shown, but the total cooking time is not displayed. In this setting, the ADJUST key does not affect in whatsoever way.

Multigrain

The setting is for cooking a mixture of grains such as brown rice, mung beans, wild rice, etc. The set default for this setting is 40 minutes of high pressure while the LESS setting is 20 minutes of cooking time and the MORE setting involves 45 minutes of just warm water soaking, then 60 minutes of cooking time on high pressure.

Steam

The setting is for steaming seafood, veggies, or reheating foods. You should not NPR (natural pressure release) on this setting, as you will be likely to overcook your food. The default here is 10 minutes of high-pressure cooking. You will require about 1 to 2 cups of water for steaming and make sure you use a basket or a steamer rack as this setting can burn food which is in direct contact with the pot.

Manual

This button allows you to manually set your pressure and cooking time (the maximum time is 240 minutes). You can best apply the button when you have a recipe indicating that you should cook on high pressure for a specified number of minutes.

Sauté

This setting is for open lid browning, sautéing, or simmering.

For regular browning: NORMAL - 160 degrees C (320 degrees F)
For darker browning: MORE - 170 degrees C (338 degrees F)
For light browning: LESS - 105 degrees C (221 degrees F)

Slow Cook

This setting converts your Instant Pot into a slow cooker, which can run to up to 40 hours. But the default is normal heat for 4 hours of cook time.

Yogurt

There are three programs on this setting: making yogurt, making Jiu Niang (fermented rice) and pasteurizing milk. The default of this setting is 8 hours of incubation. To pasteurize milk, adjust to MORE and to ferment rice or proof bread, adjust to LESS.

Timer (For Delayed Cooking)

Usually, many people confuse this setting with an actual cooking timer, which crushes their expectations regarding the cooker.

To use this setting the right way:

Start by selecting your cooking program (e.g. STEAM or any other function except the YOGURT and SAUTE) and then press on the TIMER button. Use the '+' and '-' for setting the delayed hours. Press on the TIMER setting again to change the minutes.

The time that you have set is the delayed time before the program begins. It is where you can set the pot to start cooking a few hours before arriving home or wake up so that you find freshly prepared dinner, lunch, or breakfast. You should allow for both sufficient cooking time and downtime before serving.

Top 5 Benefits of Instant Pot

Fast Cooking

The Instant Pot uses pressure to cook food, and instead of cooking beans for 3 hours, you can have bean soup or bean chili ready in 45 minutes. It means you will not have to stand over the kitchen counter and check the doneness of beans because, with the Instant Pot, you will always have perfectly cooked beans and legumes. You reduce the cooking time by 70%, which reduces the total preparation time as well.

Preserves Nutrients

Because you are cooking in a well-sealed container, the aroma, flavor, and nutrients remain within the food. Cooking with less amount of water or steam also helps the food retain their vitamins and minerals. In addition, you do not have to add water to prevent food from burning. Vegetables like broccoli and asparagus do not lose their bright color because they do not experience direct heat exposure. Meat has to cook to fall-off-the-bone tenderness. Beans and legumes are softer, and they taste better prepared in an Instant Pot.

Researchers have shown that when cooking with pressure, there is even distribution of heat, it all cooks at the same time, so no need for extension cooking.

Saves Energy

The Instant Pot is built in such a way that it does not require a gas or electric stove to cook for more extended periods. With slow cooker option in Instant Pot, you may prepare your food for a more extended period, but with little use of energy. Statistics show that Instant Pot saves energy up to 70% as compared to the other cooking appliances and methods.

Kills Harmful Microorganisms

The Instant Pot uses pressure cooking and temperatures higher than boiling water, which is useful in killing microorganisms. Therefore, another use of the Instant Pot includes acting as a sterilizer for baby bottles and jam pots. When speaking about harmful microorganisms, most people think about chicken and salmonella. Unfortunately, many ignore mycotoxins from the corn and beans. With high pressure cooking these microorganisms that may cause even liver cancer, a safe environment is created, and therefore foods from the Instant Pot is entirely safe to consume.

Safe to Use

Many think that Instant Pot is dangerous and that it may explode. It is entirely false, and with proper use of the Instant Pot, you will only experience positive things. The Instant Pot is easy and straightforward to use and just read your manual before operating.

Cheap

Yes, the Instant Pots are cheap although you may think otherwise. The Instant Pot is an appliance with different options; it can be used for stewing, as a rice cooker, a yogurt maker, a pressure cooker, a slow cooker, a steamer, and an option to keep the food warm. If you were to buy all these appliances one by one, you would go much over the Instant Pot price.

As you can see, the Instant Pot has many benefits, and if you do not own one, now it is the time.

FAQs of Instant Pot

Is the Instant Pot the Same as a Pressure Cooker?

No, it is not the same. While a pressure cooker only pressure cooks, the Instant Pot is a cooker with many functions like a pressure cooker, yogurt maker, slow cooker, warming pot, and rice cooker.

What are the Drawbacks of Using Instant Pot to Cook?

The main drawback is that you cannot adjust, taste, or inspect the food when the cooking process starts. You have to wait for the set time to elapse.

Can I Pressure Fry with My Instant Pot?

Pressure frying is not recommended for electric pressure cookers because the splattering oil may melt the cooker gasket.

Is It Safe to Use The Instant Pot?

Yes, the Instant Pot is very safe to use. It has passed many UL certifications on safety.

Is the Cooking Process Faster When Using Instant Pot?

Using pressure to cook will always save you time. However, in some foods such as shrimps and broccoli, you may not notice this. When cooking foods such as pork, you will see that time is significantly cut.

What Is the Working Pressure of the Instant Pot?

It ranges from 10.15 to 11.6 psi.

What are the Accessories You Recommend for Instant Pot?

Some of the recommended accessories include steaming racks, meat thermometers, steamer baskets, trivets, etc.

How Do I Quick Release?

When cooking has finished, unseal the venting knob to the venting position. It will take just a short time (usually a few minutes) for the pressure to be released.

How Do I Natural Release?

When cooking has finished, you wait for the valve to drop completely before opening the cover. Turn the knob to vent, and the pressure will be released. It takes 10 to 25 minutes.

Do You Use the CHICKEN Button or The MANUAL Button for Chicken?

It depends. If your recipe calls for one, use it. If you are doing a whole huge chicken, it's best to use the MANUAL setting. To get a more particular flavor, try the POULTRY setting.

Are There Any Directions on How to Use the MANUAL Function?
   The MANUAL function does what it says, and it will cook the food naturally for the desired time. Just set the time, and then press it, and it will cook the food once it has built up.

The Pot Isn't Heating Up on MANUAL. What Is Going On?
   MANUAL adjusts the cooking time. However, if the contents are frozen, you will start to notice that the countdown will only happen when you attain the pressure. In addition, take a look at the liquid you have in the pot as well; it might cause the pressure to be lacking.

How Long Does It Take to Warm Up Before Cooking?
   From 5 to 7 minutes. Use the warm liquid to help bring the pressure up faster.

Do You Need to Do An Initial Test Run?
   Yes, it is lovely to do a test run, simply because you will understand how to use this better. Often, people do not understand, so try using the water to test how fast it heats up before it cooks.

How Do You Get Low-Pressure?
   It is simple. There is a PRESSURE button, and first, you can press MANUAL, and then press the PRESSURE button until it's low. You can then press the TIMER button to adjust the time.

Can You Change the Heat on SAUTE Mode?
   You sure can. You press the ADJUST button, and then choose the three levels of temperature. Most people use it on NORMAL, but occasionally, if you want to boil something, put it on MORE.

Chapter 2 Breakfast and Brunch Recipe

Apple Cinnamon Oatmeal
Prep Time: 6 mins, Cook Time: 8 mins, Servings: 4
Ingredients:
- 1 tsp. cinnamon powder
- 1 chopped apple
- 1 cup steel-cut oats
- ¼ tsp. ground nutmeg
- 3 cups water
- Salt, to taste

Instructions:
1. Add all the ingredients to your Instant Pot and stir to combine.
2. Lock the lid. Select the Manual mode and set the cooking time for 8 minutes at High Pressure.
3. Once cooking is complete, do a natural pressure release for 5 minutes. Carefully open the lid.
4. Divide the oatmeal among four serving bowls and serve warm.

Nutritional info:
Calories 171, Fat 2.6g, Carbs 32.6g, Protein: 5.1g

Cashew and Mango Oatmeal
Prep Time: 8 mins, Cook Time: 3 mins, Servings: 2
Ingredients:
- 1 cup old-fashioned rolled oats
- 2 tbsps. unsweetened flaked coconut
- 2 tbsps. brown sugar
- 2 cups water
- 2 tbsps. chopped cashews
- ½ cup chopped mango

Instructions:
1. Put the oats and coconut in the Instant Pot, then sprinkle with the brown sugar. Pour in the water. Stir to mix well.
2. Lock the lid. Set to Manual mode, then set the timer for 3 minutes at High Pressure.
3. Once the timer goes off, perform a natural pressure release. Carefully open the lid.
4. Transfer the oatmeal in a serving bowl, then fold in the cashews and mango before serving.

Nutritional info:
Calories 276, Carbs 45.6g, Protein 7.1g, Fat 8.4g

Chocolate Oatmeal
Prep Time: 12 mins, Cook Time: 10 mins, Servings: 6
Ingredients:
- 2½ tbsps. cocoa powder
- 2 cups oatmeal
- 1 tsp. cinnamon powder
- 6 cups water
- 1 cup milk

Instructions:
1. In the Instant Pot, mix the milk, oatmeal, cocoa powder, cinnamon powder, and water.
2. Lock the lid. Select the Manual mode and cook for 10 minutes at High Pressure.
3. Once cooking is complete, do a natural pressure release for 10 minutes. Carefully open the lid.
4. Stir the oatmeal again and divide into bowls to serve.

Nutritional info:
Calories 110, Fat 4g, Carbs 8g, Protein 5g

Espresso Oatmeal
Prep Time: 12 mins, Cook Time: 10 mins, Servings: 4
Ingredients:
- 1 tsp. espresso powder
- 2½ cups water
- 2 tbsps. sugar
- 1 cup milk
- 1 cup steel-cut oats

Instructions:
1. Add all the ingredients to the Instant Pot and stir well.
2. Lock the lid. Select the Manual mode and cook for 6 minutes at High Pressure.
3. Once cooking is complete, do a natural pressure release for 5 minutes. Carefully open the lid.
4. Stir your oatmeal again, divide into bowls and serve warm.

Nutritional info:
Calories 120, Fat 2g, Carbs 10g, Protein 5g

Strawberry Oatmeal
Prep Time: 6 mins, Cook Time: 3 mins, Servings: 2
Ingredients:
- 1 tbsp. ground flaxseed
- 3 cups water
- ¼ cup sliced strawberries
- 1 cup steel-cut oats

Instructions:
1. Pour the water into the Instant Pot.
2. Stir in the oats and lock the lid. Select the Manual mode and cook for 3 minutes at High Pressure.
3. Once cooking is complete, do a natural pressure release for 10 minutes. Carefully open the lid.
4. Pour the oatmeal into a serving bowl. Top with the strawberries and flaxseed, then serve.

Nutritional info:
Calories 320, Fat 5g, Carbs 54g, Protein 12g

Peaches Oatmeal

Prep Time: 12 mins, Cook Time: 15 mins, Servings: 8

Ingredients:
- 3½ cups water
- 4 cups rolled oats
- 3½ cups milk
- 4 peaches, pitted and chopped
- ⅓ cup sugar

Instructions:
1. In the Instant Pot, combine the water, milk, oats, sugar, and peaches, and stir to mix.
2. Lock the lid. Press the Manual mode on the Instant Pot and cook for 15 minutes at High Pressure.
3. Once cooking is complete, do a natural pressure release for 10 minutes. Carefully open the lid.
4. Give it a good stir and ladle into bowls, then serve.

Nutritional info:
Calories 152, Fat 4g, Carbs 8g, Protein 4g

Pumpkin Spice Oatmeal

Prep Time: 6 mins, Cook Time: 10 mins, Servings: 2

Ingredients:
- ¼ tsp. ground cinnamon
- ⅛ tsp. ground pumpkin spice
- 1 cup steel-cut oats
- 1 tbsp. sugar
- 1 cup almond milk
- 1½ cups water

Instructions:
1. Place all ingredients into your Instant Pot and mix well.
2. Lock the lid. Select the Manual mode and set the cooking time for 6 minutes at High Pressure.
3. Once cooking is complete, do a natural pressure release for 5 minutes. Carefully open the lid.
4. Ladle into two serving bowls and serve.

Nutritional info:
Calories 377, Fat 6.6g, Carbs 69.4g, Protein: 10.7g

Blueberry Breakfast Bowl

Prep Time: 1 hour 10 mins, Cook Time: 2 mins, Servings: 4

Ingredients:
- 1 cup apple juice
- 3 tbsps. blueberries
- 1½ cups water
- 1 tbsp. honey
- 1½ cups quinoa

Instructions:
1. In the Instant Pot, stir together the water with quinoa.
2. Lock the lid. Select the Manual mode and set the cooking time for 2 minutes at High Pressure.
3. Once cooking is complete, do a natural pressure release for 10 minutes, then release any remaining pressure. Carefully open the lid.
4. Divide the quinoa into four bowls. Drizzle each bowl evenly with honey and apple juice. Sprinkle the blueberries on top and serve.

Nutritional info:
Calories 172, Fat 5g, Carbs 5g, Protein 6g

Cauliflower and Barley Bowls

Prep Time: 12 mins, Cook Time: 30 mins, Servings: 4

Ingredients:
- ½ cup grated Parmesan cheese, divided
- 3 tbsps. extra virgin olive oil, divided
- 3 cups chicken stock
- 1 cup pearl barley
- 1 head cauliflower
- Salt and pepper, to taste

Instructions:
1. Press the Sauté button on the Instant Pot and heat 2 tablespoons olive oil.
2. Add the cauliflower, salt and pepper, and sauté for 6 to 8 minutes, stirring occasionally.
3. Add half of the Parmesan cheese, stir, and cook for 3 to 4 minutes more.
4. Add the remaining olive oil, barley, and stock, and whisk well.
5. Lock the lid. Select the Manual mode and set the cooking time for 15 minutes at High Pressure.
6. Once cooking is complete, do a natural pressure release for 7 minutes, then release any remaining pressure. Carefully open the lid.
7. Sprinkle with the remaining Parmesan cheese. Divide into bowls and serve warm.

Nutritional info:
Calories 252, Fat 4g, Carbs 20g, Protein 6g

Cheesy Cauliflower Bowls

Prep Time: 12 mins, Cook Time: 4 mins, Servings: 6

Ingredients:
- 1 tbsps. chopped parsley
- ½ cup vegetable stock
- 3 tbsps. olive oil
- 1 head cauliflower, cut into florets
- ⅓ cup grated Parmesan cheese

Instructions:
1. In a bowl, combine the olive oil with cauliflower florets, and toss well.
2. Transfer to the Instant Pot and add stock.

3. Lock the lid. Select the Manual mode and set the cooking time for 4 minutes at High Pressure.
4. Once cooking is complete, do a quick pressure release. Carefully open the lid.
5. Add the parsley and Parmesan cheese, and stir to combine. Serve immediately.

Nutritional info:
Calories 120, Fat 2g, Carbs 5g, Protein 3g

Breakfast Banana Bread
Prep Time: 12 mins, Cook Time: 45 mins, Servings: 8

Ingredients:
- ⅓ cup honey
- ½ tsp. baking soda
- 2 bananas, peeled and chopped
- 1½ cups steel-cut oats
- 4 whisked eggs
- 1½ cups water

Instructions:
1. In a blender, add the oats, bananas, eggs, honey, and baking soda, and pulse until completely mixed. Pour the mixture into a loaf pan.
2. Add 1½ cups water and trivet to the Instant Pot. Place the loaf pan on the trivet.
3. Lock the lid. Select the Manual mode and set the cooking time for 45 minutes at High Pressure.
4. Once cooking is complete, do a quick pressure release. Carefully open the lid.
5. Let cool for 5 minutes and serve.

Nutritional info:
Calories 192, Fat 5g, Carbs 6g, Protein 2g

Zucchini Toast
Prep Time: 12 mins, Cook Time: 8 mins, Servings: 2

Ingredients:
- ½ zucchini, sliced
- ¼ tsp. black pepper
- 1 tbsp. olive oil
- ½ tsp. salt
- 4 whole-grain bread slices, toasted

Instructions:
1. In a bowl, toss the zucchini slices with salt. Set aside.
2. Select the Sauté mode on the Instant Pot and heat the olive oil.
3. Add the zucchini slices and sauté for about 6 minutes until softened, stirring occasionally. Season with black pepper.
4. Divide the zucchini slices evenly among bread slices and serve warm.

Nutritional info:
Calories 248, Fat 9g, Carbs 32g, Protein 8g

Cauliflower Breakfast Hash
Prep Time: 6 mins, Cook Time: 7 mins, Servings: 4

Ingredients:
- 4 eggs
- 4 chopped jalapeño peppers
- 1 tbsp. olive oil
- 3 minced garlic cloves
- 1 grated cauliflower head, liquid squeezed out
- Salt and pepper, to taste
- ½ cup water

Instructions:
1. Press the Sauté button on the Instant Pot and heat the oil.
2. Stir in the garlic and sauté for 1 minute until fragrant.
3. Stir in the grated cauliflower, pepper and salt.
4. Pour in ½ cup water and spread the cauliflower mixture evenly in the bottom of the Instant Pot.
5. Make four wells in the cauliflower and gently crack an egg into each well.
6. Sprinkle with jalapeño peppers.
7. Lock the lid. Select the Manual mode and set the cooking time for 6 minutes at High Pressure.
8. Once cooking is complete, do a quick pressure release. Carefully open the lid.
9. Cool for a few minutes and serve on plates.

Nutritional info:
Calories 113, Carbs 6.2g, Protein, 4.6g, Fat 9.5g

Potato and Spinach Hash
Prep Time: 12 mins, Cook Time: 10 mins, Servings: 4

Ingredients:
- ¼ tsp. salt
- 1 small yellow onion, chopped
- 3 baked sweet potatoes, peeled and cubed
- 11 oz. baby spinach
- 12 oz. chopped chorizo

Instructions:
1. Set the Instant Pot to Sauté and add the chorizo and onion. Cook for 2 to 3 minutes.
2. Add the potato cubes, baby spinach and salt, and stir to combine.
3. Lock the lid. Select the Manual mode and cook for 7 minutes at High Pressure.
4. Once cooking is complete, do a quick pressure release. Carefully open the lid.
5. Divide the mixture between plates and serve.

Nutritional info:

Calories 192, Fat 4g, Carbs 6g, Protein 2g

Sweet Potato Hash

Prep Time: 12 mins, Cook Time: 10 mins, Servings: 4
Ingredients:
- 1 yellow onion, chopped
- ½ lb. ground pork sausage
- 1 sweet potato, cubed
- 1 tbsp. Italian seasoning
- 6 eggs, beaten
- 2 cups water

Instructions:
1. Set the Instant Pot to Sauté. Add the onion, sausage, and sweet potato to the pot, and stir to incorporate.
2. Cook for 5 minutes and transfer to a baking dish. Set aside.
3. In a bowl, mix the eggs with Italian seasoning, and whisk well. Pour the eggs over the sausage mixture.
4. Add 2 cups water and trivet to your Instant Pot. Place the baking dish on the trivet.
5. Lock the lid. Select the Manual mode and cook for 5 minutes at High Pressure.
6. Once cooking is complete, do a quick pressure release. Carefully open the lid.
7. Remove from the pot and serve hot.

Nutritional info:
Calories 216, Fat 6g, Carbs 12g, Protein 5g

Banana and Raisin Porridge

Prep Time: 12 mins, Cook Time: 6 mins, Servings: 4
Ingredients:
- 3 cups rice milk
- 1 cup buckwheat
- ¼ cup raisins
- 1 tsp. cinnamon powder
- 1 banana, peeled and sliced

Instructions:
1. In the Instant Pot, mix the buckwheat with banana, milk, cinnamon and raisins, and stir to incorporate.
2. Lock the lid. Select the Manual mode and set the cooking time for 6 minutes at High Pressure.
3. Once cooking is complete, do a natural pressure release for 5 minutes, then release any remaining pressure. Carefully open the lid.
4. Give the porridge a good stir and divide into bowls to serve.

Nutritional info:
Calories 182, Fat 4g, Carbs 6g, Protein 7g

Millet and Oats Porridge

Prep Time: 12 mins, Cook Time: 13 mins, Servings: 8
Ingredients:
- 2 cored and chopped apples
- ½ cup rolled oats
- 3 cups water
- ½ tsp. ginger powder
- 1 cup millet

Instructions:
1. Set the Instant Pot to Sauté and add the millet. Stir and toast for 3 minutes.
2. Add the oats, water, ginger and apples to the Instant Pot, and whisk to combine.
3. Lock the lid. Select the Manual mode and cook for 10 minutes at High Pressure.
4. Once cooking is complete, do a natural pressure release for 7 minutes, then release any remaining pressure. Carefully open the lid.
5. Stir the porridge again and ladle into bowls to serve.

Nutritional info:
Calories 200, Fat 2g, Carbs 4g, Protein 5g

Pearl Barley Porridge

Prep Time: 12 mins, Cook Time: 12 mins, Servings: 6
Ingredients:
- 3 tbsps. lemon juice
- 1 red bell pepper, chopped
- 1 onion, sliced
- 1 cup pearl barley
- 3 cups vegetable stock

Instructions:
1. Add the barley and stock to the Instant Pot and stir well.
2. Press the Manual button and set the cooking time for 12 minutes at High Pressure.
3. Once cooking is complete, do a natural pressure release for 6 minutes. Carefully open the lid.
4. Transfer to a bowl and stir in the remaining ingredients, then serve.

Nutritional info:
Calories 62, Fat 1g, Carbs 9g, Protein 1g

Pomegranate Porridge

Prep Time: 6 mins, Cook Time: 3 mins, Servings: 4
Ingredients:
- 2 pomegranates seeds
- 2 tbsps. sugar
- 2 cups shredded coconut
- 1 cup pomegranate juice
- 2 cup water

Instructions:
1. In the Instant Pot, combine the coconut with water and pomegranate juice, and whisk well.

2. Lock the lid. Select the Manual mode and cook for 3 minutes at High Pressure.
3. Once cooking is complete, do a natural pressure release for 5 minutes, then release any remaining pressure. Carefully open the lid.
4. Add the pomegranate seeds and sugar and give a good stir. Ladle into bowls and serve warm.

Nutritional info:
Calories 153, Fat 3g, Carbs 10g, Protein 4g

Squash Porridge with Apples
Prep Time: 12 mins, Cook Time: 8 mins, Servings: 4
Ingredients:
- 2 tbsps. maple syrup
- 4 small apples, cored and chopped
- ½ cup water
- 2 tbsps. cinnamon powder
- 1 squash, peeled and chopped

Instructions:
1. In the Instant Pot, mix the apples with squash, cinnamon, maple syrup and water, and whisk to combine.
2. Lock the lid. Select the Porridge mode and set the cooking time for 8 minutes at High Pressure.
3. Once cooking is complete, do a natural pressure release for 5 minutes, then release any remaining pressure. Carefully open the lid.
4. Stir the porridge one more time, then divide into bowls and serve.

Nutritional info:
Calories 162, Fat 5g, Carbs 8g, Protein 2g

Eggs and Bacon Breakfast Risotto
Prep Time: 12 mins, Cook Time: 12 mins, Servings: 2
Ingredients:
- 1½ cups chicken stock
- 2 poached eggs
- 2 tbsps. grated Parmesan cheese
- 3 chopped bacon slices
- ¾ cup Arborio rice

Instructions:
1. Set your Instant Pot to Sauté and add the bacon and cook for 5 minutes until crispy, stirring occasionally.
2. Carefully stir in the rice and let cook for an additional 1 minute.
3. Add the chicken stock and stir well.
4. Lock the lid. Select the Manual mode and set the cooking time for 6 minutes at Low Pressure.
5. Once cooking is complete, do a quick pressure release. Carefully open the lid.
6. Add the Parmesan cheese and keep stirring until melted. Divide the risotto between two plates. Add the eggs on the side and serve immediately.

Nutritional info:
Calories 214, Fat 5g, Carbs 12g, Protein 5g

French Eggs
Prep Time: 12 mins, Cook Time: 8 mins, Servings: 4
Ingredients:
- ¼ tsp. salt
- 4 bacon slices
- 1 tbsp. olive oil
- 4 tbsps. chopped chives
- 4 eggs
- 1½ cups water

Instructions:
1. Grease 4 ramekins with a drizzle of oil and crack an egg into each ramekin.
2. Add a bacon slice on top and season with salt. Sprinkle the chives on top.
3. Add 1½ cups water and steamer basket to your Instant Pot. Transfer the ramekins to the basket.
4. Lock the lid. Select the Manual mode and set the cooking time for 8 minutes at High Pressure.
5. Once cooking is complete, do a quick pressure release. Carefully open the lid.
6. Serve your baked eggs immediately.

Nutritional info:
Calories 182, Fat 5, Carbs 10, Protein 5

Ham and Spinach Frittata
Prep Time: 3 mins, Cook Time: 10 mins, Servings: 8
Ingredients:
- 1 cup diced ham
- 2 cups chopped spinach
- 8 eggs, beaten
- ½ cup coconut milk
- 1 onion, chopped
- 1 tsp. salt

Instructions:
1. Put all the ingredients into the Instant Pot. Stir to mix well.
2. Lock the lid. Set to Manual mode, then set the timer for 10 minutes at High Pressure.
3. Once the timer goes off, perform a natural pressure release for 5 minutes. Carefully open the lid.
4. Transfer the frittata on a plate and serve immediately.

Nutritional info:
Calories 63, Carbs 5.0g, Protein 8.0g, Fat 3.0g

Mini Frittata
Prep Time: 12 mins, Cook Time: 5 mins, Servings: 6
Ingredients:
- 1 chopped red bell pepper

- 1 tbsp. almond milk
- ¼ tsp. salt
- 2 tbsps. grated Cheddar cheese
- 5 whisked eggs
- 1½ cups water

Instructions:
1. In a bowl, combine the salt, eggs, cheese, almond milk, and red bell pepper, and whisk well. Pour the egg mixture into 6 baking molds.
2. Add 1½ cups water and steamer basket to your Instant Pot. Transfer the baking molds to the basket.
3. Lock the lid. Select the Manual mode and cook for 5 minutes at High Pressure.
4. Once cooking is complete, do a quick pressure release. Carefully open the lid. Serve hot.

Nutritional info:
Calories 200, Fat 4g, Carbs 7g, Protein 6g

Eggs En Cocotte

Prep Time: 10 mins, Cook Time: 20 mins, Servings: 4
Ingredients:
- 1 cup water
- 1 tbsp. butter
- 4 tbsps. heavy whipping cream
- 4 eggs
- 1 tbsp. chives
- Salt and pepper, to taste

Instructions:
1. Arrange a steamer rack in the Instant Pot, then pour in the water.
2. Grease four ramekins with butter.
3. Divide the heavy whipping cream in the ramekins, then break each egg in each ramekin.
4. Sprinkle them with chives, salt, and pepper.
5. Arrange the ramekins on the steamer rack.
6. Lock the lid. Set to the Manual mode, then set the timer for 20 minutes at High Pressure.
7. Once the timer goes off, perform a natural pressure release for 10 minutes, then release any remaining pressure. Carefully open the lid.
8. Transfer them on a plate and serve immediately.

Nutritional info:
Calories 166, Carbs 3.1g, Protein 9.7g, Fat 12.7g

Cheesy Bacon Quiche

Prep Time: 5 mins, Cook Time: 10 mins, Servings: 6
Ingredients:
- 2 tbsps. olive oil
- 6 eggs, lightly beaten
- 1 cup milk
- Salt and pepper, to taste
- 2 cups Monterey Jack cheese, grated
- 1 cup bacon, cooked and crumbled

Instructions:
1. Grease the Instant Pot with olive oil.
2. Combine the eggs, milk, salt, and pepper in a large bowl. Stir to mix well.
3. Put the cheese and bacon in the pot, then pour the egg mixture over. Stir to mix well.
4. Lock the lid. Set to Manual mode, then set the timer for 10 minutes at High Pressure.
5. Once the timer goes off, perform a natural pressure release for 5 minutes. Carefully open the lid.
6. Transfer the quiche on a plate and serve.

Nutritional info:
Calories 396, Carbs 5.5g, Protein 23.7g, Fat 31.3g

Veggie Quiche

Prep Time: 12 mins, Cook Time: 20 mins, Servings: 6
Ingredients:
- ½ cup milk
- 1 red bell pepper, chopped
- 2 green onions, chopped
- Salt, to taste
- 8 whisked eggs
- 1 cup water

Instructions:
1. In a bowl, combine the whisked eggs with milk, bell pepper, onions and salt, and stir well. Pour the egg mixture into a pan.
2. In your Instant Pot, add the water and trivet. Place the pan on the trivet and cover with tin foil.
3. Lock the lid. Select the Manual mode and cook for 20 minutes at High Pressure.
4. Once cooking is complete, do a quick pressure release. Carefully open the lid.
5. Slice the quiche and divide between plates to serve.

Nutritional info:
Calories 200, Fat 3g, Carbs 7g, Protein 6g

Western Omelet

Prep Time: 12 mins, Cook Time: 30 mins, Servings: 4
Ingredients:
- ½ cup half-and-half
- 4 chopped spring onions
- 6 whisked eggs
- ¼ tsp. salt
- 8 oz. bacon, chopped
- 1½ cups water

Instructions:
1. Place the steamer basket in the Instant Pot and pour in 1½ cups water.
2. In a bowl, combine the eggs with half-and-half, bacon, spring onions and salt, and whisk well. Pour the egg mixture into a soufflé dish and transfer to the steamer basket.
3. Lock the lid. Select the Steam mode and cook for 30 minutes at High Pressure.
4. Once cooking is complete, do a quick pressure release. Carefully open the lid.
5. Allow to cool for 5 minutes before serving.

Nutritional info:
Calories 200, Fat 6g, Carbs 12g, Protein 6g

Breakfast Rice Pudding

Prep Time: 12 mins, Cook Time: 12 mins, Servings: 6
Ingredients:
- 1 cup coconut cream
- ¼ cup maple syrup
- 1¼ cups water
- 1 cup basmati rice
- 2 cups almond milk

Instructions:
1. In the Instant Pot, mix together the milk with water, rice, cream and maple syrup.
2. Lock the lid. Select the Manual mode and cook for 12 minutes at Low Pressure.
3. Once cooking is complete, do a natural pressure release for 5 minutes, then release any remaining pressure. Carefully open the lid.
4. Stir the pudding again and divide into bowls to serve.

Nutritional info:
Calories 251, Fat 5g, Carbs 6g, Protein 5g

Bread Pudding

Prep Time: 12 mins, Cook Time: 15 mins, Servings: 8
Ingredients:
- ½ cup maple syrup
- 1 bread loaf, cubed
- ½ cup butter
- 2 cups coconut milk
- 4 eggs
- 2 cups water

Instructions:
1. In a blender, blend the coconut milk with eggs, butter and maple syrup until smooth.
2. Transfer the mixture to a pudding pan and add the bread cubes. Cover the pan with tin foil.
3. Add 2 cups water and trivet to your Instant Pot. Place the pudding pan on the trivet.
4. Lock the lid. Select the Manual mode and cook for 15 minutes at High Pressure.
5. Once cooking is complete, do a quick pressure release. Carefully open the lid.
6. Allow to cool for 5 minutes before serving.

Nutritional info:
Calories 271, Fat 4g, Carbs 12g, Protein 10g

Strawberry and Orange Juice Compote

Prep Time: 10 mins, Cook Time: 15 mins, Servings: 4
Ingredients:
- 2 lbs. fresh strawberries, rinsed, trimmed, and cut in half
- 2 oz. fresh orange juice
- 1 vanilla bean, chopped
- ½ tsp. ground ginger
- ¼ cup sugar
- Toast, for serving

Instructions:
1. Put all the ingredients into the Instant Pot. Stir to mix well.
2. Lock the lid. Set to the Manual Mode, then set the timer for 15 minutes at High Pressure.
3. When the timer goes off, perform a natural pressure release for 10 minutes. Carefully open the lid.
4. Allow to cool and thicken before serving with the toast.

Nutritional info:
Calories 152, Fat 1.6g, Carbs 35.5g, Protein 2.4g

Banana Quinoa

Prep Time: 5 mins, Cook Time: 12 mins, Servings: 2
Ingredients:
- ½ cup peeled and sliced banana
- ¾ cup quinoa, soaked in water for at least 1 hour
- 1 (8 oz.) can almond milk
- 2 tbsps. honey
- 1 tsp. vanilla extract
- Pinch of salt
- ¾ cup water

Instructions:
1. Combine all the ingredients in the Instant Pot. Stir to mix well.
2. Lock the lid. Set to Rice mode, then set the timer for 12 minutes at Low Pressure.
3. Once the timer goes off, perform a quick pressure release. Carefully open the lid.

4. Serve immediately.

Nutritional info:
Calories 371, Carbs 41.4g, Protein 7.3g, Fat 20.4g

Creamy Tomatoes and Quinoa
Prep Time: 12 mins, Cook Time: 12 mins, Servings: 6

Ingredients:
- 1 tbsp. grated ginger
- 1 (28 oz) can tomatoes, chopped
- ¼ cup quinoa
- 14 oz. coconut milk
- 1 small yellow onion, chopped

Instructions:
1. In the Instant Pot, mix the onion with quinoa, tomatoes, milk and ginger, and stir well.
2. Lock the lid. Select the Manual mode and cook for 12 minutes at High Pressure.
3. Once cooking is complete, do a natural pressure release for 5 minutes, then release any remaining pressure. Carefully open the lid.
4. Stir the mixture one more time and divide into bowls to serve.

Nutritional info:
Calories 260, Fat 9g, Carbs 30g, Protein 7g

Strawberry Quinoa
Prep Time: 12 mins, Cook Time: 2 minute, Servings: 4

Ingredients:
- 2¼ cups water
- 2 tbsps. honey
- 2 cups chopped strawberries
- ¼ tsp. pumpkin pie spice
- 1 ½ cups quinoa

Instructions:
1. In the Instant Pot, mix the quinoa with honey, water, spice, and strawberries. Stir to combine.
2. Lock the lid. Select the Manual mode and set the cooking time for 2 minutes at High Pressure.
3. Once cooking is complete, do a natural pressure release for 10 minutes, then release any remaining pressure. Carefully open the lid.
4. Let the quinoa rest for 10 minutes. Give a good stir and serve immediately.

Nutritional info:
Calories 162, Fat 3g, Carbs 6g, Protein 3g

Blackberry Egg Cake
Prep Time: 12 mins, Cook Time: 8 mins, Servings: 3

Ingredients:
- Zest from ½ an orange
- ½ cup fresh blackberries
- 1 tbsp. coconut oil
- 3 tbsps. coconut flour
- 5 eggs, whisked
- 1 cup water
- Pinch salt

Instructions:
1. Place a steamer basket in the Instant Pot and pour in a cup of water.
2. In a mixing bowl, combine the eggs, coconut oil, and coconut flour until well combined. Season with a pinch of salt.
3. Add the blackberries and orange zest.
4. Pour into muffin cups.
5. Place the muffin cups in the steamer basket.
6. Lock the lid. Press the Steam button and set the cooking time for 8 minutes at High Pressure.
7. Once cooking is complete, do a quick pressure release. Carefully open the lid.
8. Allow to cool for 5 minutes before serving.

Nutritional info:
Calories 172, Carbs 11.4g, Protein 5.6g, Fat 16.9g

Special Pancake
Prep Time: 12 mins, Cook Time: 30 mins, Servings: 4

Ingredients:
- 2½ tsps. baking powder
- 2 eggs, beaten
- 2 tbsps. sugar
- 1½ cups milk
- 2 cups white flour

Instructions:
1. In a bowl, mix the flour with eggs, milk, sugar, and baking powder. Stir to incorporate.
2. Spread out the mixture onto the bottom of the Instant Pot.
3. Lock the lid. Select the Manual mode and cook for 30 minutes at High Pressure.
4. Once cooking is complete, do a quick pressure release. Carefully open the lid.
5. Let the pancake cool for a few minutes before slicing to serve.

Nutritional info:
Calories 251, Fat 5g, Carbs 6g, Protein 3g

Broccoli and Egg Casserole
Prep Time: 5 mins, Cook Time: 15 mins, Servings: 6

Ingredients:
- 6 eggs, beaten
- ⅓ cup all-purpose flour
- 3 cups cottage cheese
- ¼ cup butter, melted
- Salt and pepper, to taste
- 2 tbsps. chopped onions

- 3 cups broccoli florets

Instructions:
1. Combine the eggs, flour, cheese, butter, salt, and pepper in a large bowl. Stir to mix well.
2. Put the onions and broccoli in the Instant Pot. Pour the egg mixture over. Stir to combine well.
3. Lock the lid. Set to Manual mode, then set the timer to 15 minutes at High pressure.
4. Once the timer goes off, perform a natural pressure release for 10 minutes, then release any remaining pressure. Carefully open the lid.
5. Transfer them on a plate and serve immediately.

Nutritional info:
Calories407, Carbs 15.8g, Protein 27.8g, Fat 25.7g

Cheesy Egg and Bacon Muffins

Prep Time: 12 mins, Cook Time: 8 mins, Servings: 4

Ingredients:
- 4 cooked bacon slices, crumbled
- 4 tbsps. shredded Cheddar cheese
- ¼ tsp. salt
- 1 green onion, chopped
- 4 eggs, beaten
- 1½ cups water

Instructions:
1. In a bowl, mix the eggs with cheese, bacon, onion and salt, and whisk well. Pour the egg mixture evenly into four muffin cups.
2. Add 1½ cups water and steamer basket to the Instant Pot. Place the muffin cups in the basket.
3. Lock the lid. Select the Manual mode and set the cooking time for 8 minutes at High Pressure.
4. Once cooking is complete, do a quick pressure release. Carefully open the lid.
5. Divide the muffins between plates and serve warm.

Nutritional info:
Calories 182, Fat 7g, Carbs 8g, Protein 12g

Pumpkin and Apple Butter

Prep Time: 12 mins, Cook Time: 10 mins, Servings: 6

Ingredients:
- 30 oz. pumpkin purée
- 4 apples, cored, peeled, and cubed
- 12 oz. apple cider
- 1 cup sugar
- 1 tbsp. pumpkin pie spice

Instructions:
1. In the Instant Pot, stir together the pumpkin purée with apples, apple cider, sugar, and pumpkin pie spice.
2. Lock the lid. Select the Manual mode and cook for 10 minutes at High Pressure.
3. Once cooking is complete, do a quick pressure release. Carefully open the lid.
4. Remove from the pot and serve in bowls.

Nutritional info:
Calories 182, Fat 6g, Carbs 8g, Protein 2g

Breakfast Cobbler

Prep Time: 12 mins, Cook Time: 15 mins, Servings: 2

Ingredients:
- 2 tbsps. honey
- ¼ cup shredded coconut
- 1 plum, pitted and chopped
- 3 tbsps. coconut oil, divided
- 1 apple, cored and chopped

Instructions:
1. In the Instant Pot, combine the plum with apple, half of the coconut oil, and honey, and blend well.
2. Lock the lid. Select the Manual mode and cook for 10 minutes at High Pressure.
3. Once cooking is complete, do a quick pressure release. Carefully open the lid.
4. Transfer the mixture to bowls and clean your Instant Pot.
5. Set your Instant Pot to Sauté and heat the remaining coconut oil. Add the coconut, stir, and toast for 5 minutes.
6. Sprinkle the coconut over fruit mixture and serve.

Nutritional info:
Calories 172, Fat 7g, Carbs 6g, Protein 2g

Tofu and Sweet Potato Mix

Prep Time: 12 mins, Cook Time: 10 mins, Servings: 4

Ingredients:
- 2 tbsps. red pepper sauce
- 1 lb. cubed extra-firm tofu
- 2 tsps. sesame oil
- ⅓ cup vegetable stock
- 1 cup chopped sweet potato

Instructions:
1. Select the Sauté mode and heat the sesame oil.
2. Add the sweet potato, stir, and cook for 2 minutes.
3. Add the tofu and stock, stir, and cook for 2 minutes more.
4. Lock the lid. Select the Manual mode and cook for 3 minutes at High Pressure.
5. Once cooking is complete, do a quick pressure release. Carefully open the lid.

6. Pour in the red pepper sauce and stir to incorporate. Serve immediately.

Nutritional info:
Calories 172, Fat 7g, Carbs 20g, Protein 6g

Brown Rice and Chickpeas Medley
Prep Time: 12 mins, Cook Time: 25 mins, Servings: 4
Ingredients:
- 1½ cups brown rice
- 1 tbsp. olive oil
- 1 cup chickpeas
- 14 oz. tomatoes, chopped
- 1 red onion, chopped

Instructions:
1. Set your Instant Pot to Sauté and heat the olive oil.
2. Add the onions, stir, and cook for 3 minutes until translucent.
3. Add the tomatoes, chickpeas, and rice, and stir well.
4. Lock the lid. Select the Manual mode and cook for 20 minutes at Low Pressure.
5. Once cooking is complete, do a natural pressure release for 10 minutes, then release any remaining pressure. Carefully open the lid.
6. Let the mixture cool for 5 minutes before serving.

Nutritional info:
Calories 253, Fat 4g, Carbs 9g, Protein 7g

Breakfast Arugula Salad
Prep Time: 12 mins, Cook Time: 15 mins, Servings: 6
Ingredients:
- 2 blood oranges, peeled and sliced
- 2 cups water
- 4 oz. arugula
- 1 tsp. sunflower oil
- 1 cup kamut grains, soaked

Instructions:
1. In the Instant Pot, combine the kamut grains with sunflower oil and water, and whisk well.
2. Lock the lid. Select the Manual mode and set the cooking time for 15 minutes at High Pressure.
3. Once cooking is complete, do a natural pressure release for 10 minutes, then release any remaining pressure. Carefully open the lid.
4. Drain the kamut grains and transfer to a large bowl. Add the arugula and oranges, and toss well. Serve immediately.

Nutritional info:
Calories 163, Fat 6g, Carbs 7g, Protein 3g

Cranberry Beans Salad
Prep Time: 12 mins, Cook Time: 15 mins, Servings: 4
Ingredients:
- 3 tbsps. olive oil
- 1 ½ cups fresh green beans
- 5 tbsps. apple cider vinegar
- ½ red onion, chopped
- 1 cup cranberry beans, soaked and drained
- 1 cup water

Instructions:
1. Add 1 cup water and steamer basket to your Instant Pot.
2. Place the cranberry beans and green beans in the basket.
3. Lock the lid. Select the Manual mode and cook for 15 minutes at High Pressure.
4. Once cooking is complete, do a quick pressure release. Carefully open the lid.
5. Drain all beans and transfer them to a salad bowl. Add the onions, vinegar, and olive oil, and gently toss to combine. Serve immediately.

Nutritional info:
Calories 170, Fat 4g, Carbs 15g, Protein 6g

Swiss Chard Salad
Prep Time: 12 mins, Cook Time: 5 mins, Servings: 4
Ingredients:
- ¼ tsp. red pepper flakes
- 1 bunch Swiss chard, sliced
- ¼ cup toasted pine nuts
- 1 tbsp. balsamic vinegar
- 2 tbsps. olive oil

Instructions:
1. Set your Instant Pot to Sauté and heat the olive oil.
2. Add the chard, stir, and cook for 2 minutes until tender.
3. Add pepper flakes and vinegar and stir well.
4. Lock the lid. Select the Steam mode and cook for 3 minutes at High Pressure.
5. Sprinkle with the pine nuts and divide into bowls to serve.

Nutritional info:
Calories 110, Fat 2g, Carbs 6g, Protein 4g

Pineapple and Peas Breakfast Curry
Prep Time: 12 mins, Cook Time: 20 mins, Servings: 4
Ingredients:
- 4 cups water
- 1 cup peas, soaked and drained
- 1 tsp. curry powder
- 1 cup canned pineapple, sliced
- ¼ cup cashew butter

Instructions:

1. In the Instant Pot, stir together the peas and water.
2. Lock the lid. Select the Manual mode and cook for 16 minutes at High Pressure.
3. Once cooking is complete, do a quick pressure release. Carefully open the lid.
4. Drain the peas and transfer to a bowl.
5. Clean the pot and set it to Sauté. Add the peas, curry powder, pineapple and cashew butter, and stir for 1 minute.
6. Lock the lid. Select the Manual mode and cook for 2 minutes at High Pressure.
7. Once cooking is complete, do a quick pressure release. Carefully open the lid.
8. Serve warm.

Nutritional info:
Calories 181, Fat 6g, Carbs 15g, Protein 8g

Garlic Eggplants with Tomato Sauce

Prep Time: 12 mins, Cook Time: 9 mins, Servings: 3
Ingredients:
- 3 minced garlic cloves
- 1 cup tomato sauce
- 1 tbsp. olive oil
- 1 tbsp. garlic powder
- 4 cups cubed eggplant

Instructions:
1. Press the Sauté button on the Instant Pot and heat the olive oil.
2. Add the garlic, stir, and cook for 2 minutes until tender.
3. Add the eggplant, garlic powder, and tomato sauce, and stir well.
4. Lock the lid. Select the Manual mode and cook for 7 minutes at High Pressure.
5. Once cooking is complete, do a quick pressure release. Carefully open the lid.
6. Transfer to three bowls and serve warm.

Nutritional info:
Calories 172, Fat 4g, Carbs 7g, Protein 4g

Celeriac and Bacon Mix

Prep Time: 12 mins, Cook Time: 10 mins, Servings: 6
Ingredients:
- 2 tbsps. chicken stock
- 2 tsps. dried parsley
- 4 oz. shredded Cheddar cheese
- 3 bacon strips
- 2 lbs. peeled and cubed celeriac

Instructions:
1. Set the Instant Pot to Sauté and cook the bacon for 2 minutes.
2. Add the parsley, celeriac and stock, and stir.
3. Lock the lid. Select the Manual mode and cook for 6 minutes at High Pressure.
4. Once cooking is complete, do a quick pressure release. Carefully open the lid.
5. Add the cheese and keep stirring until melted. Serve warm.

Nutritional info:
Calories 164, Fat 3g, Carbs 6g, Protein 7g

Turkey Breast and Avocado Breakfast

Prep Time: 12 mins, Cook Time: 7 mins, Servings: 4
Ingredients:
- 4 whisked eggs
- 4 avocado slices
- 2 tbsps. olive oil
- 2 tbsps. vegetable stock
- 4 cooked turkey breast slices

Instructions:
1. Set the Instant Pot to Sauté and heat the olive oil.
2. Add the turkey and brown for 2 minutes, then transfer to a plate.
3. Add the eggs and vegetable stock to the pot and whisk well.
4. Lock the lid. Select the Manual mode and cook for 5 minutes at High Pressure.
5. Once cooking is complete, do a quick pressure release. Carefully open the lid.
6. Divide the eggs and avocado slices next to turkey breast slices and serve.

Nutritional info:
Calories 185, Fat 2g, Carbs 16g, Protein 6g

Breakfast Coconut Yogurt

Prep Time: 20 mins, Cook Time: 8 hours, Servings: 4
Ingredients:
- 2 cans coconut cream
- 1 package yogurt starter
- 1 tbsp. gelatin

Instructions:
1. Pour the coconut cream into the Instant Pot.
2. Lock the lid. Select the Yogurt mode, then bring to a boil at High Pressure.
3. When the coconut cream boils, perform a natural pressure release. Carefully open the lid.
4. Add the yogurt starter and stir to mix well.
5. Lock the lid. Set the timer for 8 hours to ferment at High Pressure.

6. When the timer goes off, perform a normal release for 10 minutes, then release any remaining pressure. Carefully open the lid.
7. Stir in the gelatin and keep stirring until smooth.
8. Pour the yogurt in a jar or a glass and put in the refrigerator for at least 6 hours before serving.

Nutritional info:
Calories 352, Fat 21.9g, Carbs 15.2g, Protein 6.3g

Fruit Yogurt

Prep Time: 30 mins, Cook Time: 8 hours, Servings: 4

Ingredients:
- 3 cups milk
- 1 tbsp. vanilla bean paste
- 1 cup Greek yogurt
- 1 cup puréed fruit of your choice
- ¼ cup sugar

Instructions:
1. Pour the milk into the Instant Pot.
2. Lock the lid. Set to the Adjust mode, then pasteurize the milk for 45 minutes.
3. Once the pasteurizing is complete, perform a natural pressure release. Carefully open the lid.
4. Pour in the vanilla bean paste and Greek yogurt.
5. Lock the lid. Set to Yogurt mode, then set the timer for 8 hours at High pressure.
6. Once the timer goes off, perform a natural pressure release for 10 minutes, then release any remaining pressure. Carefully open the lid.
7. Pour the yogurt in a jar or a glass, then put in the refrigerator to chill for at least 1 hour.
8. Remove the yogurt from the refrigerator and mix in the puréed fruits and sugar before serving.

Nutritional info:
Calories 172, Carbs 24.6g, Protein 3.8g, Fat 2.3g

Super Thick Cashew and Almond Milk Yogurt

Prep Time: 10 mins, Cook Time: 8 hours, Servings: 4

Ingredients:
- ⅓ cup raw cashews
- 2 tbsps. arrowroot powder
- 4 cups almond milk
- ¼ cup yogurt with live culture
- 1 tbsp. maple syrup

Instructions:
1. Combine the cashews, arrowroot powder, and almond milk in a food processor. Process until the mixture in creamy and smooth.
2. Pour the mixture in a saucepan and simmer for 5 minutes over medium heat. Keep stirring.
3. Turn off the heat and allow to cool.
4. Pour the mixture into the Instant Pot, then mix in the yogurt.
5. Lock the lid. Set to the Yogurt mode, then set the timer for 8 hours at High Pressure.
6. When the timer goes off, perform a natural pressure release for 10 minutes, then release any remaining pressure. Carefully open the lid.
7. Pour the yogurt in four mason jars, then put them in the refrigerator to chill for at least an hour.
8. Remove the jars from the refrigerator. Drizzle the yogurt with maple syrup and serve chilled.

Nutritional info:
Calories 285, Carbs 36.5g, Protein 4.6g, Fat 14.7g

Chapter 3 Desserts Recipe

Tapioca Pudding

Prep Time: 12 mins, Cook Time: 15 mins, Servings: 4

Ingredients:
- 1 cup water
- 1¼ cups almond milk
- ¼ cup rinsed and drained seed tapioca pearls
- ½ cup sugar
- ½ tsp. lemon zest

Instructions:
1. Pour the water into the Instant Pot.
2. Add the steamer basket inside the pot.
3. In a heat-proof bowl, mix all the ingredients until the sugar has dissolved.
4. Cover with foil and put the bowl on top of the basket.
5. Lock the lid. Set the Instant Pot to Manual mode, then set the timer for 10 minutes at High Pressure.
6. When the timer goes off, perform a natural release for 5 minutes, then release any remaining pressure. Carefully open the lid.
7. Serve immediately or refrigerate for several hours and serve chilled.

Nutritional info:
Calories 187, Fat 2.5g, Carbs 28.9g, Protein: 2.5g

Chocolate Chia Pudding

Prep Time: 6 mins, Cook Time: 3 hours, Servings: 4

Ingredients:
- 2 tbsps. cacao powder
- ¼ tsp. salt
- ¼ cup chia seeds
- ½ tsp. liquid stevia
- 1 cup freshly squeezed coconut milk

Instructions:
1. Pour all the ingredients in the Instant Pot and stir to mix well.
2. Lock the lid. Set the Instant Pot to Slow Cook mode, then set the timer for 3 hours at High Pressure.
3. When the timer goes off, perform a natural release for 10 minutes, then release any remaining pressure. Carefully open the lid.
4. Serve immediately or refrigerate for several hours and serve chilled.

Nutritional info:
Calories 346, Carbs 21.2g, Protein 8.4g, Fat 27.5g

Coconut Pudding

Prep Time: 6 mins, Cook Time: 3 hours, Servings: 2

Ingredients:
- 1 tsp. erythritol
- ½ cup coconut milk
- A dash of vanilla extract
- ½ tsp. cinnamon powder
- ¼ cup dried coconut flakes
- Salt, to taste
- ½ cup water

Instructions:
1. Put all ingredients in the Instant Pot.
2. Mix until well combined.
3. Lock the lid. Set the Instant Pot to Slow Cook mode, then set the timer for 3 hours at High Pressure.
4. When the timer goes off, perform a natural release for 10 minutes, then release any remaining pressure. Carefully open the lid.
5. Serve immediately or refrigerate for several hours and serve chilled.

Nutritional info:
Calories 188, Carbs 9.3g, Protein 1.7g, Fat 17.3g

Cream and Cinnamon Puddings

Prep Time: 20 mins, Cook Time: 15 mins, Servings: 6

Ingredients:
- 2 cups fresh cream
- 1 tsp. cinnamon powder
- Zest of 1 orange
- 5 tbsps. sugar
- 6 egg yolks
- 2 cups water

Instructions:
1. Set the pot on Sauté mode and heat it up.
2. Add cream, cinnamon and orange zest and sauté for a few minutes and leave aside for 20 minutes.
3. Using a bowl, combine the sugar and egg yolks. Pour the egg yolk mixture in the cream mixture, whisk well, strain the mixture, divide it into ramekins and cover them with tin foil.
4. Clean the pot, add the water, add steamer basket, add ramekins.
5. Lock the lid. Set the Instant Pot to Manual mode, then set the timer for 10 minutes at High Pressure.
6. When the timer goes off, perform a natural release for 5 minutes, then release any remaining pressure. Carefully open the lid.
7. Refrigerate the puddings for several hours, then serve chilled.

Nutritional info:
Calories 211, Fat 8g, Carbs 20g, Protein 10g

Lemon and Maple Syrup Pudding

Prep Time: 12 mins, Cook Time: 5 mins, Servings: 7

Ingredients:
- ½ cup maple syrup
- 3 cups milk
- Lemon zest from 2 grated lemons

- 2 tbsps. gelatin
- Juice of 2 lemons
- 1 cup water

Instructions:
1. In the blender, mix milk with lemon juice, lemon zest, maple syrup and gelatin, pulse really well and divide into ramekins.
2. In the Instant Pot, set in the water, add steamer basket, add ramekins inside.
3. Lock the lid. Set the Instant Pot to Manual mode, then set the timer for 5 minutes on High Pressure.
4. When the timer goes off, perform a natural release. Carefully open the lid.
5. Refrigerate and serve the puddings chilled.

Nutritional info:
Calories 151, Fat 3g, Carbs 18g, Protein 3g

Pineapple Pudding

Prep Time: 12 mins, Cook Time: 5 mins, Servings: 8

Ingredients:
- 1 cup rice
- 1 tbsp. avocado oil
- 14 oz. milk
- Sugar, to taste
- 8 oz. chopped canned pineapple

Instructions:
1. In the Instant Pot, mix oil, milk and rice, stir.
2. Lock the lid. Set the Instant Pot to Manual mode, then set the timer for 3 minutes at Low Pressure.
3. When the timer goes off, perform a natural release. Carefully open the lid.
4. Add sugar and pineapple, stir.
5. Lock the lid, then set the timer for 2 minutes at Low Pressure.
6. When the timer goes off, perform a natural release. Carefully open the lid.
7. Divide into dessert bowls and serve.

Nutritional info:
Calories 154, Fat 4g, Carbs 14g, Protein 4g

Coconut Cream and Cinnamon Pudding

Prep Time: 12 mins, Cook Time: 10 mins, Servings: 6

Ingredients:
- Zest of 1 grated lemon
- 2 cups coconut cream
- 5 tbsps. sugar
- 6 tbsps. flour
- 1 tsp. cinnamon powder
- 1 cup water

Instructions:
1. Set the Instant Pot on Sauté mode and add coconut cream, cinnamon and orange zest, then stir.
2. Simmer for 3 minutes then transfer to a bowl and leave aside.
3. Add flour and sugar, stir well and divide this into ramekins.
4. Add the water to the Instant Pot, add steamer basket, add ramekins.
5. Lock the lid. Set the Instant Pot to Manual mode, then set the timer for 10 minutes at Low Pressure.
6. When the timer goes off, perform a natural release for 5 minutes, then release any remaining pressure. Carefully open the lid.
7. Serve cold.

Nutritional info:
Calories 170, Fat 5g, Carbs 8g, Protein 10g

Coconut and Avocado Pudding

Prep Time: 2 hours, Cook Time: 2 mins, Servings: 3

Ingredients:
- 14 oz. canned coconut milk
- 1 tbsp. cocoa powder
- 1 avocado, pitted, peeled and chopped
- 4 tbsps. sugar
- ½ cup avocado oil

Instructions:
1. In a bowl, mix oil with cocoa powder and half of the sugar, stir well, transfer to a lined container, keep in the fridge for 1 hour and chop into small pieces.
2. In the Instant Pot, mix coconut milk with avocado and the rest of the sugar, blend using an immersion blender.
3. Lock the lid. Set the Instant Pot to Manual mode, then set the timer for 2 minutes at High Pressure.
4. When the timer goes off, perform a natural release. Carefully open the lid.
5. Add chocolate chips, stir, divide pudding into bowls and keep in the fridge until you serve it.

Nutritional info:
Calories 140, Fat 3g, Carbs 3g, Protein 4g

Cocoa and Milk Pudding

Prep Time: 50 mins, Cook Time: 3 mins, Servings: 4

Ingredients:
- 2 cups hot coconut milk
- 4 tbsps. sugar
- ½ tsp. cinnamon powder
- 4 tbsps. cocoa powder
- 2 tbsps. gelatin
- 1 cup plus 2 tbsps. water

Instructions:

1. In a bowl, mix the milk with sugar, cinnamon and cocoa powder and stir well.
2. In a bowl, mix gelatin with 2 tablespoons of water, stir well, add to cocoa mix, stir and divide into ramekins.
3. Add 1 cup of water to the Instant Pot, add the steamer basket and ramekins inside.
4. Lock the lid. Set the Instant Pot to Manual mode, then set the timer for 4 minutes at High Pressure.
5. When the timer goes off, perform a natural release. Carefully open the lid.
6. Serve puddings cold.

Nutritional info:
Calories 120, Fat 2g, Carbs 4g, Protein 3g

Cream Cheese Pudding
Prep Time: 12 mins, Cook Time: 20 mins, Servings: 2 minutes

Ingredients:
- ¼ tsp. vanilla extract
- 1½ tsps. caramel extract
- 2 eggs
- 2 oz. cream cheese
- 1½ tbsps. sugar
- 1 cup water

Instructions:
1. Mix cream cheese with eggs, caramel extract, vanilla extract and sugar in a blender and pulse well to divide into greased ramekins.
2. In the Instant Pot, set in the water, add steamer basket and ramekins inside.
3. Lock the lid. Set the Instant Pot to Manual mode, then set the timer for 20 minutes at High Pressure.
4. When the timer goes off, perform a natural release for 10 minutes, then release any remaining pressure. Carefully open the lid.
5. Serve the puddings cold.

Nutritional info:
Calories 174, Fat 7g, Carbs 2g, Protein 4g

Cinnamon Butter Bites
Prep Time: 6 mins, Cook Time: 5 hours, Servings: 12

Ingredients:
- 5 eggs, beaten
- 1 cup all-purpose flour
- 1 grass-fed unsalted butter stick
- 1 tbsp. cinnamon
- ¼ cup liquid stevia
- ¼ cup olive oil
- Salt, to taste

Instructions:
1. Mix all ingredients in a mixing bowl, except for the olive oil.
2. Grease the Instant Pot with olive oil.
3. Pour in the batter.
4. Lock the lid. Set the Instant Pot to Slow Cook mode, then set the timer for 5 hours at High Pressure.
5. When the timer goes off, perform a natural release for 10 minutes, then release any remaining pressure. Carefully open the lid.
6. Serve immediately.

Nutritional info:
Calories 161, Carbs 1.2g, Protein 4.5g, Fat 15.5g

Keto Almond Bread
Prep Time: 12 mins, Cook Time: 5 hours, Servings: 10

Ingredients:
- 1½ tsps. baking powder
- 1½ cups erythritol
- 3 eggs, beaten
- 2½ cups all-purpose flour
- ¼ cup olive oil
- Salt, to taste

Instructions:
1. Mix all ingredients in a mixing bowl.
2. Once properly mixed, pour the batter in the greased Instant Pot.
3. Lock the lid. Set the Instant Pot to Slow Cook mode, then set the timer for 5 hours at High Pressure.
4. When the timer goes off, perform a natural release for 10 minutes, then release any remaining pressure. Carefully open the lid.
5. Serve immediately.

Nutritional info:
Calories 67, Carbs 0.6g, Protein 0.9g, Fat 6.9g

Apple Bread
Prep Time: 12 mins, Cook Time: 1 hour, Servings: 4

Ingredients:
- 1 tbsp. baking powder
- 3 eggs
- 1½ cups sweetened condensed milk
- 2½ cups white flour
- 3 apples, peeled, cored and chopped
- 1 tbsp. melted coconut oil
- 1 cup water

Instructions:
1. In a bowl, mix the baking powder with eggs and whisk well.
2. Add the milk, flour and apple pieces, whisk well and pour into a loaf pan greased with coconut oil.
3. In the Instant Pot, add the water. Arrange a trivet in the pot, then place the loaf pan on the trivet.

4. Lock the lid. Set the Instant Pot to Slow Cook mode, then set the timer for 1 hour at High Pressure.
5. When the timer goes off, perform a natural release for 10 minutes, then release any remaining pressure. Carefully open the lid.
6. Leave apple bread to cool down, slice and serve.

Nutritional info:
Calories 211, Fat 2g, Carbs 14g, Protein 4g

Bulletproof Hot Choco
Prep Time: 6 mins, Cook Time: 5 mins, Servings: 1
Ingredients:
- 2 tbsps. coconut oil, divided
- ½ cup coconut milk
- ½ cup water
- 2 tbsps. unsweetened cocoa powder
- Dash of cinnamon
- 1 tsp. erythritol

Instructions:
1. Place 1 tablespoon of coconut oil and milk in the Instant Pot and pour in the water.
2. Lock the lid. Set the Instant Pot to Manual mode, then set the timer for 5 minutes at High Pressure.
3. When the timer goes off, perform a quick release.
4. Open the lid and press the Sauté button.
5. Add 1 tablespoon of coconut oil, cocoa powder, cinnamon and erythritol. Stir to combine well and the mixture has a thick consistency.
6. Transfer the mixture on a baking sheet, then put the sheet in the refrigerator for several hours. Serve chilled.

Nutritional info:
Calories 534, Carbs 12.9g, Protein 4.7g, Fat 57.2g

Coconut Boosters
Prep Time: 2 hours, Cook Time: 5 mins, Servings: 5
Ingredients:
- 1 cup coconut oil
- ½ cup chia seeds
- 1 tsp. vanilla extract
- 1 tsp. erythritol
- ¼ cup unsweetened dried coconut flakes

Instructions:
1. Press the Sauté button on the Instant Pot.
2. Heat the coconut oil and add the chia seeds, vanilla extract, erythritol, and coconut flakes and sauté for 5 minutes.
3. Allow to cool and remove the mixture from the pot. Form the mixture into balls and set on a baking sheet.
4. Allow to set in the refrigerator for 2 hours before serving.

Nutritional info:
Calories 480, Carbs 9.4g, Protein 2.9g, Fat 50g

Keto Brownies
Prep Time: 12 mins, Cook Time: 5 hours, Servings: 9
Ingredients:
- 2 tsps. erythritol
- ¼ cup all-purpose flour
- ½ cup coconut oil
- ⅓ cup dark chocolate chips
- 5 beaten eggs
- Salt, to taste
- 2 tbsps. olive oil

Instructions:
1. Place all the ingredients in a mixing bowl, except for the olive oil.
2. Make sure they are well combined.
3. Grese the Instant Pot with olive oil. Pour the mixture into the greased Instant Pot.
4. Lock the lid. Set the Instant Pot to Slow Cook mode, then set the timer for 5 hours at High Pressure.
5. When the timer goes off, perform a natural release for 10 minutes, then release any remaining pressure. Carefully open the lid.
6. Transfer the brownies on a platter and slice to serve.

Nutritional info:
Calories 214, Carbs 3.4g, Protein 5.4g, Fat 20.7g

Chocolate Mug Cake
Prep Time: 12 mins, Cook Time: 10 mins, Servings: 1
Ingredients:
- 1 cup water
- 6 drops liquid stevia
- 1½ tbsps. cocoa powder
- 1 egg, beaten
- ¼ tsp. baking powder
- ¼ cup almond powder
- Salt, to taste

Instructions:
1. Place a steam rack in the Instant Pot and pour in the water.
2. In a bowl, add all the remaining ingredients.
3. Mix until well combined.
4. Pour into a heat-proof mug.
5. Place the mug on the steam rack.
6. Lock the lid. Set the Instant Pot to Steam mode, then set the timer for 10 minutes at High Pressure.
7. When the timer goes off, perform a quick release. Carefully open the lid.

8. Serve the cake immediately.

Nutritional info:
Calories 149, Carbs 5.8g, Protein 6.8g, Fat 10.5g

Chocolate Cake
Prep Time: 12 mins, Cook Time: 6 mins, Servings: 3

Ingredients:
- 4 tbsps. self-raising flour
- 1 egg
- 4 tbsps. sugar
- 4 tbsps. milk
- 1 tbsp. cocoa powder
- 1 tbsp. melted coconut oil
- 1 cup water

Instructions:
1. In a bowl, combine the flour, egg, sugar, milk and cocoa powder, stir well and set the mixture to a cake pan greased with coconut oil.
2. Add the water to the Instant Pot, add steamer basket, add cake inside.
3. Lock the lid. Set the Instant Pot to Manual mode, then set the timer for 6 minutes at High Pressure.
4. When the timer goes off, perform a natural release for 5 minutes, then release any remaining pressure. Carefully open the lid.
5. Serve the cake warm.

Nutritional info:
Calories 261, Fat 5g, Carbs 20g, Protein 4g

Dates and Ricotta Cake
Prep Time: 30 mins, Cook Time: 20 mins, Servings: 6

Ingredients:
- 1 lb. softened ricotta cheese
- 4 eggs
- 4 oz. honey
- 6 oz. dates, soaked and drained
- Juice of 2 oranges
- 1 cup water

Instructions:
1. In a bowl, mix soft ricotta with eggs and whisk well.
2. Add honey, dates, and orange juice, whisk, pour into a cake pan and cover with tin foil.
3. Add the water to the Instant Pot, add steamer basket, add cake pan.
4. Lock the lid. Set the Instant Pot to Manual mode, then set the timer for 20 minutes at High Pressure.
5. When the timer goes off, perform a natural release for 10 minutes, then release any remaining pressure. Carefully open the lid.
6. Allow cake to cool down, slice and serve.

Nutritional info:
Calories 212, Fat 7g, Carbs 20g, Protein 9g

Simple Banana Cake
Prep Time: 12 mins, Cook Time: 1 hour, Servings: 4

Ingredients:
- 1 tsp. nutmeg powder
- 2 cups flour
- 1 tsp. cinnamon powder
- ¼ cup sugar
- 4 bananas, peeled and mashed
- 1 cup water

Instructions:
1. In a bowl, mix sugar with flour, bananas, cinnamon and nutmeg, stir, pour into a greased cake pan and cover with tin foil.
2. In the Instant Pot, set in the water, add steamer basket, add cake pan.
3. Lock the lid. Set the Instant Pot to Manual mode, then set the timer for 1 hour at High Pressure.
4. When the timer goes off, perform a natural release for 10 minutes, then release any remaining pressure. Carefully open the lid.
5. Slice and divide between plates to serve cold.

Nutritional info:
Calories 300, Fat 10g, Carbs 45g, Protein 4g

Simple Pumpkin and Yogurt Cake
Prep Time: 12 mins, Cook Time: 45 mins, Servings: 12

Ingredients:
- ½ cup Greek yogurt
- 1½ cups all-purpose flour
- ¾ cup sugar
- ½ tsp. baking powder
- 8 oz. canned pumpkin purée
- 3 tbsps. butter
- 1½ cups water

Instructions:
1. In a bowl, combine the yogurt, flour, sugar, baking powder and pumpkin purée, whisk well and pour into a cake pan coat with butter.
2. Add the water to the Instant Pot, add trivet inside, add cake pan.
3. Lock the lid. Set the Instant Pot to Manual mode, then set the timer for 45 minutes at High Pressure.
4. When the timer goes off, perform a natural release for 10 minutes, then release any remaining pressure. Carefully open the lid.
5. Leave cake to cool down, slice and serve.

Nutritional info:
Calories 201, Fat 3g, Carbs 15g, protein 4g

Ginger Cookies Cheesecake

Prep Time: 15 mins, Cook Time: 15 mins, Servings: 6

Ingredients:
- 16 oz. soft cream cheese
- ½ cup crumbled ginger cookies
- ½ cup sugar
- 2 eggs
- 2 cups water
- 2 tsps. melted butter

Instructions:
1. Grease a cake pan with the butter, add cookie crumbs and spread them evenly.
2. In a bowl, beat cream cheese with a mixer.
3. Add eggs and sugar and stir very well.
4. Add the water to the Instant Pot, add steamer basket, add cake pan inside.
5. Lock the lid. Set the Instant Pot to Manual mode, then set the timer for 15 minutes at High Pressure.
6. When the timer goes off, perform a natural release for 10 minutes. Carefully open the lid.
7. Keep cheesecake in the fridge for a few hours before serving it.

Nutritional info:
Calories 394, Fat 12g, Carbs 20g, Protein 6g

Coconut Pancake

Prep Time: 12 mins, Cook Time: 40 mins, Servings: 4

Ingredients:
- 1½ cups coconut milk
- 2 cups self-raising flour
- 2 eggs
- 1 tbsp. olive oil
- 2 tbsps. sugar

Instructions:
1. In a bowl, mix eggs with sugar, milk and flour and whisk until you obtain a batter.
2. Grease the Instant Pot with oil, add the batter, spread into the pot.
3. Lock the lid. Set the Instant Pot to Manual mode, then set the timer for 40 minutes at Low Pressure.
4. When the timer goes off, perform a natural release for 10 minutes, then release any remaining pressure. Carefully open the lid.
5. Slice pancake, divide between plates and serve cold.

Nutritional info:
Calories 162, Fat 3, Carbs 7g, Protein 3g

Ketogenic Vanilla Jell-O

Prep Time: 2 hours, Cook Time: 6 mins, Servings: 6

Ingredients:
- 1 cup boiling water
- 2 tbsps. unsweetened gelatin powder
- 1 tsp. vanilla extract
- 1 cup heavy cream
- 3 tbsps. erythritol

Instructions:
1. Place the boiling water in the Instant Pot.
2. Press the Sauté button on the Instant Pot. Bring the water to a simmer.
3. Add the gelatin powder and allow to dissolve.
4. Add the remaining ingredients.
5. Pour the mixture into Jell-O molds.
6. Place in the refrigerator to set for 2 hours.

Nutritional info:
Calories 105, Carbs 5.2g, Protein 3.3g, Fat 7.9g

Nut-Free Keto Fudge

Prep Time: 6 mins, Cook Time: 4 hours, Servings: 15

Ingredients:
- 4 tbsps. erythritol
- ½ tsp. baking powder
- 6 eggs, beaten
- ¼ cup cocoa powder
- 1 butter stick, melted
- ¼ tsp. salt

Instructions:
1. Mix all ingredients in a bowl. Stir to combine well.
2. Pour the mixture into the Instant Pot.
3. Lock the lid. Set the Instant Pot to Slow Cook mode, then set the timer for 4 hours at High Pressure.
4. When the timer goes off, perform a natural release for 10 minutes, then release any remaining pressure. Carefully open the lid.
5. Divide the fudges and serve immediately.

Nutritional info:
Calories 131, Carbs 1.3g, Protein 4.3g, Fat 12.2g

Easy Sweet Soufflé

Prep Time: 12 mins, Cook Time: 30 mins, Servings: 6

Ingredients:
- 8 oz. chocolate, melted
- 1 tsp. vanilla extract
- ¼ cup sugar
- 3 egg yolks, beaten
- ¼ tsp. cream of tartar
- 1 cup water

Instructions:
1. In a bowl, mix melted chocolate with vanilla, sugar, egg yolks and cream of tartar, whisk well and divide into greased ramekins.
2. Set up the Instant Pot. Add the water, add steamer basket, add ramekins.

3. Lock the lid. Set the Instant Pot to Manual mode, then set the timer for 30 minutes at High Pressure.
4. When the timer goes off, perform a natural release for 10 minutes, then release any remaining pressure. Carefully open the lid.
5. Leave soufflé to cool down and serve.

Nutritional info:
Calories 190, Fat 2g, Carbs 7g, Protein 3g

Tasty Blackberry Pie

Prep Time: 12 mins, Cook Time: 35 mins, Servings: 6

Ingredients:
- ⅓ cup tapioca pearls
- 2 tbsps. sugar
- 4 cups blackberries
- 2 tbsps. soft butter
- 1 graham cracker pie crust
- 1½ cups water

Instructions:
1. In a bowl, mix tapioca with sugar, blackberries and butter and whisk until sugar melts and pour the mixture into pie crust.
2. Add the water to the Instant Pot, arrange the steamer basket in the pot, then add the pie.
3. Lock the lid. Set the Instant Pot to Manual mode, then set the timer for 35 minutes at High Pressure.
4. When the timer goes off, perform a natural release for 10 minutes, then release any remaining pressure. Carefully open the lid.
5. Let the pie cool down, slice, divide between plates and serve.

Nutritional info:
Calories 251, Fat 3g, Carbs 7g, Protein 8g

Easy Lemon Pie

Prep Time: 12 mins, Cook Time: 10 mins, Servings: 8

Ingredients:
- 8 oz. cream cheese
- 15 oz. canned lemon pie filling
- ½ cup sugar
- 1 graham cracker pie crust
- 8 oz. heavy whipping cream
- 1½ cups water

Instructions:
1. In a bowl, mix cream cheese with lemon pie filling and sugar, whisk well, spread into pie crust.
2. Put the pie crust in a baking pan, then top with cream.
3. Add the water to the Instant Pot. Arrange the trivet in the pot, then place the baking pan on the trivet.

4. Lock the lid. Set the Instant Pot to Manual mode, then set the timer for 10 minutes at High Pressure.
5. When the timer goes off, perform a natural release for 5 minutes. Carefully open the lid.
6. Leave the pie aside to cool down, slice and serve.

Nutritional info:
Calories 233, Fat 4g, Carbs 6g, Protein 3g

Cherry Pie

Prep Time: 12 mins, Cook Time: 30 mins, Servings: 16

Ingredients:
- 1 yellow cake mix
- ½ cup butter
- 20 oz. canned cherries
- 2 tbsps. blueberries
- ½ cup chopped walnuts
- 1½ cups water

Instructions:
1. In a bowl, combine cake mix with butter, stir until you obtain a crumbly mixture and use a pie pan to press it down.
2. In a separate bowl, mix cherries with blueberries and walnuts, stir and spread over the crust.
3. Add the water to the Instant Pot, add steamer basket, add pie inside.
4. Lock the lid. Set the Instant Pot to Manual mode, then set the timer for 30 minutes at High Pressure.
5. When the timer goes off, perform a natural release for 10 minutes, then release any remaining pressure. Carefully open the lid.
6. Set the pie aside to cool down, slice and divide between plates. Serve.

Nutritional info:
Calories 261, Fat 3g, Carbs 12g, Protein 3g

Peanut Butter Cups

Prep Time: 12 mins, Cook Time: 4 mins, Servings: 12

Ingredients:
- 8 oz. chocolate pudding mix
- 4 cups milk
- 12 oz. heavy whipping cream
- 10 oz. prepared and cubed cake
- 16 oz. mini peanut butter cups
- 1½ cups water

Instructions:
1. In a bowl, mix the chocolate pudding mix with milk and whipped cream and whisk.
2. Divide cake cubes in small ramekins, add chocolate mixture and top with peanut butter cups.

3. Add the water to the Instant Pot, add trivet inside, add ramekins.
4. Lock the lid. Set the Instant Pot to Manual mode, then set the timer for 4 minutes at High Pressure.
5. When the timer goes off, perform a quick release. Carefully open the lid.
6. Leave cups to cool down a bit and serve.

Nutritional info:
Calories 177, Fat 2g, Carbs 6g, Protein 7g

Simple Cake Bars
Prep Time: 12 mins, Cook Time: 20 mins, Servings: 12

Ingredients:
- 1 yellow cake mix
- ½ cup milk
- 1 egg, whisked
- ⅓ cup canola oil
- 1 cup baking chips
- 1½ cups water

Instructions:
1. In a bowl, mix cake mix with milk, eggs, oil and baking chips, stir well, pour into a baking pan and spread well.
2. Add the water to the Instant Pot, add trivet, add baking pan inside.
3. Lock the lid. Set the Instant Pot to Manual mode, then set the timer for 20 minutes at High Pressure.
4. When the timer goes off, perform a natural release for 8 to 10 minutes. Carefully open the lid.
5. Leave cake to cool down, cut into medium bars and serve.

Nutritional info:
Calories 276, Fat 6g, Carbs 8g, Protein 3g

White Chocolate Mousse
Prep Time: 12 mins, Cook Time: 3 mins, Servings: 6

Ingredients:
- 12 oz. chopped white chocolate
- 12 oz. chopped black chocolate
- 2 cups heavy cream
- 1 tbsp. sugar
- 1 tsp. vanilla extract

Instructions:
1. In the Instant Pot, mix white and black chocolate with cream. Stir to combine well.
2. Lock the lid. Set the Instant Pot to Manual mode, then set the timer for 3 minutes at High Pressure.
3. When the timer goes off, perform a quick release. Carefully open the lid.
4. Add the sugar and vanilla, stir until the sugar melts, divide into bowls and serve cold.

Nutritional info:
Calories 176, Fat 4g, Carbs 12g, Protein 3g

Simple Ricotta Mousse
Prep Time: 12 mins, Cook Time: 8 mins, Servings: 4

Ingredients:
- ⅔ cup maple syrup
- ¼ cup chopped pecans
- 1¼ cups ricotta cheese
- ½ cup heavy cream
- ½ cup mascarpone cheese

Instructions:
1. In the Instant Pot, mix the maple syrup with pecans and ricotta, stir.
2. Lock the lid. Set the Instant Pot to Manual mode, then set the timer for 3 minutes at High Pressure.
3. When the timer goes off, perform a quick release. Carefully open the lid.
4. Add the heavy cream and mascarpone, stir to mix well. Divide into bowls, let stand to cool down and serve.

Nutritional info:
Calories 182, Fat 3g, Carbs 10g, Protein 4g

Special Cookies
Prep Time: 12 mins, Cook Time: 10 mins, Servings: 20

Ingredients:
- 17 oz. chocolate cookie mix
- ¼ cup canola oil
- 1 egg
- 1½ cups chopped chocolate covered coffee beans
- 1 cup chopped macadamia nuts
- 1 cup water

Instructions:
1. In a bowl, mix chocolate cookie mix with oil, egg, coffee beans and nuts, whisk well and make the mixture into 20 small cookies.
2. Add the water to the Instant Pot, add steamer basket, add cookies inside.
3. Lock the lid. Set the Instant Pot to Manual mode, then set the timer for 10 minutes at High Pressure.
4. When the timer goes off, perform a quick release. Carefully open the lid.
5. Set the cookies aside to cool down and serve them.

Nutritional info:
Calories 200, Fat 3g, Carbs 6g, Protein 4g

Lemon Cookies
Prep Time: 12 mins, Cook Time: 15 mins, Servings: 30

Ingredients:
- 1 egg, whisked
- 18 oz. lemon cake mix
- 1 cup crisp rice cereal

- ½ cup butter
- 1 tsp. lemon zest
- 1 cup water

Instructions:
1. In a bowl, mix the egg with cake mix, rice cereal, butter and lemon zest, whisk well, shape cookies out of this mix and arrange on a baking sheet.
2. Set up the Instant Pot. Add the water, arrange the trivet in the pot, place the baking sheet on the trivet.
3. Lock the lid. Set the Instant Pot to Manual mode, then set the timer for 15 minutes at Low Pressure.
4. When the timer goes off, perform a natural release for 10 minutes, then release any remaining pressure. Carefully open the lid.
5. Leave cookies to cool down and serve them.

Nutritional info:
Calories 221, Fat 3g, Carbs 6g, Protein 3g

Delicious Berry Cobbler

Prep Time: 12 mins, Cook Time: 35 mins, Servings: 12

Ingredients:
- 1 package cake mix
- 1¼ cups milk
- ½ cup canola oil
- 40 oz. canned raspberry filling
- 1½ cups water
- Vanilla ice cream

Instructions:
1. In a bowl, combine the cake mix with milk and oil and whisk well.
2. In a pie pan, spread the raspberry filling on top of the cake mix mixture.
3. Add the water to the Instant Pot, add steamer basket, add cake pan.
4. Lock the lid. Set the Instant Pot to Manual mode, then set the timer for 35 minutes at High Pressure.
5. When the timer goes off, perform a quick release. Carefully open the lid.
6. Set the cobbler aside to cool down, add vanilla ice cream on top and serve.

Nutritional info:
Calories 227, Fat 4g, Carbs 8g, Protein 3g

Baked Custard

Prep Time: 12 mins, Cook Time: 15 mins, Servings: 6

Ingredients:
- 2 egg yolks
- 3 eggs
- ¾ cup sugar
- 2 cups heated heavy cream
- ¼ cup heated Irish cream liqueur
- 1½ cups water

Instructions:
1. In a bowl, mix egg yolks with eggs and sugar and whisk until sugar melts.
2. Add cream and liqueur, whisk well and divide into ramekins.
3. Add the water to the Instant Pot. Arrange the steamer basket in the pot, put in the custard.
4. Lock the lid. Set the Instant Pot to Manual mode, then set the timer for 15 minutes at High Pressure.
5. When the timer goes off, perform a natural release for 10 minutes, then release any remaining pressure. Carefully open the lid.
6. Leave custards to cool down and serve.

Nutritional info:
Calories 191, Fat 3g, Carbs 9g, Protein 4g

Rhubarb and Strawberries Mix

Prep Time: 12 mins, Cook Time: 6 mins, Servings: 6

Ingredients:
- 3 cups sliced rhubarb
- ⅓ cup sugar
- ¼ cup orange juice
- 2 cups halved strawberries
- 1 cup whipping cream

Instructions:
1. In the Instant Pot, mix the rhubarb with sugar and orange juice, stir.
2. Lock the lid. Set the Instant Pot to Manual mode, then set the timer for 6 minutes at High Pressure.
3. When the timer goes off, perform a quick release. Carefully open the lid.
4. Pulse the mixture with an immersion blender, cool down a bit, add strawberries and whipping cream, divide into bowls and serve cold.

Nutritional info:
Calories 222, Fat 5g, Carbs 10g, Protein 3g

Winter Cherry Mix

Prep Time: 12 mins, Cook Time: 5 mins, Servings: 6

Ingredients:
- Sugar, to taste
- 2 tbsps. water
- 2 tbsps. cornstarch
- 16 oz. cherries, pitted
- 2 tbsps. lemon juice

Instructions:
1. In the Instant Pot, mix cherries with sugar and lemon juice, stir.
2. Lock the lid. Set the Instant Pot to Manual mode, then set the timer for 3 minutes at High Pressure.
3. When the timer goes off, perform a natural release. Carefully open the lid.

4. In a bowl, mix water with cornstarch, stir well, add to the pot, set the pot on Sauté mode, add the rest of the cherries, stir, cook for 2 minutes, divide into bowls and serve cold.

Nutritional info:
Calories 161, Fat 4g, Carbs 8g, Protein 6g

Stuffed Strawberries

Prep Time: 12 mins, Cook Time: 2 mins, Servings: 24
Ingredients:
- 11 oz. soft cream cheese
- ¼ tsp. almond extract
- ½ cup sugar
- 24 strawberries
- 1 cup water
- 1 tbsp. grated chocolate

Instructions:
1. In a bowl, mix the cream cheese with almond extract and sugar, stir until sugar melts and stuff strawberries with this mix.
2. Add the water to the Instant Pot, add steamer basket, arrange strawberries inside.
3. Lock the lid. Set the Instant Pot to Manual mode, then set the timer for 2 minutes at High Pressure.
4. When the timer goes off, perform a quick release. Carefully open the lid.
5. Divide strawberries on dessert plates. Spread with chocolate on top and serve them cold.

Nutritional info:
Calories 200, Fat 4g, Carbs 6g, Protein 3g

Glazed Fruits

Prep Time: 12 mins, Cook Time: 12 mins, Servings: 6
Ingredients:
- ½ cup honey
- ½ cup balsamic vinegar
- ¼ tsp. salt
- 6 peaches, pitted and halved
- Vanilla ice cream

Instructions:
1. Set the Instant Pot on Sauté mode, add honey and balsamic vinegar, sauté for 2 minutes.
2. Add the salt and peaches, stir.
3. Lock the lid. Set the Instant Pot to Manual mode, then set the timer for 10 minutes at High Pressure.
4. When the timer goes off, perform a quick release. Carefully open the lid.
5. Divide into bowls, leave aside to cool down, add vanilla ice cream on top and serve.

Nutritional info:
Calories 169, Fat 2g, Carbs 7g, Protein 3g

Apples and Wine Sauce

Prep Time: 12 mins, Cook Time: 10 mins, Servings: 6
Ingredients:
- 6 apples, peeled and cored
- 1 cup red wine
- 1 tsp. cinnamon powder
- ¼ cup raisins
- ½ cup sugar

Instructions:
1. In the Instant Pot, add apples, wine, cinnamon, raisins and sugar.
2. Lock the lid. Set the Instant Pot to Manual mode, then set the timer for 10 minutes at High Pressure.
3. When the timer goes off, perform a natural release for 5 minutes, then release any remaining pressure. Carefully open the lid.
4. Divide apples on dessert plates and serve warm.

Nutritional info:
Calories 200, Fat 3g, Carbs 34g, Protein 3g

Poached Pears

Prep Time: 12 mins, Cook Time: 10 mins, Servings: 6
Ingredients:
- 1 cup red wine
- ½ cup sugar
- 2 tsps. vanilla extract
- ¼ tsp. cinnamon
- 6 green pears

Instructions:
1. In the Instant Pot, mix the wine with sugar, vanilla, cinnamon and pears.
2. Lock the lid. Set the Instant Pot to Manual mode, then set the timer for 10 minutes at High Pressure.
3. When the timer goes off, perform a quick release. Carefully open the lid.
4. Let the pears cool and transfer them to bowls. Reserve the wine sauce remains in the Instant Pot.
5. Drizzle wine sauce all over and serve.

Nutritional info:
Calories 172, Fat 5g, Carbs 20g, Protein 4g

Flavored Pears

Prep Time: 12 mins, Cook Time: 10 mins, Servings: 4
Ingredients:
- 11 oz. currant jelly
- 26 oz. grape juice
- Juice and zest of 1 lemon
- 4 pears
- 2 rosemary springs

Instructions:
1. Transfer the currant jelly and grape juice to the Instant Pot and add lemon zest and juice before stirring.
2. Add pears and rosemary springs.

3. Lock the lid. Set the Instant Pot to Manual mode, then set the timer for 10 minutes at High Pressure.
4. When the timer goes off, perform a quick release. Carefully open the lid.
5. Arrange pears on plates and serve them cold with the cooking juice on top.

Nutritional info:
Calories 172, Fat 4g, Carbs 17g, Protein 12g

Lemon and Orange Jam
Prep Time: 12 mins, Cook Time: 30 mins, Servings: 8
Ingredients:
- Juice and zest of 2 lemons
- 1 lb. oranges, halved, peeled and grated
- 1 tsp. vanilla extract
- 2 cups water
- ½ cup sugar

Instructions:
1. In the Instant Pot, mix the lemon juice and zest with orange, vanilla extract, water.
2. Lock the lid. Set the Instant Pot to Manual mode, then set the timer for 15 minutes at High Pressure.
3. When the timer goes off, perform a natural release for 10 minutes, then release any remaining pressure. Carefully open the lid.
4. Add the sugar, set the pot on Sauté mode, cook until sugar dissolves, divide into jars and serve cold.

Nutritional info:
Calories 87, Fat 1g, Carbs 13g, Protein 2g

Easy Plum Jam
Prep Time: 20 mins, Cook Time: 8 mins, Servings: 12
Ingredients:
- 1 tsp. vanilla extract
- 3 lbs. plums, pitted and roughly chopped
- 2 tbsps. lemon juice
- 1 cup water
- 1 cup sugar

Instructions:
1. In the Instant Pot, combine plums with sugar and vanilla extract, stir and leave aside for 20 minutes
2. Add lemon juice and water, stir.
3. Lock the lid. Set the Instant Pot to Manual mode, then set the timer for 8 minutes at High Pressure.
4. When the timer goes off, perform a natural release for 5 minutes, then release any remaining pressure. Carefully open the lid.
5. Divide into bowls and serve cold.

Nutritional info:
Calories 191, Fat 3g, Carbs 12g, Protein 4g

Ginger and Peach Marmalade
Prep Time: 12 mins, Cook Time: 5 mins, Servings: 6
Ingredients:
- 3 tbsps. grated ginger
- ½ cup sugar
- 4½ cups peeled and cubed peaches
- 1 box fruit pectin
- ½ tsp. vanilla extract

Instructions:
1. Set the Instant Pot on Sauté mode, add peaches, ginger, vanilla extract and pectin, stir, bring to a boil, add sugar, stir.
2. Lock the lid. Set the Instant Pot to Manual mode, then set the timer for 5 minutes at High Pressure.
3. When the timer goes off, perform a natural release. Carefully open the lid.
4. Divide jam into jars and serve.

Nutritional info:
Calories 87, Fat 4g, Carbs 9g, Protein 2g

Strawberry and Chia Marmalade
Prep Time: 12 mins, Cook Time: 4 mins, Servings: 6
Ingredients:
- 4 tbsps. sugar
- 2 tbsps. chia seeds
- 2 lbs. halved strawberries
- Zest of 1 grated lemon
- ½ tsp. vanilla extract

Instructions:
1. In the Instant Pot, mix sugar with strawberries, vanilla extract, lemon zest and chia seeds, stir.
2. Lock the lid. Set the Instant Pot to Manual mode, then set the timer for 4 minutes at High Pressure.
3. When the timer goes off, perform a natural release. Carefully open the lid.
4. Stir again, divide into cups and serve cold

Nutritional info:
Calories 110, Fat 2g, Carbs 2g, Protein 3g

Peach and Cinnamon Compote
Prep Time: 12 mins, Cook Time: 5 mins, Servings: 6
Ingredients:
- 2 tbsps. grape nuts cereal
- 8 peaches, chopped
- 1 tsp. ground cinnamon
- 6 tbsps. sugar
- 1 tsp. vanilla extract

Instructions:
1. Put peaches in the Instant Pot, add sugar, cinnamon and vanilla extract, stir well.

2. Lock the lid. Set the Instant Pot to Manual mode, then set the timer for 5 minutes at High Pressure.
3. When the timer goes off, perform a natural release. Carefully open the lid.
4. Add grape nuts, stir, divide into bowls and serve cold.

Nutritional info:
Calories 121, Fat 4g, Carbs 17g, Protein 4g

Blueberry and Coconut Sweet Bowls

Prep Time: 12 mins, Cook Time: 6 mins, Servings: 1

Ingredients:
- 1 cup vanilla yogurt
- 1 cup coconut milk
- 1 cup blueberries
- 2 tsps. sugar
- 1 cup unsweetened and flaked coconut
- 1½ cups water

Instructions:
1. Combine milk with coconut, yogurt, blueberries and sugar in a heat-proof dish and stir well then cover with tin foil.
2. Add the water to the Instant Pot, add trivet, add dish.
3. Lock the lid. Set the Instant Pot to Manual mode, then set the timer for 6 minutes at High Pressure.
4. When the timer goes off, perform a natural release for 5 minutes, then release any remaining pressure. Carefully open the lid.
5. Divide into bowls and serve cold.

Nutritional info:
Calories 142, Fat 2g, Carbs 4g, Protein 6g

Cocoa and Walnuts Sweet Cream

Prep Time: 12 mins, Cook Time: 2 mins, Servings: 6

Ingredients:
- 2 oz. avocado oil
- 4 tbsps. cocoa powder
- 1 tsp. vanilla extract
- 1 cup chopped walnuts
- 4 tbsps. sugar

Instructions:
1. Put the avocado oil with cocoa, vanilla, walnuts and sugar in a large bowl.
2. Blend with an immersion blender.
3. Pour the mixture in the Instant Pot.
4. Lock the lid. Set the Instant Pot to Manual mode, then set the timer for 2 minutes at High Pressure.
5. When the timer goes off, perform a natural release. Carefully open the lid.
6. Divide into small bowls and keep in the fridge until you serve it.

Nutritional info:
Calories 120, Fat 4g, Carbs 9g, Protein 2g

Chapter 4 Fish and Seafood Recipe

Lemony Salmon

Prep Time: 6 mins, Cook Time: 3 mins, Servings: 2

Ingredients:
- ¼ cup lemon juice
- Cooking spray
- Salt and pepper, to taste
- 2 salmon fillets, frozen
- 1 cup water

Instructions:
1. Add the water and steamer rack to the Instant Pot. Spray the rack with cooking spray.
2. Place the salmon fillets in the steamer rack. Season with salt and pepper.
3. Drizzle with lemon juice.
4. Lock the lid. Select the Steam mode and cook for 3 minutes at Low Pressure.
5. Once cooking is complete, do a quick pressure release. Carefully open the lid.
6. Remove from the pot and serve on a plate.

Nutritional info:
Calories 172, Fat 6.7g, Carbs 2.6g, Protein 24.6g

Savory Salmon with Dill

Prep Time: 12 mins, Cook Time: 10 mins, Servings: 2

Ingredients:
- 2 tbsps. dill
- ⅓ cup olive oil
- 1 tbsp. fresh lemon juice
- 2 tbsps. butter
- 2 salmon fillets
- 1 cup water
- Salt and pepper, to taste

Instructions:
1. Add the water and steam rack to the Instant Pot.
2. Put the remaining ingredients in a heatproof dish and stir well.
3. Place the dish on the steam rack.
4. Lock the lid. Select the Steam mode and cook for 10 minutes at Low Pressure.
5. Once cooking is complete, do a quick pressure release. Carefully open the lid.
6. Divide the salmon fillets among two serving plates and serve.

Nutritional info:
Calories 914, Carbs 4.1g, Protein 63.2g, Fat, 80.9g

Salmon with Basil Pesto

Prep Time: 6 mins, Cook Time: 6 mins, Servings: 6

Ingredients:
- 3 garlic cloves, minced
- 1½ lbs. salmon fillets
- 2 cups basil leaves
- 2 tbsps. freshly squeezed lemon juice
- ½ cup olive oil
- Salt and pepper, to taste

Instructions:
1. Make the pesto sauce: Put the basil leaves, olive oil, lemon juice, and garlic in a food processor, and pulse until smooth.
2. Season with salt and pepper.
3. Place the salmon fillets in the Instant Pot and add the pesto sauce.
4. Lock the lid. Select the Manual mode and set the cooking time for 6 minutes at Low Pressure.
5. Once cooking is complete, do a quick pressure release. Carefully open the lid.
6. Divide the salmon among six plates and serve.

Nutritional info:
Calories 336, Carbs 0.9g, Protein 20.5g, Fat 28.1g

Salmon Tandoori

Prep Time: 2 hours, Cook Time: 6 mins, Servings: 4

Ingredients:
- 1½ lbs. salmon fillets
- 3 tbsps. coconut oil
- Salt and pepper, to taste
- 1 tbsp. tandoori spice mix

Instructions:
1. In a bowl, add all the ingredients. Toss well until the fish is fully coated. Allow the fish to marinate for 2 hours in the fridge.
2. Place the marinated salmon in the Instant Pot.
3. Lock the lid. Select the Manual mode and cook for 6 minutes at Low Pressure. Flip the fish halfway through the cooking time.
4. Once cooking is complete, do a quick pressure release. Carefully open the lid.
5. Remove from the pot and serve on a plate.

Nutritional info:
Calories 354, Carbs 1.4g, Protein 22.4g, Fat 35.2g

Simple Steamed Salmon Fillets

Prep Time: 6 mins, Cook time: 10 mins, Servings: 3

Ingredients:
- 1 cup water
- 2 tbsps. freshly squeezed lemon juice
- 2 tbsps. soy sauce
- 10 oz. salmon fillets

- Salt and pepper, to taste
- 1 tsp. toasted sesame seeds

Instructions:
1. Set a trivet in the Instant Pot and pour the water into the pot.
2. Using a heat-proof dish, combine all ingredients.
3. Place the heat-proof dish on the trivet.
4. Lock the lid. Select the Manual mode and cook for 10 minutes at Low Pressure.
5. Once cooking is complete, do a quick pressure release. Carefully open the lid.
6. Garnish with toasted sesame seeds and serve.

Nutritional info:
Calories 160, Fat 7.4g, Carbs 2.6g, Protein 20.1g

Instant Pot Curried Salmon

Prep Time: 6 mins, Cook Time: 8 mins, Servings: 4

Ingredients:
- 2 cups coconut milk
- 2 tbsps. coconut oil
- 1 onion, chopped
- 1 lb. raw salmon, diced
- 1½ tbsps. minced garlic

Instructions:
1. Press the Sauté button on the Instant Pot and heat the oil.
2. Sauté the garlic and onions until fragrant, about 2 minutes.
3. Add the diced salmon and stir for 1 minute.
4. Pour in the coconut milk.
5. Lock the lid. Select the Manual mode and cook for 4 minutes at Low Pressure.
6. Once cooking is complete, do a quick pressure release. Carefully open the lid.
7. Let the salmon cool for 5 minutes before serving.

Nutritional info:
Calories 524, Carbs 10.3g, Protein 26.7g, Fat 43.6g

Lemon Pepper Salmon

Prep Time: 15 mins, Cook time: 5 mins, Servings: 4

Ingredients:
- 1 cup water
- 1 tsp. ground dill
- 1 tsp. ground tarragon
- 1 tsp. ground basil
- 4 salmon fillets
- 2 tbsps. olive oil
- Salt, to taste
- 4 lemon slices
- 1 carrot, sliced
- 1 zucchini, sliced

Instructions:
1. In the Instant Pot, add the water, dill, tarragon, and basil.
2. Place the steamer basket inside.
3. Set in the salmon. Drizzle with a tablespoon of olive oil, pepper and salt. Top with lemon slices.
4. Lock the lid. Select the Steam mode and cook for 3 minutes at Low Pressure.
5. Once cooking is complete, do a quick pressure release. Carefully open the lid.
6. Transfer the fish to a plate and discard the lemon slices.
7. Drizzle the Instant Pot with remaining olive oil. Add the carrot and zucchini to the Instant Pot. Set to Sauté mode, then sauté for 2 minutes or until the vegetables are tender.
8. Serve the salmon with the veggies.
9. Garnish with fresh lemon wedges.

Nutritional info:
Calories 252, Fat 11.1g, Carbs 3.8g, Protein 35.3g

Chili-Garlic Salmon

Prep Time: 3 mins, Cook time: 7 mins, Servings: 4

Ingredients:
- ¼ cup soy sauce
- 4 salmon fillets
- 5 tbsps. organic sugar-free chili sauce
- Salt and pepper, to taste
- ¼ cup water
- 3 tbsps. chopped green onions

Instructions:
1. In the Instant Pot, add all the ingredients except for the green onions.
2. Lock the lid. Select the Manual mode and cook for 7 minutes at Low Pressure.
3. Once cooking is complete, do a quick pressure release. Carefully open the lid.
4. Garnish with green onions and serve.

Nutritional info:
Calories 409, Fat 14.4g, Carbs 0.9g, Protein 65.4g

Steamed Herbed Red Snapper

Prep Time: 3 mins, Cook time: 12 mins, Servings: 4

Ingredients:
- 1 cup water
- 4 red snapper fillets
- 1½ tsps. chopped fresh herbs
- ¼ tsp. paprika
- 3 tbsps. freshly squeezed lemon juice
- Salt and pepper, to taste

Instructions:
1. Set a trivet in the Instant Pot and pour the water into the pot.

2. Mix all ingredients in a heat-proof dish that will fit in the Instant Pot. Combine to coat the fish with all ingredients.
3. Place the heat-proof dish on the trivet.
4. Lock the lid. Select the Manual mode and cook for 12 minutes at Low Pressure.
5. Once cooking is complete, do a quick pressure release. Carefully open the lid.
6. Serve warm.

Nutritional info:
Calories 226, Fat 3g, Carbs 2.1g, Protein 45.6g

Steamed Greek Snapper
Prep Time: 6 mins, Cook time: 10 mins, Servings: 4
Ingredients:
- 1 cup water
- 12 snapper fillets
- 3 tbsps. olive oil
- 2 tbsps. Greek yogurt
- 1 garlic clove, minced
- Salt and pepper, to taste

Instructions:
1. Set a trivet in the Instant Pot and pour the water into the pot.
2. In a mixing bowl, combine the olive oil, garlic, and Greek yogurt. Sprinkle salt and pepper for seasoning.
3. Apply Greek yogurt mixture to the fish fillets. Place the fillets on the trivet.
4. Lock the lid. Select the Steam mode and cook for 10 minutes at Low Pressure.
5. Once cooking is complete, do a quick pressure release. Carefully open the lid.
6. Serve warm.

Nutritional info:
Calories 250, Fat 6.3g, Carbs 0.4g, Protein 44.8g

Cod with Orange Sauce
Prep Time: 12 mins, Cook Time: 7 mins, Servings: 4
Ingredients:
- 1 cup white wine
- 1 small ginger piece, grated
- 4 spring onions, finely chopped
- Juice of 1 orange
- 4 boneless cod fillets

Instructions:
1. In the Instant Pot, combine the wine with ginger, spring onions and orange juice, stir, add steamer basket, add cod fillets inside.
2. Lock the lid. Select the Manual mode, then set the timer for 7 minutes at Low Pressure.
3. Once the timer goes off, do a quick pressure release. Carefully open the lid.
4. Divide fish on plates, drizzle orange juice all over and serve.

Nutritional info:
Calories 172, Fat 5g, Carbs 7g, Protein 7g

Steamed Lemon Mustard Salmon
Prep Time: 8 mins, Cook time: 10 mins, Servings: 4
Ingredients:
- 1 cup water
- 1 garlic clove, minced
- 4 skinless salmon fillets
- 2 tbsps. Dijon mustard
- Salt and pepper, to taste
- 2 tbsps. freshly squeezed lemon juice

Instructions:
1. Set a trivet in the Instant Pot and pour the water into the pot.
2. In a bowl, mix lemon juice, mustard, and garlic. Sprinkle salt and pepper for seasoning.
3. Top the salmon fillets with the mustard mixture. Place the fish fillets on the trivet.
4. Lock the lid. Select the Steam mode and cook for 10 minutes at Low Pressure.
5. Once cooking is complete, do a quick pressure release. Carefully open the lid.
6. Serve warm.

Nutritional info:
Calories 402, Fat 14.8g, Carbs 2.2g, Protein 65.3g

Quick Salmon
Prep Time: 12 mins, Cook Time: 5 mins, Servings: 4
Ingredients:
- 1 cup water
- ¼ cup lemon juice
- 1 tbsp. butter
- ¼ tsp. salt
- 4 boneless salmon fillets
- 1 bunch dill, chopped

Instructions:
1. Place the water in the Instant Pot, add lemon juice, add steamer basket, add salmon inside, season with some salt, sprinkle dill and drizzle melted butter.
2. Lock the lid. Select the Manual mode and cook for 5 minutes at Low Pressure.
3. Once cooking is complete, do a quick pressure release. Carefully open the lid.
4. Divide salmon between plates and serve with a side dish.

Nutritional info:
Calories 412, Fat 12g, Carbs 27g, Protein 12g

Lemon Pepper Salmon

Prep Time: 12 mins, Cook Time: 10 mins, Servings: 4

Ingredients:
- 1 cup water
- 1 lemon, sliced
- 1 red bell pepper, julienned
- 1 lb. boneless salmon fillets
- Black pepper, to taste
- 3 tsps. melted butter

Instructions:
1. Set the water in the Instant Pot, add steamer basket, add salmon fillets, season them with black pepper, drizzle melted butter all over, divide bell pepper and lemon slices on top.
2. Lock the lid. Select the Manual mode and cook for 7 minutes at Low Pressure.
3. Once cooking is complete, do a quick pressure release. Carefully open the lid.
4. Divide salmon and bell pepper on plates, top with lemon slices and serve.

Nutritional info:
Calories 281, Fat 8g, Carbs 16g, Protein 6g

Flounder with Dill and Capers

Prep Time: 3 mins, Cook time: 10 mins, Servings: 4

Ingredients:
- 1 cup water
- 1 tbsp. chopped fresh dill
- 4 lemon wedges
- 2 tbsps. chopped capers
- 4 flounder fillets
- Salt and pepper, to taste

Instructions:
1. In the Instant Pot, set in a steamer basket and pour the water into the pot.
2. Sprinkle salt and pepper to the flounder fillets. Sprinkle with dill and chopped capers on top. Add lemon wedges on top for garnish.
3. Place the fillets on the trivet.
4. Lock the lid. Select the Steam mode and cook for 10 minutes at Low Pressure.
5. Once cooking is complete, do a quick pressure release. Carefully open the lid.
6. Serve warm.

Nutritional info:
Calories 135, Fat 3.6g, Carbs 5.5g, Protein 21.3g

Italian Salmon with Lemon Juice

Prep Time: 6 mins, Cook Time: 8 mins, Servings: 5

Ingredients:
- 1½ lbs. salmon fillets
- 2 tbsps. butter
- 3 tbsps. olive oil
- 1 tbsp. Italian herb seasoning mix
- 3 tbsps. freshly squeezed lemon juice
- Salt and pepper, to taste
- ⅓ cup water

Instructions:
1. Place all ingredients in the Instant Pot and stir well.
2. Lock the lid. Select the Manual mode and set the cooking time for 8 minutes at Low Pressure. Flip the fish halfway through the cooking time.
3. Once cooking is complete, do a quick pressure release. Carefully open the lid.
4. Divide the salmon among plates and serve.

Nutritional info:
Calories 328, Carbs 1.6g, Protein 22.5g, Fat 28.3g

Thai Fish Curry

Prep Time: 6 mins, Cook Time: 6 mins, Servings: 6

Ingredients:
- 1½ lbs. salmon fillets
- 2 cups fresh coconut milk
- ¼ cup chopped cilantro
- ⅓ cup olive oil
- 2 tbsps. curry powder
- Salt and pepper, to taste

Instructions:
1. In the Instant Pot, add all the ingredients. Give a good stir.
2. Lock the lid. Select the Manual mode and set the cooking time for 6 minutes at Low Pressure.
3. Once cooking is complete, do a quick pressure release. Carefully open the lid. Set warm.

Nutritional info:
Calories 470, Carbs 5.6g, Protein 25.5g, Fat 39.8g

Coconut Curry Cod

Prep Time: 4 mins, Cook time: 8 mins, Servings: 4

Ingredients:
- 2 tsps. curry powder
- 2 tsps. grated ginger
- 4 cod fillets
- 1½ cups coconut milk
- 1 cilantro sprig, chopped
- Salt and pepper, to taste

Instructions:
1. In the Instant Pot, set in all ingredients excluding the cilantro. Give a good stir to combine.
2. Lock the lid. Select the Steam mode and cook for 8 minutes at Low Pressure.
3. Once cooking is complete, do a quick pressure release. Carefully open the lid.

4. Garnish with chopped cilantro before serving.

Nutritional info:
Calories 291, Fat 22.1g, Carbs 5.7g, Protein 19.7g

Cod Meal

Prep Time: 6 mins, Cook Time: 5 mins, Servings: 2

Ingredients:
- 1 cup water
- 2 tbsps. ghee
- 1 fresh large fillet cod
- Salt and pepper, to taste

Instructions:
1. Cut fillet into 3 pieces. Coat with the ghee and season with salt and pepper.
2. Pour the water into the pot and place steamer basket/trivet inside.
3. Arrange the fish pieces over the basket/trivet.
4. Lock the lid. Select the Manual mode and cook for 5 minutes at Low Pressure.
5. Once cooking is complete, do a quick pressure release. Carefully open the lid.
6. Serve warm.

Nutritional info:
Calories 197, Carbs 2g, Fat 12g, Protein 19.5g

Tuna Salad with Lettuce

Prep Time: 12 mins, Cook Time: 10 mins, Servings: 4

Ingredients:
- 2 tbsps. olive oil
- ½ lb. tuna, sliced
- 1 tbsp. fresh lemon juice
- 2 eggs
- 1 head lettuce
- Salt and pepper, to taste
- 1 cup water

Instructions:
1. In a large bowl, season the tuna with lemon juice, salt and pepper. Transfer the tuna to a baking dish.
2. Add the eggs, water, and steamer rack to the Instant Pot. Place the baking dish on the steamer rack.
3. Lock the lid. Select the Steam mode and set the cooking time for 10 minutes at Low Pressure.
4. Once cooking is complete, do a quick pressure release. Carefully open the lid.
5. Allow the eggs and tuna to cool. Peel the eggs and slice into wedges. Set aside.
6. Assemble the salad by shredding the lettuce in a salad bowl. Toss in the cooled tuna and eggs.
7. Sprinkle with olive oil, then serve.

Nutritional info:
Calories 260, Carbs 6.3g, Protein 17.2g, Fat 19.9g

Steamed Chili-Rubbed Tilapia

Prep Time: 6 mins, Cook time: 10 mins, Servings: 4

Ingredients:
- 1 cup water
- ½ tsp. garlic powder
- 1 lb. skinless tilapia fillet
- 2 tbsps. extra virgin olive oil
- Salt and pepper, to taste
- 2 tbsps. chili powder

Instructions:
1. Set a trivet in the Instant Pot and pour the water into the pot.
2. Season the tilapia fillets with salt, pepper, chili powder, and garlic powder. Drizzle with olive oil on top.
3. Place in the steamer basket.
4. Lock the lid. Select the Steam mode and cook for 10 minutes at Low Pressure.
5. Once cooking is complete, do a quick pressure release. Carefully open the lid.
6. Serve warm.

Nutritional info:
Calories 211, Fat 10g, Carbs 2g, Protein 26g

Halibut and Broccoli Casserole

Prep Time: 6 mins, Cook Time: 6 mins, Servings: 6

Ingredients:
- 1 tbsp. Dijon mustard
- 1¼ cup full-fat coconut cream
- 2 tbsps. olive oil
- 1½ lbs. halibut fillets, sliced
- 1 cup broccoli florets
- Salt and pepper, to taste

Instructions:
1. In the Instant Pot, add all the ingredients. Give a good stir.
2. Lock the lid. Select the Manual mode and set the cooking time for 8 minutes at Low Pressure.
3. Once cooking is complete, do a quick pressure release. Carefully open the lid.
4. Let the fish and broccoli cool for 5 minutes before serving.

Nutritional info:
Calories 419, Carbs 3.7g, Protein 18.4g, Fat 37.7g

Halibut with Pesto

Prep Time: 12 mins, Cook time: 8 mins, Servings: 4

Ingredients:
- 2 tbsps. extra virgin olive oil
- 1 tbsp. freshly squeezed lemon juice
- 1 cup basil leaves
- 2 garlic cloves, minced
- 4 halibut fillets

- ¼ cup water
- Salt and pepper, to taste

Instructions:
1. Place the halibut fish in the Instant Pot. Set aside.
2. In a food processor, pulse the basil, olive oil, garlic, and lemon juice until coarse. Sprinkle salt and pepper for seasoning.
3. Spread pesto sauce over halibut fillets. Add the water.
4. Lock the lid. Select the Manual mode and cook for 8 minutes at Low Pressure.
5. Once cooking is complete, do a quick pressure release. Carefully open the lid.
6. Serve warm.

Nutritional info:
Calories 401, Fat 8.4g, Carbs 0.8g, Protein 75.8g

Halibut En Papillote
Prep Time: 12 mins, Cook time: 10 mins, Servings: 4

Ingredients:
- 1 cup water
- 1 cup chopped tomatoes
- 1 thinly sliced shallot
- 4 halibut fillets
- ½ tbsp. grated ginger
- Salt and pepper, to taste

Instructions:
1. In the Instant Pot, set in a steamer basket and pour the water into the pot.
2. Get a large parchment paper and place the fillet in the middle. Season with salt and pepper. Add the grated ginger, tomatoes, and shallots. Fold the parchment paper to create a pouch and crimp the edges.
3. Place the parchment paper containing the fish.
4. Lock the lid. Select the Steam mode and cook for 10 minutes at Low Pressure.
5. Once cooking is complete, do a quick pressure release. Carefully open the lid.
6. Serve warm.

Nutritional info:
Calories 383, Fat 5.5g, Carbs 2.7g, Protein 76.3g

Red Curry Halibut
Prep Time: 3 mins, Cook time: 10 mins, Servings: 4

Ingredients:
- 2 tbsps. chopped cilantro
- 4 skinless halibut fillets
- 3 green curry leaves
- 1 cup chopped tomatoes
- 1 tbsp. freshly squeezed lime juice
- Salt and pepper, to taste

Instructions:
1. Place all ingredients in the Instant Pot. Give a good stir to combine the ingredients.
2. Lock the lid. Select the Manual mode and cook for 10 minutes at Low Pressure.
3. Do a quick pressure release.

Nutritional info:
Calories 379, Fat 5.5g, Carbs 1.8g, Protein 76.1g

Thyme-Sesame Crusted Halibut
Prep Time: 6 mins, Cook time: 8 mins, Servings: 4

Ingredients:
- 1 cup water
- 1 tsp. dried thyme leaves
- 1 tbsp. toasted sesame seeds
- 8 oz. halibut, sliced
- Salt and pepper, to taste
- 1 tbsp. freshly squeezed lemon juice

Instructions:
1. Set a trivet in the Instant Pot and pour the water into the pot.
2. Season the halibut with lemon juice, salt, and pepper. Sprinkle with dried thyme leaves and sesame seeds.
3. Place the fish on the trivet.
4. Lock the lid. Select the Steam mode and cook for 8 minutes at Low Pressure.
5. Once cooking is complete, do a quick pressure release. Carefully open the lid.
6. Serve warm.

Nutritional info:
Calories 246, Fat 17.7g, Carbs 4.2g, Protein 17.5g

Steamed Cod with Ginger and Scallions
Prep Time: 6 mins, Cook time: 12 mins, Servings: 4

Ingredients:
- 1 cup water
- 6 scallions, chopped
- 2 tbsps. grated ginger
- 4 skinless cod fillets
- Salt and pepper, to taste
- 2 tbsps. soy sauce
- 3 tbsps. freshly squeezed lemon juice

Instructions:
1. Set a trivet in the Instant Pot and pour the water into the pot.
2. Place the cod fillets in a heat-proof dish that will fit inside the Instant Pot.
3. Pour the lemon juice, soy sauce, and ginger over the fish. Add salt and pepper for seasoning. Sprinkle with scallions last.
4. Place the dish on the trivet.

5. Lock the lid. Select the Steam mode and cook for 12 minutes at Low Pressure.
6. Once cooking is complete, do a quick pressure release. Carefully open the lid.
7. Serve warm.

Nutritional info:
Calories 94, Fat 0.6g, Carbs 3.2g, Protein 18.3g

Cheddar Creamy Haddock
Prep Time: 12 mins, Cook Time: 10 mins, Servings: 3
Ingredients:
- 12 oz. haddock fillets
- 3 tbsps. diced onions
- 1 tbsp. butter
- Salt and pepper, to taste
- ½ cup heavy cream
- 5 oz. grated Cheddar cheese

Instructions:
1. Heat the Instant Pot on Sauté mode.
2. Add the butter and onions to the Instant Pot. Sauté until onions become translucent and softened, 3 minutes.
3. Season the fish with salt and pepper. Add the fish in the pot and cook for 2 minutes per side.
4. Add the cream and the cheese.
5. Lock the lid. Select the Manual mode and cook for 5 minutes at Low Pressure.
6. Once cooking is complete, do a quick pressure release. Carefully open the lid.
7. Serve immediately.

Nutritional info:
Calories 192, Carbs 5g, Fat 17.5g, Protein 18g

Yogurt Fish Patties
Prep Time: 12 mins, Cook Time: 8 mins, Servings: 4
Ingredients:
- 1 tsp. baking soda
- ¼ cup fat-free Greek yogurt
- 1 small onion, chopped
- 1 lb. fish fillets, chopped
- 3 tbsps. all-purpose flour
- 1 tbsp. olive oil

Instructions:
1. In a mixing bowl, thoroughly mix fish, yogurt, onion, flour, and baking soda.
2. Make 6 balls and press them to make patties.
3. Press Sauté. Grease the pot with olive oil.
4. Set in the patties and cook each side for 4 minutes. Serve warm.

Nutritional info:
Calories 288, Fat 14g, Carbs 30g, Protein 11g

Steamed Tilapia
Prep Time: 12 mins, Cook Time: 10 mins, Servings: 4
Ingredients:
- ¼ cup chopped scallions
- 1 tbsp. Chinese black bean paste
- 1 tbsp. peanut oil
- 1 lb. tilapia fillets
- 3 tbsps. soy sauce
- 1 cup water

Instructions:
1. In a bowl, mix soy sauce with black bean paste and whisk well.
2. Add fish, toss and leave aside for 10 minutes.
3. Set the Instant Pot on Sauté mode, add oil, heat it up.
4. Add scallions, sauté for 2 minutes and transfer to a bowl.
5. Clean the pot, add the water, add steamer basket, add fish fillets inside, sprinkle scallions on top.
6. Lock the lid. Select the Manual mode and cook for 3 minutes at Low Pressure.
7. Once cooking is complete, do a quick pressure release. Carefully open the lid.
8. Divide everything between plates and serve with a side salad.

Nutritional info:
Calories 152, Fat 2g, Carbs 12g, Protein 5g

Lemon White Fish
Prep Time: 3 mins, Cook Time: 6 mins, Servings: 4
Ingredients:
- 1 tbsp. olive oil
- 4 white fish fillets
- Juice and zest of 1 lemon
- 1 cup fish stock
- 1 thumb-size ginger, grated
- Salt and pepper, to taste
- 4 spring onions, chopped

Instructions:
1. Except for the spring onions, add all the ingredients to the Instant Pot.
2. Lock the lid. Select the Manual mode and set the cooking time for 6 minutes at Low Pressure.
3. Once cooking is complete, do a quick pressure release for 5 minutes. Carefully open the lid.
4. Sprinkle the spring onions on top for garnish before serving.

Nutritional info:
Calories 234, Fat 15g, Carbs 3g, Protein 22g

Wild Alaskan Cod with Cherry Tomatoes
Prep Time: 3 mins, Cook Time: 8 mins, Servings: 4

Ingredients:
- 1 large wild Alaskan Cod fillet
- 1 cup chopped cherry tomatoes
- Salt and pepper, to taste
- 2 tbsps. butter

Instructions:
1. Except for the butter, add all the ingredients to the Instant Pot.
2. Lock the lid. Select the Manual mode and set the cooking time for 8 minutes at Low Pressure.
3. Once cooking is complete, do a quick pressure release. Carefully open the lid.
4. Stir in the butter and serve warm.

Nutritional info:
Calories 134, Fat 6g, Carbs 1g, Protein 17g

Buttery Smoked Cod with Scallions
Prep Time: 5 mins, Cook Time: 3 mins, Servings: 2

Ingredients
- ½ lemon, sliced
- ½ cup water
- 2 fillets smoked cod
- 2 tbsps. chopped scallions
- 2 tsps. butter
- Sea salt and ground black pepper, to taste

Instructions:
1. Add the lemon and water to the Instant Pot, then put the steamer rack on top.
2. Transfer the smoked cod fillets to the steamer basket.
3. Add the scallions, butter, salt, and black pepper to the fillets.
4. Lock the lid. Select the Steam mode and cook for 3 minutes at Low Pressure.
5. Once cooking is complete, do a quick pressure release. Carefully open the lid.
6. Remove from the pot to a plate and serve warm.

Nutritional info:
Calories 236, Fat 5g, Carbs 4g, Protein 41g

Easy Mahi Mahi with Enchilada Sauce
Prep Time: 3 mins, Cook Time: 8 mins, Servings: 2

Ingredients:
- 2 fresh Mahi Mahi fillets
- ¼ cup commercial enchilada sauce
- Salt and pepper, to taste
- 2 tbsps. butter

Instructions:
1. Add all the ingredients, except for the butter, to the Instant Pot.
2. Lock the lid. Select the Manual mode and cook for 8 minutes at Low Pressure.
3. Once cooking is complete, do a quick pressure release. Carefully open the lid.
4. Stir in the butter and serve on plates.

Nutritional info:
Calories 369, Fat 27g, Carbs 11g, Protein 20g

Sardine and Plum Tomato Curry
Prep Time: 10 mins, Cook Time: 8 hours, Servings: 4

Ingredients:
- 1 tbsp. olive oil
- 1 lb. fresh sardines, cubed
- ½ cup tomato puree
- ½ large onion, sliced
- 2 plum tomatoes, chopped finely
- 1 garlic clove, minced
- Salt and ground black pepper, to taste

Instructions:
1. Select the Sauté button on your Instant Pot and heat the olive oil. Add the sardines and sauté for 2 minutes.
2. Add the remaining ingredients to the Instant Pot and stir to combine.
3. Lock the lid. Select the Slow Cook mode and cook for 8 hours at Low Pressure.
4. Once cooking is complete, do a quick pressure release. Carefully open the lid.
5. Give the cooked curry a good stir and serve.

Nutritional info:
Calories 297, Fat 16g, Carbs 6g, Protein 29g

Lemon-Butter Grouper
Prep Time: 10 mins, Cook Time: 4 mins, Servings: 4

Ingredients:
- 1½ cups water
- 4 grouper fillets
- 2 tbsps. fresh lemon juice
- 4 tbsps. butter
- 2 garlic cloves, smashed
- ½ tsp. dried basil
- ½ tsp. sweet paprika
- Sea salt and ground black pepper, to taste

Instructions:
1. Add the water and steamer basket to the Instant Pot.
2. Arrange the grouper fillets in the steamer basket and add the remaining ingredients.
3. Lock the lid. Select the Manual mode and set the cooking time for 4 minutes at Low Pressure.

4. Once cooking is complete, do a quick pressure release. Carefully open the lid.
5. Transfer the fillets to four plates and serve warm.

Nutritional info:
Calories 345, Fat 15g, Carbs 1g, Protein 50g

Sole Fillets with Pickle-Mayo Sauce
Prep Time: 5 mins, Cook Time: 3 mins, Servings: 4
Ingredients:
- 1½ lbs. sole fillets
- 1 tsp. paprika
- Sea salt and ground black pepper, to taste
- 1½ cups water
- 1 tbsp. pickle juice
- ½ cup mayonnaise
- 2 cloves garlic, smashed

Instructions:
1. On a clean work surface, season the sole fillets with paprika, salt, and pepper.
2. Add the water and steamer basket to the Instant Pot. Arrange the sole fillets in the steamer basket.
3. Lock the lid. Select the Manual mode and set the cooking time for 3 minutes at Low Pressure.
4. Meanwhile, make the sauce: Mix together the pickle juice, mayo, and smashed garlic in a bowl until well combined.
5. Once cooking is complete, do a quick pressure release. Carefully open the lid.
6. Remove the fillets from the pot and serve alongside the sauce.

Nutritional info:
Calories 210, Fat 11g, Carbs 4g, Protein 24g

Orange-Butter Sea Bass
Prep Time: 3 mins, Cook Time: 18 mins, Servings: 2
Ingredients:
- 1 tbsp. safflower oil
- ½ lb. sea bass
- Sea salt, to taste
- ¼ tsp. white pepper
- 1 cup water
- ½ orange, juiced
- 1 tbsp. tamari sauce
- 1 clove garlic, minced
- 1 tbsp. melted butter
- ½ tsp. dried dill weed

Instructions:
1. Press the Sauté button on the Instant Pot and heat the safflower oil.
2. Sear the sea bass for about 2 minutes on each side. Sprinkle the salt and white pepper to season.
3. Add the water and steamer rack to the Instant Pot, then transfer the sea bass to the steamer rack.
4. Lock the lid. Select the Steam mode and cook for 10 minutes at Low Pressure.
5. Once cooking is complete, do a quick pressure release. Carefully open the lid. Transfer the sea bass to a plate and set aside.
6. Add the orange juice, tamari sauce, garlic, butter, and dill weed to the cooking liquid in the Instant Pot, and stir to incorporate.
7. Press the Sauté button again and allow to simmer, or until the sauce is thickened.
8. Spoon the sauce over the sea bass and serve warm.

Nutritional info:
Calories 226, Fat 14g, Carbs 3g, Protein 22g

Sea Bass Risotto with Leeks
Prep Time: 5 mins, Cook Time: 7 mins, Servings: 4
Ingredients
- 2 tbsps. melted butter
- ½ cup leeks, sliced
- 2 cups basmati rice
- 1½ lbs. sea bass fillets, diced
- 2 garlic cloves, minced
- 2 cups vegetable broth
- 1 cup water
- ½ tsp. ground black pepper
- Salt, to taste

Instructions:
1. Press the Sauté button on your Instant Pot and heat the butter.
2. Add the sliced leeks and cook for 2 to 3 minutes, stirring constantly.
3. Add the remaining ingredients to the pot and mix well.
4. Lock the lid. Select the Manual mode and set the cooking time for 4 minutes at Low Pressure.
5. Once cooking is complete, do a quick pressure release. Carefully open the lid.
6. Transfer the fish to a large plate and serve.

Nutritional info:
Calories 22, Fat 32g, Carbs 41g, Protein 1g

Creamy Shrimp Pasta
Prep Time: 12 mins, Cook Time: 15 mins, Servings: 8
Ingredients:
- 12 oz. linguine pasta
- 1 small red onion, diced

- 12 oz. shrimps, peeled and deveined
- 1 tsp. butter
- ⅓ cup heavy cream
- 4 cups water

Instructions:
1. Add the water and pasta to the Instant Pot.
2. Lock the lid. Select the Manual mode and cook for 7 minutes at High Pressure.
3. Once cooking is complete, do a quick pressure release. Carefully open the lid.
4. Drain the pasta and transfer to a container.
5. Press the Sauté button and heat the butter until melted.
6. Add the shrimp and cook for 2 minutes per side. Add the mix with the pasta.
7. Add the onions; cook for 5 minutes until turn translucent and softened.
8. Stir in the cream; cook for 2 to 3 minutes more.
9. Serve the pasta with the cream sauce.

Nutritional info:
Calories 134, Fat 5g, Carbs 9g, Protein 14g

Shrimp Green Curry

Prep Time: 12 mins, Cook Time: 60 mins, Servings: 5
Ingredients:
- 7 oz. cleaned and deveined shrimps
- 4 tbsps. Thai basil leaves
- 2 tbsps. green curry paste
- 1 tsp. coconut oil
- 4 tsps. fish sauce

Instructions:
1. Press the Sauté bottom on the Instant Pot.
2. Add and heat the oil in the Instant Pot.
3. Add the chili and shrimp; sauté for 2 minutes.
4. Add the fish sauce, paste, and basil; cook for 1 minute more.
5. Lock the lid. Select the Manual mode and cook for 60 minutes at Low Pressure.
6. Once cooking is complete, do a quick pressure release. Carefully open the lid.
7. Transfer the cooked recipe on serving plates.
8. Serve the recipe warm.

Nutritional info:
Calories 62, Fat 1g, Carbs 2g, Protein 13g

Chili-Lime Shrimps

Prep Time: 2 mins, Cook time: 4 mins, Servings: 4
Ingredients:
- 1½ lbs. peeled and deveined raw shrimp
- 1 tbsp. chili powder
- Salt and pepper, to taste
- 1 tbsp. coconut oil
- 2 tbsps. freshly squeezed lime juice

Instructions:
1. Place all ingredients in the Instant Pot.
2. Lock the lid. Select the Manual mode and cook for 4 minutes at Low Pressure.
3. Once cooking is complete, do a quick pressure release. Carefully open the lid.
4. Serve warm.

Nutritional info:
Calories 206, Fat 5.7g, Carbs 1.7g, Protein 34.9g

Szechuan Shrimps

Prep Time: 3 mins, Cook time: 6 mins, Servings: 4
Ingredients:
- 1 tbsp. julienned ginger
- 1½ lbs. unpeeled raw shrimps
- 3 tbsps. soy sauce
- 2 tbsps. crushed red pepper
- Salt and pepper, to taste
- 3 tbsps. chopped green scallions

Instructions:
1. Place all ingredients in the Instant Pot.
2. Lock the lid. Select the Manual mode and cook for 6 minutes at Low Pressure.
3. Once cooking is complete, do a quick pressure release. Carefully open the lid.
4. Garnish with green scallions and serve.

Nutritional info:
Calories 179, Fat 2.3g, Carbs 2.1g, Protein 35.1g

Simple Shrimp

Prep Time: 12 mins, Cook Time: 3 mins, Servings: 3
Ingredients:
- ½ cup chicken stock
- ½ cup white wine
- 2 tbsps. olive oil
- 1 tbsp. minced garlic
- 2 lbs. shrimp, deveined and peeled

Instructions:
1. Set the Instant Pot on Sauté mode, add oil, heat it up.
2. Add garlic and sauté for 30 seconds.
3. Add shrimp, wine and stock, stir.
4. Lock the lid. Select the Manual mode and cook for 3 minutes at Low Pressure.
5. Once cooking is complete, do a quick pressure release. Carefully open the lid.

6. Divide into bowls and serve.
Nutritional info:
Calories 190, Fat 2g, Carbs 7g, Protein 2g

Shrimps with Mango Basil
Prep Time: 6 mins, Cook time: 5 mins, Servings: 4
Ingredients:
- 1 cup chopped basil
- Salt and pepper, to taste
- 1 large ripe mange, peeled and cubed
- ¼ cup turmeric powder
- 1 lb. raw shrimp, peeled and deveined

Instructions:
1. Place the mango cubes in a blender or food processor and pulse until smooth.
2. Place the shrimps, basil, and turmeric powder in the Instant Pot. Sprinkle with salt and pepper. Mix until well combined.
3. Pour over the mango purée and mix.
4. Lock the lid. Select the Manual mode and cook for 5 minutes at Low Pressure.
5. Once cooking is complete, do a quick pressure release. Carefully open the lid.
6. Serve warm.

Nutritional info:
Calories 158, Fat 5g, Carbs 6g, Protein 16g

Simple Curried Shrimps
Prep Time: 6 mins, Cook time: 4 mins, Servings: 4
Ingredients:
- 1 tbsp. extra virgin olive oil
- 1½ lb. raw shrimp, peeled and deveined
- 2 oranges, peeled and separated
- 1 tbsp. curry powder
- Salt and pepper, to taste

Instructions:
1. Press the Sauté button on the Instant Pot and heat the olive oil.
2. Toast the curry powder for a minute until fragrant. Add the shrimps and oranges. Sprinkle salt and pepper for seasoning.
3. Lock the lid. Select the Manual mode and cook for 4 minutes at Low Pressure.
4. Once cooking is complete, do a quick pressure release. Carefully open the lid.
5. Serve warm.

Nutritional info:
Calories 188, Fat 5g, Carbs 1g, Protein 24g

Shrimp Scampi
Prep Time: 3 mins, Cook time: 6 mins, Servings: 4
Ingredients:
- 2 tsps. chopped garlic
- Salt and pepper, to taste
- 1 lb. peeled and deveined raw shrimp
- ¼ cup low-sodium organic chicken broth
- 2 tsps. chopped parsley

Instructions:
1. Place all ingredients in the Instant Pot.
2. Lock the lid. Select the Manual mode and cook for 6 minutes at Low Pressure.
3. Once cooking is complete, do a quick pressure release. Carefully open the lid.
4. Serve warm.

Nutritional info:
Calories 123, Fat 1.7g, Carbs 1.8g, Protein 23.7g

Instant Pot Lemon Shrimps
Prep Time: 8 mins, Cook time: 6 mins, Servings: 4
Ingredients:
- ¼ cup soy sauce
- ½ cup freshly squeezed lemon juice
- Fresh rosemary sprig
- 1½ lbs. peeled and deveined shrimps
- Salt and pepper, to taste
- Parsley, for garnish

Instructions:
1. Combine all the ingredients in the Instant Pot.
2. Lock the lid. Select the Steam mode and cook for 6 minutes at Low Pressure.
3. Once cooking is complete, do a quick pressure release. Carefully open the lid.
4. Press the Sauté button and continue cooking until the sauce has reduced to half.
5. Garnish with parsley and serve.

Nutritional info:
Calories 184, Fat 2.4g, Carbs 3.7g, Protein 35.8g

Shrimp Boil
Prep Time: 12 mins, Cook Time: 35 mins, Servings: 4
Ingredients:
- 2 lbs. peeled and deveined shrimp
- 1 tsp. crushed red pepper
- 1 chopped sweet onion
- 1 cup chicken stock
- 1 tbsp. old bay seasoning

Instructions:
1. In the Instant Pot, mix stock with old bay seasoning, red pepper, onion and shrimp, stir.
2. Lock the lid. Select the Manual mode and cook for 30 minutes on Low Pressure.

3. Once cooking is complete, do a quick pressure release. Carefully open the lid.
4. Divide into bowls and serve.

Nutritional info:
Calories 162, Fat 2g, Carbs 6g, Protein 4g

Fast Shrimp Scampi

Prep Time: 12 mins, Cook Time: 4 mins, Servings: 4

Ingredients:
- 1 cup chicken stock
- 2 tbsps. butter
- Juice of 1 lemon
- 1 lb. shrimp, peeled and deveined
- 2 shallots, chopped

Instructions:
1. Set the Instant Pot on Sauté mode, add butter, heat it up.
2. Add shallots and sauté for 1 to 2 minutes.
3. Add shrimp, lemon juice and stock, stir.
4. Lock the lid. Select the Manual mode and cook for 2 minutes at Low Pressure.
5. Once cooking is complete, do a quick pressure release. Carefully open the lid.
6. Divide into bowls and serve.

Nutritional info:
Calories 182, Fat 5g, Carbs 12g, Protein 5g

Spicy Prawns

Prep Time: 6 mins, Cook Time: 5 mins, Servings: 4

Ingredients:
- 1 tbsp. red pepper flakes
- 3 garlic cloves, minced
- 3 tbsps. olive oil
- ½ lb. prawns
- 1 tbsp. butter, melted
- ¼ cup water
- Salt and pepper, to taste

Instructions:
1. Place all the ingredients in the Instant Pot.
2. Lock the lid. Select the Manual mode and cook for 5 minutes at Low Pressure.
3. Once cooking is complete, do a quick pressure release. Carefully open the lid.
4. Transfer to a large plate and serve.

Nutritional info:
Calories 174, Carbs 2.4g, Protein 8.9g, Fat 15.2g

Delicious and Simple Octopus

Prep Time: 12 mins, Cook Time: 15 mins, Servings: 4

Ingredients:
- ¼ tsp. sweet paprika
- 2 lbs. octopus, rinsed
- Salt and black pepper, to taste
- ¼ tsp. chili powder

Instructions:
1. Season octopus with salt and pepper, add to the Instant Pot.
2. Add enough water to cover, then add chili powder and paprika, stir a bit.
3. Lock the lid. Select the Manual mode and cook for 15 minutes at Low Pressure.
4. Once cooking is complete, do a quick pressure release. Carefully open the lid.
5. Cut the octopus and serve.

Nutritional info:
Calories 112, Fat 6g, Carbs 7g, Protein 3g

Teriyaki Scallops

Prep Time: 12 mins, Cook Time: 4 mins, Servings: 3

Ingredients:
- ½ cup soy sauce
- 1 lb. sea scallops
- 1 tbsp. chopped chives
- 1 tbsp. avocado oil
- 3 tbsps. maple syrup

Instructions:
1. Set the Instant Pot on Sauté mode, add oil, heat it up.
2. Add scallops and sear for 1 minute on each side.
3. Add maple syrup, soy sauce and chives, toss to combine well.
4. Lock the lid. Select the Manual mode and cook for 2 minutes at Low Pressure.
5. Once cooking is complete, do a quick pressure release. Carefully open the lid.
6. Divide between plates and serve scallops immediately.

Nutritional info:
Calories 300, Fat 5g, Carbs 8g, Protein 12g

Sea Scallops with Champagne Butter Sauce

Prep Time: 5 mins, Cook Time: 5 mins, Servings: 3

Ingredients:
- 1 lb. sea scallops
- 1 cup vegetable broth
- ½ cup Champagne
- 2 tbsps. butter
- ½ tsp. cayenne pepper
- ¼ tsp. pink peppercorns, crushed
- Sea salt and ground black pepper, to taste

Instructions:
1. Place all the ingredients in the Instant Pot.

2. Lock the lid. Select the Manual mode and set the cooking time for 3 minutes at Low Pressure.
3. Once cooking is complete, do a quick pressure release. Carefully open the lid.
4. Using a slotted spoon, transfer the scallops to a platter and set aside.
5. Set your Instant Pot to Sauté and cook the sauce, stirring constantly, or until the sauce is reduced by half.
6. Pour the sauce over the scallops and serve immediately.

Nutritional info:
Calories 166, Fat 8g, Carbs 5g, Protein 17g

Buttery Steamed Lobster Tails
Prep Time: 5 mins, Cook Time: 3 mins, Servings: 6
Ingredients
- 1 cup water
- ¾ lb. lobster tails, halved
- ½ tsp. red pepper flakes
- Sea salt and freshly ground black pepper, to taste
- ¼ stick butter, at room temperature

Instructions:
1. Add the water and steamer basket to your Instant Pot. Arrange the lobster tails (shell-side down) in the steamer basket.
2. Lock the lid. Select the Steam mode and set the cooking time for 3 minutes at Low Pressure.
3. Once cooking is complete, do a quick pressure release. Carefully open the lid.
4. Remove the lobster tails from the pot to a large plate.
5. Sprinkle with the red pepper flakes, salt, and black pepper. Spread the butter over the lobster tails and serve.

Nutritional info:
Calories 234, Fat 13g, Carbs 0g, Protein 28g

Instant Pot Boiled Mussels
Prep Time: 8 mins, Cook time: 10 mins, Servings: 4
Ingredients:
- 1 tbsp. extra virgin olive oil
- 1 onion, sliced
- 2 lbs. black mussels, cleaned and soaked
- 2 tbsps. lemon juice
- Salt and pepper, to taste

Instructions:
1. Press the Sauté button on the Instant Pot and heat the oil.
2. Sauté the onion for 1 minute until fragrant.
3. Add the mussels and drizzle with lemon juice, sprinkle with salt and pepper. Stir until well combined.
4. Lock the lid. Select the Manual mode and cook for 10 minutes at Low Pressure.
5. Once cooking is complete, do a quick pressure release. Carefully open the lid.
6. Serve warm.

Nutritional info:
Calories 144, Fat 4.4g, Carbs 6.7g, Protein 19.2g

Mussels with White Wine and Shallots
Prep Time: 10 mins, Cook Time: 5 mins, Servings: 4
Ingredients:
- 2 lbs. fresh mussels
- 1 tbsp. extra-virgin olive oil
- 3 large shallots, minced
- 2 garlic cloves, minced
- ½ cup water
- ½ cup dry white wine
- Juice of ½ lemon

Instructions:
1. Scrub and de-beard the mussels. Place the mussels in a large bowl of cold water, discarding any shells that are not tightly closed. Set aside.
2. Set your Instant Pot to Sauté and heat the olive oil.
3. Add the shallots and garlic and cook for 2 minutes, stirring occasionally.
4. Put the mussels, water, and wine in the Instant Pot and give a good stir.
5. Lock the lid. Select the Manual mode and set the cooking time for 3 minutes at Low Pressure.
6. Once cooking is complete, do a quick pressure release. Carefully open the lid.
7. Remove the mussels from the pot to a platter. Pour the wine broth over the mussels and serve drizzled with the lemon juice.

Nutritional info:
Calories 260, Fat 2g, Carbs 10g, Protein 27g

Tomato Mussels
Prep Time: 8 mins, Cook Time: 8 mins, Servings: 2
Ingredients:
- 1 cup diced tomatoes
- 2 lbs. cleaned and rinsed fresh mussels
- ½ cup white wine
- Salt, to taste
- ½ tbsp. ground black pepper
- ½ tbsp. dried parsley

Instructions:

1. Put the tomatoes into the Instant Pot with the juices and add the wine, salt, pepper, and parsley.
2. Place the mussels in a steamer basket and lower it to the liquid.
3. Lock the lid. Select the Manual mode and cook for 3 minutes at Low Pressure.
4. Once cooking is complete, do a quick pressure release. Carefully open the lid.
5. Serve warm.

Nutritional info:
Calories 274, Carbs 5.5g, Fat 8.5g, Protein 32g

Lemon Blue Crab with Herbs
Prep Time: 10 mins, Cook Time: 3 mins, Servings: 2
Ingredients
- 1 lb. frozen blue crab
- ½ cup water
- ⅓ cup dry white wine
- 1 sprig thyme
- 1 sprig rosemary
- Sea salt and ground black pepper, to taste
- ½ lemon, cut into wedges

Instructions:
1. Place all the ingredients except for the lemon wedges in the Instant Pot.
2. Lock the lid. Select the Manual mode and cook for 3 minutes at High Pressure.
3. Once cooking is complete, do a quick pressure release. Carefully open the lid.
4. Garnish with the lemon wedges on top and serve.

Nutritional info:
Calories 362, Fat 17g, Carbs 4g, Protein 2g

Steamed Crab Legs
Prep Time: 6 mins, Cook Time: 12 mins, Servings: 4
Ingredients:
- ¼ cup butter
- 1½ cups water
- 1 tbsp. lemon juice
- 2 lbs. king crab legs

Instructions:
1. Add the water and steamer basket to the Instant Pot. Arrange the crab legs in the basket.
2. Lock the lid. Select the Steam mode and cook for 12 minutes at Low Pressure.
3. Once cooking is complete, do a quick pressure release. Carefully open the lid.
4. Drizzle with lemon juice and let the butter melt on top of the legs before serving.

Nutritional info:
Calories 199, Fat 16g, Carbs 1.2g, Protein: 12.7g

Boiled Garlic Clams
Prep Time: 7 mins, Cook time: 6 mins, Servings: 4
Ingredients:
- 1 cup water
- ½ cup freshly chopped parsley
- 2 tbsps. olive oil
- 6 garlic cloves
- 50 scrubbed small clams
- Salt and pepper, to taste

Instructions:
1. Press the Sauté button on the Instant Pot and heat the olive oil. Sauté the garlic until fragrant and slightly browned.
2. Add the clams, water, and parsley. Sprinkle salt and pepper for seasoning.
3. Lock the lid. Select the Manual mode and cook for 6 minutes at Low Pressure.
4. Once cooking is complete, do a quick pressure release. Carefully open the lid.
5. Serve warm.

Nutritional info:
Calories 89, Fat 2.8g, Carbs 0.9g, Protein 11.3g

Chapter 5 Poultry Recipe

Salsa Chicken

Prep Time: 6 mins, Cook Time: 6 mins, Servings: 2

Ingredients:
- ½ cup chicken broth
- ½ cup salsa
- 1 lb. chicken breast fillets
- 1 oz. taco seasoning mix

Instructions:
1. On a clean work surface, rub the chicken with taco seasoning.
2. Add the chicken to the Instant Pot. Pour in the chicken broth and salsa.
3. Lock the lid. Select the Manual mode and cook for 6 minutes at High Pressure.
4. Once cooking is complete, do a natural pressure release for 5 minutes, then release any remaining pressure. Carefully open the lid.
5. Remove from the pot to a large plate. Shred the chicken and pour salsa on top before serving.

Nutritional info:
Calories 300, Fat 4.8g, Carbs 13.9g, Protein 45.9g

Garlicky Greek Chicken

Prep Time: 6 mins, Cook Time: 12 mins, Servings: 4

Ingredients:
- 1 tsp. dried oregano
- 1 sliced lemon
- 3 tbsps. extra-virgin olive oil
- 1 lb. chicken thighs
- 3 minced garlic cloves
- ½ cup of water
- Salt and pepper, to taste

Instructions:
1. Put all the ingredients in the Instant Pot and stir well.
2. Lock the lid. Select the Poultry mode and cook for 12 minutes at High Pressure.
3. Once cooking is complete, do a natural pressure release for 6 minutes, then release any remaining pressure. Carefully open the lid.
4. Let the chicken thighs cool for 5 minutes, then serve.

Nutritional info:
Calories 298, Carbs 2.1g, Protein 16.5g, Fat 23.3g

Cajun Chicken with Zucchini

Prep Time: 12 mins, Cook Time: 10 to 15 mins, Servings: 6

Ingredients:
- 1 lb. skinless chicken drumsticks
- ½ tsp. Cajun seasoning
- 1 small red bell pepper, sliced
- 1½ tsps. olive oil, divided
- 1 small zucchini, sliced

Instructions:
1. Select the Sauté mode and heat 1 teaspoon olive oil.
2. Add the chicken drumsticks and bell pepper and cook for 4 to 5 minutes per side until evenly browned. Transfer to a plate and set aside.
3. Heat the remaining olive oil in the Instant Pot.
4. Add the zucchini slices and Cajun and sauté for 2 to 3 minutes until crisp.
5. Remove from the pot and serve the chicken with zucchini on a plate.

Nutritional info:
Calories 154, Fat 8g, Carbs 3g, Protein 17g

Chicken Peas Rice

Prep Time: 12 mins, Cook Time: 15 mins, Servings: 4

Ingredients:
- 1 chopped small onion
- 4 oz. chicken breasts
- 2 cups white rice
- 1 tsp. olive oil
- ½ cup green peas
- 2 cups water

Instructions:
1. Press the Sauté button on the Instant Pot and heat the oil.
2. Add the chicken breasts and sauté for 6 to 7 minutes until lightly browned. Set aside on a plate.
3. Add the onions and cook 3 to 4 minutes until translucent.
4. Add the rice, 2 cups water, and green peas, and mix well.
5. Lock the lid. Select the Manual mode and cook for 4 minutes at Low Pressure.
6. Once cooking is complete, do a natural pressure release for 5 minutes, then release any remaining pressure. Carefully open the lid.
7. Serve the rice with the chicken breasts.

Nutritional info:
Calories 274, Fat 5g, Carbs 23g, Protein 34g

Chicken Coconut Curry

Prep Time: 12 mins, Cook Time: 30 mins, Servings: 6

Ingredients:
- 2 large onions, chopped
- 7 oz. chicken breasts
- 2 tbsps. green curry paste
- 1 tbsp. olive oil
- ¾ cup reduced-fat coconut milk
- 2 cups water

Instructions:

1. Press the Sauté button on the Instant Pot and heat the oil.
2. Add the chicken breast and sauté for 2 to 3 minutes per side.
3. Stir in the onions and cook for 3 to 4 minutes more until softened.
4. Pour in the milk and 2 cups water. Add the curry paste and stir well.
5. Lock the lid. Select the Manual mode and cook for 10 minutes at High Pressure.
6. Once cooking is complete, do a natural pressure release for 5 minutes, then release any remaining pressure. Carefully open the lid.
7. Remove from the pot and serve on plates.

Nutritional info:
Calories 232, Fat 7g, Carbs 1g, Protein 34g

Classic Lemon Chicken
Prep Time: 12 mins, Cook Time: 10 mins, Servings: 4
Ingredients:
- 4 chicken thighs
- 2 tbsps. fresh lemon juice
- 1 medium red onion, sliced
- 2 tsps. olive oil
- 1 garlic clove, crushed
- 1 cup water

Instructions:
1. Line a baking pan with parchment paper and set aside.
2. In a mixing bowl, thoroughly mix olive oil and lemon juice. Add the chicken thighs and toss to coat. Transfer to the baking pan and top with the garlic and onion slices.
3. Pour 1 cup water into the Instant Pot. Arrange a steamer basket inside it and place the baking pan on the basket.
4. Lock the lid. Select the Manual mode and cook for 6 minutes at High Pressure.
5. Once cooking is complete, do a quick pressure release. Carefully open the lid.
6. Allow to cool for 5 minutes before serving.

Nutritional info:
Calories 173, Fat 11g, Carbs 4g, Protein 14g

Garlicky Chicken
Prep Time: 12 mins, Cook time: 15 mins, Servings: 4
Ingredients:
- 5 garlic cloves, minced
- 4 chicken breasts, halved
- 3 tbsps. coconut oil
- Salt and pepper, to taste
- 1 cup water

Instructions:

1. Press the Sauté button on the Instant Pot and heat the coconut oil. Sauté the garlic for 3 minutes until fragrant, then stir in the chicken breasts. Sprinkle pepper and salt for seasoning. Pour in the water.
2. Lock the lid. Select the Manual mode and cook for 6 minutes at High Pressure.
3. Once cooking is complete, do a natural pressure release for 5 minutes, then release any remaining pressure. Carefully open the lid.
4. Serve the chicken while warm.

Nutritional info:
Calories 591, Fat 37.5g, Carbs 1.1g, Protein 60.8g

Instant Pot Pesto Chicken
Prep Time: 12 mins, Cook time: 10 mins, Servings: 4
Ingredients:
- 4 chicken breasts
- ¼ cup extra virgin olive oil
- Salt and pepper, to taste
- 2 cups basil leaves
- 5 sun-dried tomatoes
- 1 cup water, if needed

Instructions:
1. Put the basil leaves, olive oil, and tomatoes in the food processor until smooth. Season with salt and people to taste. Add a cup of water if needed.
2. Place the chicken in the Instant Pot. Pour the sauce over the chicken.
3. Lock the lid. Select the Manual mode and cook for 8 minutes at High Pressure.
4. Once cooking is complete, do a natural pressure release for 6 minutes, then release any remaining pressure. Carefully open the lid.
5. Transfer to a large plate and serve warm.

Nutritional info:
Calories 556, Fat 32.7g, Carbs 1.1g, Protein 60.8g

Instant Pot Emergency Broccoli Chicken
Prep Time: 12 mins, Cook time: 10 mins, Servings: 4
Ingredients:
- ¼ cup soy sauce
- 1 head broccoli florets
- 1 tbsp. coconut oil
- 1½ lbs. chicken breasts, sliced
- 3 minced garlic cloves

Instructions:
1. Press the Sauté button on the Instant Pot and heat the oil. Sauté the garlic until fragrant, about 2 minutes.

2. Stir in the chicken breasts, broccoli florets, and soy sauce.
3. Lock the lid. Select the Manual mode and cook for 8 minutes at High Pressure.
4. Once cooking is complete, do a natural pressure release for 5 minutes, then release any remaining pressure. Carefully open the lid.
5. Serve the chicken with broccoli florets on a plate.

Nutritional info:
Calories 263, Fat 15.4g, Carbs 1.8g, Protein 28.6g

Chicken Cacciatore

Prep Time: 6 mins, Cook time: 12 mins, Servings: 6

Ingredients:
- 1 bay leaf
- ½ cup pitted black olives
- 6 chicken drumsticks
- 2 cups tomato purée
- Salt and pepper, to taste
- 1 cup water

Instructions:
1. Place all ingredients in the Instant Pot and stir well.
2. Lock the lid. Select the Manual mode and cook for 12 minutes at High Pressure.
3. Once cooking is complete, do a natural pressure release for 8 minutes, then release any remaining pressure. Carefully open the lid.
4. Allow to cool for a few minutes before serving.

Nutritional info:
Calories 256, Fat 13.2g, Carbs 9.5g, Protein 25.3g

Whole Roasted Chicken with Lemon and Rosemary

Prep Time: 2 hours, Cook time: 25 to 30 mins, Servings: 12

Ingredients:
- 1 (5 to 6 pounds) whole chicken
- 6 minced garlic cloves
- Salt and pepper, to taste
- 1 sliced lemon
- 1 rosemary sprig
- 1 cup water or chicken broth

Instructions:
1. On a clean work surface, rub the chicken with the minced garlic cloves, salt and pepper.
2. Stuff the lemon slices and rosemary sprig into the cavity of the chicken. Place the chicken into the Instant Pot and add the water or chicken broth.
3. Lock the lid. Select the Poultry mode and cook for 25 to 30 minutes at High Pressure.
4. Once cooking is complete, do a natural pressure release for 15 minutes, then release any remaining pressure. Carefully open the lid.
5. Remove the chicken from the pot and shred it. Serve immediately.

Nutritional info:
Calories 248, Fat 17.2g, Carbs 0.9g, Protein 21.3g

Easy Asian Chicken

Prep Time: 12 mins, Cook time: 10 mins, Servings: 5

Ingredients:
- 3 minced garlic cloves
- ¼ cup chicken broth
- 1½ lbs. boneless chicken breasts
- 3 tbsps. soy sauce
- 1 tbsp. ginger slices

Instructions:
1. Place all ingredients in the Instant Pot. Give a good stir.
2. Lock the lid. Press the Poultry button and set the cooking time for 10 minutes.
3. Once cooking is complete, do a natural pressure release for 8 minutes, then release any remaining pressure. Carefully open the lid.
4. Garnish with chopped scallions and drizzle with sesame oil, if desired.

Nutritional info:
Calories 169, Fat 3.6g, Carbs 1.2g, Protein 30.9g

Cashew Chicken with Sautéed Vegetables

Prep Time: 15 mins, Cook time: 20 mins, Servings: 6

Ingredients:
- 2 lbs. chicken breasts, thinly sliced
- Salt and pepper, to taste
- 1 head broccoli florets
- 1 cup cubed red bell pepper
- 1 cup cashew nuts, toasted
- ½ cup water

Instructions:
1. Press the Sauté button on the Instant Pot. Stir in the chicken breasts and cook for 5 minutes. Sprinkle pepper and salt for seasoning. Pour in ½ cup water for additional moisture.
2. Press the Poultry button and set the cooking time for 10 minutes at High Pressure.
3. Once cooking is complete, do a quick pressure release. Carefully open the lid. Transfer the chicken breast to a large plate.

4. Press the Sauté button and stir in the broccoli and red bell pepper. Allow to simmer for 5 minutes. Scatter the toasted cashew nuts over the vegetables.
5. Serve the chicken breasts with sautéed vegetables on the side.

Nutritional info:
Calories 261, Fat 16.2g, Carbs 5.3g, Protein 23.7g

Chicken Curry
Prep Time: 6 mins, Cook time: 15 mins, Servings: 6
Ingredients:
- 2 cups freshly squeezed coconut milk
- 1½ lbs. boneless chicken breasts
- 2 cups chopped tomatoes
- 2 tbsps. curry powder
- 1 ginger
- Salt and pepper, to taste

Instructions:
1. Press the Sauté button on the Instant Pot. Add the chicken breasts and cook for 3 minutes until lightly golden. Season with salt and pepper.
2. Stir in the curry powder and continue cooking for 2 minutes more. Add the remaining ingredients and whisk well.
3. Press the Poultry button and set the cooking time for 10 minutes.
4. Once cooking is complete, do a natural pressure release for 6 minutes, then release any remaining pressure. Carefully open the lid.
5. Cool for 5 minutes and serve on plates.

Nutritional info:
Calories 336, Fat 22.4g, Carbs 7.4g, Protein 28.1g

Smoky Paprika Chicken
Prep Time: 5mins, Cook time: 15 mins, Servings: 6
Ingredients:
- 2 tbsps. smoked paprika
- 2 lbs. chicken breasts
- Salt and pepper, to taste
- 1 tbsp. olive oil
- ½ cup water

Instructions:
1. Press the Sauté button on the Instant Pot and heat the olive oil.
2. Stir in the chicken breasts and smoked paprika and cook for 3 minutes until lightly golden.
3. Season with salt and pepper and add ½ cup water.
4. Lock the lid. Select the Manual mode and cook for 12 minutes at High Pressure.
5. Once cooking is complete, do a natural pressure release for 8 minutes, then release any remaining pressure. Carefully open the lid.

6. Garnish with cilantro or scallions, if desired.

Nutritional info:
Calories 217, Fat 12.4g, Carbs 1.5g, Protein 34g

Spiced Chicken Drumsticks
Prep Time: 6 mins, Cook time: 15 mins, Servings: 10 to 12
Ingredients:
- ¼ tsp. dried thyme
- 1½ tbsps. paprika
- Salt and pepper, to taste
- ½ tsp. onion powder
- 12 chicken drumsticks
- 2 cups water

Instructions:
1. On a clean work surface, rub the chicken drumsticks generously with the spices. Season with salt and pepper.
2. Transfer the chicken to the Instant Pot and add the water.
3. Lock the lid. Select the Poultry mode and cook for 15 minutes at High Pressure.
4. Once cooking is complete, do a natural pressure release for 8 minutes, then release any remaining pressure. Carefully open the lid.
5. Remove from the pot to a plate and serve.

Nutritional info:
Calories 218, Fat 12.1g, Carbs 2.5g, Protein 23.8g

Chili Lime Chicken
Prep Time: 12 mins, Cook time: 6 mins, Servings:5
Ingredients:
- 6 garlic cloves, minced
- 1 tbsp. chili powder
- 1 tsp. cumin
- 1 lb. skinless and boneless chicken breasts
- 1 ½ limes, juiced
- 1 cup water

Instructions:
1. In the Instant Pot, add the chicken breasts, garlic, chili powder, cumin, lime juice, salt, pepper, and water.
2. Lock the lid. Select the Manual mode and cook for 6 minutes at High Pressure.
3. Once cooking is complete, do a natural pressure release for 5 minutes, then release any remaining pressure. Carefully open the lid.
4. Cool for 5 minutes and serve warm.

Nutritional info:
Calories 166, Fat 8.5g, Carbs 1.5g, Protein 19.3g

Lemony Fennel Chicken
Prep Time: 12 mins, Cook time: 12 mins, Servings: 8
Ingredients:
- 3 tbsps. freshly squeezed lemon juice
- 1 tsp. cinnamon
- ¼ cup fennel bulb
- 4 garlic cloves, minced
- 2 lbs. boneless and skinless chicken thighs
- Salt and pepper, to taste
- ½ cup water

Instructions:
1. Place lemon juice, cinnamon, fennel bulb, garlic, and chicken thighs in the Instant Pot. Sprinkle pepper and salt for seasoning. Add ½ cup of water for moisture.
2. Lock the lid. Select the Manual mode and cook for 12 minutes at High Pressure.
3. Once cooking is complete, do a natural pressure release for 8 minutes, then release any remaining pressure. Carefully open the lid.
4. Remove the chicken from the pot and shred it, then serve.

Nutritional info:
Calories 257, Fat 18.8g, Carbs 1.9g, Protein 187g

Creamy Chicken with Mushrooms
Prep Time: 12 mins, Cook time: 13 mins, Servings: 6
Ingredients:
- 4 garlic cloves, minced
- 1 onion, chopped
- 1 cup mushrooms, sliced
- 6 boneless chicken breasts, halved
- ½ cup coconut milk
- ½ cup water

Instructions:
1. Press the Sauté button on the Instant Pot and stir in the chicken breasts.
2. Fold in the onions and garlic and sauté for at least 3 minutes until tender. Season with salt and pepper. Add the remaining ingredients to the Instant Pot and whisk well.
3. Lock the lid. Select the Poultry mode and cook for 8 minutes at High Pressure.
4. Once cooking is complete, do a natural pressure release for 5 minutes, then release any remaining pressure. Carefully open the lid.
5. Allow to cool for 5 minutes before serving.

Nutritional info:
Calories 383, Fat 11.9g, Carbs 3.5g, Protein 62.2g

Thai Peanut Chicken
Prep Time: 6 mins, Cook time: 12 mins, Servings: 6
Ingredients:
- 2 tbsps. chopped scallions
- Salt and pepper, to taste
- 1½ cups toasted peanuts, divided
- 2 garlic cloves, minced
- 1½ lbs. chicken breasts
- 1 cup water

Instructions:
1. Place 1 cup of toasted peanuts in a food processor and pulse until smooth. This will serve as your peanut butter.
2. On a flat work surface, chop the remaining toasted peanuts finely and set aside.
3. Press the Sauté button on the Instant Pot and add the chicken breasts and garlic. Keep on stirring for 3 minutes until the meat has turned lightly golden. Sprinkle pepper and salt for seasoning.
4. Pour in the prepared peanut butter and water. Give the mixture a good stir.
5. Lock the lid. Select the Poultry mode and set the cooking time for 8 minutes at High Pressure.
6. Once cooking is complete, do a natural pressure release for 5 minutes, then release any remaining pressure. Carefully open the lid.
7. Garnish with chopped peanuts and scallions before serving.

Nutritional info:
Calories 575, Fat 34.8g, Carbs 2.5g, Protein 42g

Chinese Steamed Chicken
Prep Time: 6 mins, Coo time: 10 mins, Servings: 6
Ingredients:
- 1 tsp. grated ginger
- 1½ lbs. chicken thighs
- 1 tbsp. five-spice powder
- ¼ cup soy sauce
- 3 tbsps. sesame oil
- 1 cup water
- Salt and pepper, to taste

Instructions:
1. In the Instant Pot, stir in all the ingredients.
2. Lock the lid. Select the Poultry mode and set the cooking time for 10 minutes at High Pressure.
3. Once cooking is complete, do a natural pressure release for 7 minutes, then release any remaining pressure. Carefully open the lid.
4. Serve the chicken thighs while warm.

Nutritional info:

Calories 236, Fat 11.3g, Carbs 1.3g, Protein 31.3g

Chicken Stew with Tomatoes and Spinach

Prep Time: 13 mins, Cook time: 10 mins, Servings: 6

Ingredients:
- 1 ginger, sliced
- 3 garlic cloves, minced
- 2 cups spinach leaves
- 1 cup chopped tomatoes
- 1 lb. chicken breasts
- 1 cup water
- Salt and pepper, to taste

Instructions:
1. Press the Sauté button on the Instant Pot and add the chicken and garlic. Stir-fry for 3 minutes until the garlic becomes fragrant.
2. Add the ginger, tomatoes, spinach, and water. Season with salt and pepper.
3. Lock the lid. Select the Manual mode and set the cooking time for 6 minutes at High Pressure.
4. Once cooking is complete, do a natural pressure release for 5 minutes, then release any remaining pressure. Carefully open the lid.
5. Cool for a few minutes and serve warm.

Nutritional info:
Calories128, Fat 6.2g, Carbs 1.9g, Protein 15.6g

Crispy Chicken Wings

Prep Time: 15 mins, Cook time: 15 mins, Servings: 8

Ingredients:
- 1 tbsp. paprika
- 1 tsp. rosemary leaves
- Salt and pepper, to taste
- 2 lbs. chicken wings
- 1 cup water

Instructions:
1. Put all the ingredients in the Instant Pot and stir well.
2. Lock the lid. Select the Manual mode and set the cooking time for 15 minutes at High Pressure.
3. Once cooking is complete, do a natural pressure release for 10 minutes, then release any remaining pressure. Carefully open the lid.
4. Transfer to a plate and serve.

Nutritional info:
Calories 148, Fat 4.1g, Carbs 1.1g, Protein 25.2g

Basil and Tomatoes Chicken Soup

Prep Time: 6 mins, Cook time: 20 mins, Servings: 4

Ingredients:
- ¼ cup fresh basil leaves
- 8 chopped plum tomatoes
- 4 skinless chicken breasts, halved
- Salt and pepper, to taste
- 5 cups water

Instructions:
1. Place all ingredients into the Instant Pot. Give a good stir to mix everything.
2. Lock the lid. Select the Manual mode and set the timer to 20 minutes at High Pressure.
3. Once cooking is complete, do a natural pressure release for 10 minutes, then release any remaining pressure. Carefully open the lid.
4. Let the soup cool for 10 minutes and serve warm.

Nutritional info:
Calories 431, Fat 7.2g, Carbs 22.4g, Protein 61.7g

Mexican Shredded Chicken

Prep Time: 12 mins, Cook time: 18 mins, Servings: 4

Ingredients:
- ½ tsp. paprika
- 3 lbs. chicken breasts
- ½ tsp. dried oregano
- 1 tbsp. chili powder
- ¼ tsp. cumin powder
- Salt and pepper, to taste
- 2 cups water

Instructions:
1. Place all ingredients in the Instant Pot and whisk well.
2. Lock the lid. Select the Poultry mode and set the cooking time for 18 minutes at High Pressure.
3. Once cooking is complete, do a natural pressure release for 12 minutes, then release any remaining pressure. Carefully open the lid.
4. Remove the chicken breasts from the pot and shred them. Serve immediately.

Nutritional info:
Calories 196, Fat 10.5g, Carbs 0.1g, Protein 23.6g

Sesame Chicken

Prep Time: 6 mins, Cook time: 25 mins, Servings: 12

Ingredients:
- 1½ cup soy sauce
- 1 bay leaf
- 2 packets dried star anise flowers
- 5 lbs. chicken breasts or thighs
- 2 tbsps. toasted sesame seeds
- 2 cups water

Instructions:
1. Place the chicken breasts, soy sauce, star anise flowers, and bay leaf into the Instant Pot.

2. Lock the lid. Select the Manual mode and set the cooking time for 25 minutes at High Pressure.
3. Once cooking is complete, do a natural pressure release for 15 minutes, then release any remaining pressure. Carefully open the lid.
4. Allow the chicken breasts cool for 5 minutes and serve.

Nutritional info:
Calories 159, Fat 3.5g, Carbs 5.4g, Protein 26.7g

Eggplant and Chicken Sauté
Prep Time: 6 mins, Cook time: 10 mins, Servings: 6
Ingredients:
- 3 eggplants, sliced
- 1 tbsp. coconut oil
- 1 tsp. red pepper flakes
- 1 lb. ground chicken
- Salt and pepper, to taste

Instructions:
1. Press the Sauté button on the Instant Pot and heat the coconut oil.
2. Stir in the ground chicken and cook for 3 minutes until lightly golden.
3. Add the remaining ingredients and stir to combine.
4. Lock the lid. Select the Poultry mode and set the cooking time for 6 minutes at High Pressure.
5. Once cooking is complete, do a quick pressure release. Carefully open the lid.
6. Transfer to a large plate and serve warm.

Nutritional info:
Calories 202, Fat 8.9g, Carbs 17.5g, Protein 16.7g

Cheesy Jalapeño Chicken
Prep Time: 15 mins, Cook Time: 12 mins, Servings: 3
Ingredients:
- 1 lb. boneless chicken breast
- 3 jalapeños, sliced
- 8 oz. Cheddar cheese
- ¾ cup sour cream
- 8 oz. cream cheese
- Salt and pepper, to taste
- ½ cup water

Instructions:
1. Add ½ cup water, cream cheese, jalapeños, chicken breast, salt, and pepper to the pot. Stir to combine well.
2. Lock the lid. Select the Manual mode and set the cooking time for 12 minutes at High Pressure.
3. Once cooking is complete, do a natural pressure release for 8 minutes, then release any remaining pressure. Carefully open the lid.
4. Mix in the sour cream and Cheddar cheese, and serve warm!

Nutritional info:
Calories 528, Carbs 4.5 g, Fat 48.5 g, Protein 23 g

BBQ Chicken
Prep Time: 12 mins, Cook Time: 12 mins, Servings: 3
Ingredients:
- ½ cup barbecue sauce
- 2 lbs. chicken breasts
- 1 cup water
- 2½ tbsps. honey
- ½ cup chopped onion
- Salt and pepper, to taste

Instructions:
1. In the Instant Pot, add all the ingredients and stir well.
2. Lock the lid. Select the Manual mode and set the timer to 12 minutes at High Pressure.
3. Once cooking is complete, do a natural pressure release for 5 minutes, then release any remaining pressure. Carefully open the lid.
4. Cook for a few minutes to thicken the sauce. Serve warm.

Nutritional info:
Calories 309, Carbs 47 g, Fat 9 g, Protein 11 g

Broccoli Chicken with Parmesan
Prep Time: 8 mins, Cook Time: 5 mins, Servings: 2 to 3
Ingredients:
- ⅓ cup grated Parmesan cheese
- 1 cup chicken broth
- 2 cups broccoli florets
- ½ cup heavy cream
- 3 cups cooked and shredded chicken
- Salt and pepper, to taste

Instructions:
1. In the Instant pot, add the broth, broccoli, chicken, salt, and pepper. Using a spatula, stir the ingredients.
2. Lock the lid. Select the Steam mode and cook for 3 minutes at High Pressure.
3. Once cooking is complete, do a quick pressure release. Carefully open the lid.
4. Set your Instant Pot to Sauté and stir in the cream.
5. Cook for 2 minutes. Transfer to a large plate and serve.

Nutritional info:
Calories 317, Carbs 6 g, Fat 23.5 g, Protein 34 g

Ginger Chicken Congee
Prep Time: 12 mins, Cook Time: 25 mins, Servings: 4
Ingredients:
- 2 cups rice

- 8 medium chicken breasts
- 4 cups water
- 4-inch minced ginger piece
- 1 chicken stock cube
- Salt and pepper, to taste

Instructions:
1. Add the rice, water, chicken breasts, chicken stock, and ginger to the Instant Pot. Season with salt and pepper.
2. Lock the lid. Select the Poultry mode and set the cooking time for 25 minutes at High Pressure.
3. Once cooking is complete, do a natural pressure release for 10 minutes, then release any remaining pressure. Carefully open the lid. Serve warm.

Nutritional info:
Calories 218, Carbs 27.5 g, Fat 4 g, Protein 18 g

Chicken Yogurt Salsa
Prep Time: 15 mins, Cook Time: 15 mins, Servings: 4
Ingredients:
- 1 medium jar salsa
- ½ cup water
- 1 cup plain Greek yogurt
- 4 chicken breasts

Instructions:
1. Add all the ingredients to the Instant Pot. Using a spatula, gently stir to combine well.
2. Lock the lid. Select the Poultry mode and set the cooking time for 15 minutes at High Pressure.
3. Once cooking is complete, do a natural pressure release for 8 minutes, then release any remaining pressure. Carefully open the lid.
4. Transfer the cooked mixture to a salad bowl and serve warm.

Nutritional info:
Calories 314, Carbs 31 g, Fat 6.5 g, Protein 31 g

Lemon Garlic Chicken
Prep Time: 1 hour 20 mins, Cook time: 12 mins, Servings: 6
Ingredients:
- 3 tbsps. olive oil, divided
- 2 tsps. dried parsley
- 6 chicken breasts
- 3 minced garlic cloves
- 1 tbsp. lemon juice
- Salt and pepper, to taste

Instructions:
1. Mix together 2 tablespoons olive oil, chicken breasts, parsley, garlic cloves, and lemon juice in a large bowl. Place in the refrigerator to marinate for 1 hour.
2. Press the Sauté button on the Instant Pot and heat the remaining olive oil.
3. Cook the chicken breasts for 5 to 6 minutes per side until cooked through.
4. Allow to cool for 5 minutes before serving.

Nutritional info:
Calories 341, Fat 17.9g, Carbs 0.7g, Protein 42.4g

Broccoli Chicken with Black Beans
Prep Time: 10 mins, Cook Time: 25 mins, Servings: 4
Ingredients:
- 1 tbsp. olive oil
- 2 chicken breasts, skinless and boneless
- 1 cup broccoli florets
- 1½ cups chicken stock
- 2 tbsps. tomato sauce
- 1 cup black beans, soaked overnight and drained
- A pinch of salt and black pepper

Instructions:
1. Set your Instant Pot to Sauté and heat the olive oil. Add the chicken breasts and sauté for 5 minutes until lightly browned.
2. Add the remaining ingredients to the pot and stir well.
3. Lock the lid. Select the Poultry mode and cook for 20 minutes at High Pressure.
4. Once cooking is complete, do a natural pressure release for 10 minutes, then release any remaining pressure. Carefully open the lid.
5. Remove from the pot and serve on plates.

Nutritional info:
Calories 291, Fat 16g, Carbs 8g, Protein 16g

Thyme Chicken with Brussels Sprouts
Prep Time: 10 mins, Cook Time: 25 mins, Servings: 4
Ingredients:
- 1 tbsp. olive oil
- 2 chicken breasts, skinless, boneless and halved
- 2 cups Brussels sprouts, halved
- 1 cup chicken stock
- 2 thyme springs, chopped
- A pinch of salt and black pepper

Instructions:
1. Set your Instant Pot to Sauté and heat the olive oil. Add the chicken breasts and brown for 5 minutes.
2. Add the remaining ingredients to the pot and whisk to combine.

3. Lock the lid. Select the Poultry mode and set the cooking time for 20 minutes at High Pressure.
4. Once cooking is complete, do a natural pressure release for 10 minutes, then release any remaining pressure. Carefully open the lid.
5. Divide the chicken and Brussels sprouts among four plates and serve.

Nutritional info:
Calories 206, Fat 10g, Carbs 6g, Protein 17g

Fennel Chicken
Prep Time: 10 mins, Cook Time: 25 mins, Servings: 4
Ingredients:
- 2 tbsps. olive oil
- 2 tbsps. grated ginger
- 2 chicken breasts, skinless, boneless and halved
- 1 cup chicken stock
- 2 fennel bulbs, sliced
- 1 tbsp. basil, chopped
- A pinch of salt and black pepper

Instructions:
1. Set your Instant Pot to Sauté and heat the olive oil. Cook the ginger and chicken breasts for 5 minutes until evenly browned.
2. Add the remaining ingredients to the pot and mix well.
3. Lock the lid. Select the Poultry mode and cook for 20 minutes at High Pressure.
4. Once cooking is complete, do a natural pressure release for 10 minutes, then release any remaining pressure. Carefully open the lid.
5. Allow the chicken cool for 5 minutes before serving.

Nutritional info:
Calories 220, Fat 12g, Carbs 7g, Protein 15g

Filipino Chicken Adobo
Prep Time: 3 mins, Cook Time: 30 mins, Servings: 4
Ingredients
- 4 chicken legs
- ⅓ cup soy sauce
- ¼ cup white vinegar
- ¼ cup sugar
- 5 cloves garlic, crushed
- 2 bay leaves
- 1 onion, chopped
- Salt and pepper, to taste

Instructions:
1. Add all the ingredients to your Instant Pot and stir to combine well.
2. Lock the lid. Select the Poultry mode and cook for 30 minutes at High Pressure.
3. Once cooking is complete, do a natural pressure release for 10 minutes, then release any remaining pressure. Carefully open the lid.
4. Divide the chicken legs among four plates and serve warm.

Nutritional info:
Calories 429, Fat 15g, Carbs 16g, Protein 53g

Paprika Chicken with Tomatoes
Prep Time: 10 mins, Cook Time: 20 mins, Servings: 4
Ingredients:
- 1 tbsp. avocado oil
- 1½ lbs. chicken breast, skinless, boneless, and cubed
- 1 cup tomatoes, cubed
- 1 cup chicken stock
- 1 tbsp. smoked paprika
- 1 tsp. cayenne pepper
- A pinch of salt and black pepper

Instructions:
1. Set your Instant Pot to Sauté and heat the oil. Cook the cubed chicken in the hot oil for 2 to 3 minutes until lightly browned.
2. Add the remaining ingredients to the pot and stir well.
3. Lock the lid. Select the Poultry mode and set the cooking time for 18 minutes at High Pressure.
4. Once cooking is complete, do a natural pressure release for 10 minutes, then release any remaining pressure. Carefully open the lid.
5. Serve the chicken and tomatoes in bowls while warm.

Nutritional info:
Calories 228, Fat 9g, Carbs 7g, Protein 16g

Chicken with Artichokes and Bacon
Prep Time: 10 mins, Cook Time: 25 mins, Servings: 4
Ingredients:
- 2 chicken breasts, skinless, boneless, and halved
- 2 cups canned artichokes, drained, and chopped
- 1 cup bacon, cooked and crumbled
- 1 cup water
- 2 tbsps. tomato paste
- 1 tbsp. chives, chopped
- Salt, to taste

Instructions:
1. Mix all the ingredients in your Instant Pot until well combined.
2. Lock the lid. Select the Poultry mode and set the cooking time for 25 minutes at High Pressure.
3. Once cooking is complete, do a natural pressure release for 10 minutes, then

release any remaining pressure. Carefully open the lid.
4. Remove from the pot to a large plate and serve.

Nutritional info:
Calories 220, Fat 11g, Carbs 7g, Protein 10g

Crispy Chicken with Herbs

Prep Time: 10 mins, Cook Time: 30 mins, Servings: 2 to 3

Ingredients:
- 2 tbsps. butter, softened
- ½ head of garlic, crushed
- 1 thyme sprig, crushed
- 1 rosemary sprig, crushed
- ½ tbsp. paprika
- Salt and ground black pepper, to taste
- 1½ lbs. whole chicken, patted dry
- 2 cups water

Instructions:
1. Mix together the butter, garlic, thyme, rosemary, paprika, salt, and pepper in a shallow dish, and stir to incorporate.
2. Slather the butter mixture all over the chicken until well coated. Add the water and chicken to the Instant Pot.
3. Lock the lid. Select the Manual mode and cook for 20 minutes at High Pressure.
4. Once cooking is complete, do a natural pressure release for 10 minutes, then release any remaining pressure. Carefully open the lid.
5. Remove the chicken from the pot and place it under the broiler for 10 minutes, or until the skin is just lightly crisped. Serve warm.

Nutritional info:
Calories 492, Fat 2g, Carbs 70g, Protein 2g

Cheesy Chicken Tenders

Prep Time: 10 mins, Cook Time: 12 mins, Servings: 2

Ingredients:
- 1 tbsp. softened butter
- 1 lb. chicken tenders
- ½ cup vegetable broth
- Sea salt and freshly ground black pepper, to taste
- ¼ tsp. smoked paprika
- ½ cup Cottage cheese, crumbled
- 1 heaping tbsp. fresh chives, roughly chopped

Instructions:
1. Press the Sauté button on your Instant Pot and melt the butter. Brown the chicken tenders for 2 to 3 minutes.
2. Add the broth, salt, black pepper, and paprika to the pot and whisk well.
3. Lock the lid. Select the Manual mode and set the cooking time for 8 minutes at High Pressure.
4. Once cooking is complete, do a natural pressure release for 5 minutes, then release any remaining pressure. Carefully open the lid.
5. Add the crumbled cheese to the pot, cover, and allow to sit for 5 minutes until melted.
6. Sprinkle the fresh chives on top for garnish before serving.

Nutritional info:
Calories 357, Fat 3g, Carbs 52g, Protein 2g

Chicken Wings and Scallions and Tomato Sauce

Prep Time: 10 mins, Cook Time: 25 mins, Servings: 4

Ingredients:
- 1 tbsp. olive oil
- 6 scallions, chopped
- A pinch of salt and black pepper
- 8 chicken wings
- 8 oz. tomato sauce
- 2 cups chicken stock
- 1 tomato, chopped

Instructions:
1. Set your Instant Pot to Sauté and heat the olive oil.
2. Add the scallions, salt, and pepper and sauté for 5 minutes, stirring occasionally.
3. Stir in the chicken wings and cook for 5 minutes until lightly browned. Add the remaining ingredients to the pot and stir well.
4. Lock the lid. Select the Manual mode and set the cooking time for 15 minutes at High Pressure.
5. Once cooking is complete, do a natural pressure release for 10 minutes, then release any remaining pressure. Carefully open the lid.
6. Remove from the pot to a plate and serve hot.

Nutritional info:
Calories 223, Fat 10g, Carbs 8g, Protein 10g

Classic Chicken Wings

Prep Time: 5 mins, Cook Time: 10 mins, Servings: 4 to 5

Ingredients:
- 3 lbs. chicken wings
- 1 cup water
- Kosher salt, to taste
- 2 cups wing sauce

Instructions:
1. Add the chicken wings and water to the Instant Pot. Sprinkle with the salt.

2. Pour the wing sauce into the pot and whisk to combine.
3. Lock the lid. Select the Manual mode and cook for 10 minutes at High Pressure.
4. Once cooking is complete, do a natural pressure release for 10 minutes, then release any remaining pressure. Carefully open the lid.
5. Allow the chicken wings cool for 5 minutes before serving.

Nutritional info:
Calories 444, Fat 12g, Carbs 8g, Protein 76g

Simple Lime Turkey Wings
Prep Time: 10 mins, Cook Time: 30 mins, Servings:4
Ingredients:
- 1 tbsp. avocado oil
- 1 yellow onion, chopped
- 2 turkey wings, halved
- 4 garlic cloves, minced
- 1 cup chicken stock
- Lime juice and zest from 1 lime
- A pinch of salt and black pepper

Instructions:
1. Set your Instant Pot to Sauté and heat the avocado oil. Sauté the onion for 2 minutes until translucent, stirring occasionally.
2. Add the remaining ingredients to the pot and mix well.
3. Lock the lid. Select the Poultry mode and set the cooking time for 28 minutes at High Pressure.
4. Once cooking is complete, do a natural pressure release for 10 minutes, then release any remaining pressure. Carefully open the lid.
5. Divide the turkey wings among plates and serve.

Nutritional info:
Calories 230, Fat 10g, Carbs 8g, Protein 17g

Pomegranate-Glazed Turkey with Cranberries
Prep Time: 10 mins, Cook Time: 30 mins, Servings: 4
Ingredients:
- 2 tbsps. avocado oil
- 1 big turkey breast, skinless, boneless and sliced
- 1 cup cranberries
- 1 cup walnuts, chopped
- 1 cup pomegranate juice
- 1 bunch thyme, chopped
- A pinch of salt and black pepper

Instructions:
1. Press the Sauté button on the Instant Pot and heat the oil. Stir in the turkey slices and brown for 5 minutes.

2. Add the remaining ingredients to the pot and mix well.
3. Lock the lid. Select the Poultry mode and cook for 25 minutes at High Pressure.
4. Once cooking is complete, do a natural pressure release for 10 minutes, then release any remaining pressure. Carefully open the lid.
5. Remove from the pot and serve warm.

Nutritional info:
Calories 248, Fat 13g, Carbs 6g, Protein 16g

Balsamic Turkey and Onions
Prep Time: 10 mins, Cook Time: 30 mins, Servings: 4
Ingredients:
- 1 tbsp. olive oil
- 2 cups sliced red onions
- 2 tbsps. balsamic vinegar
- 2½ lbs. turkey breast, skinless, boneless and sliced
- 1 cup chicken stock
- 2 tbsps. cilantro, chopped
- A pinch of salt and black pepper

Instructions:
1. Set your Instant Pot to Sauté and heat the olive oil. Add the onions and balsamic vinegar and sauté for 5 minutes, stirring occasionally, or until the onions are translucent.
2. Stir in the turkey slices and brown for 5 minutes. Add the remaining ingredients to the pot and stir to incorporate.
3. Lock the lid. Select the Poultry mode and set the cooking time for 20 minutes at High Pressure.
4. Once cooking is complete, do a natural pressure release for 10 minutes, then release any remaining pressure. Carefully open the lid.
5. Transfer the turkey slices to plates and serve warm.

Nutritional info:
Calories 227, Fat 11g, Carbs 6g, Protein 18g

Allspice Turkey Drumsticks with Beer
Prep Time: 5 mins, Cook Time: 20 mins, Servings: 2
Ingredients
- 1 lb. turkey drumsticks, boneless
- 1 (6-oz) bottle beer
- 1 carrot, sliced
- 1 small leek, sliced
- ¼ tsp. ground allspice
- Sea salt and freshly ground black pepper, to taste

Instructions:

1. Place all the ingredients in the Instant Pot and stir well.
2. Lock the lid. Select the Manual mode and cook for 20 minutes at High Pressure.
3. Once cooking is complete, do a natural pressure release for 10 minutes, then release any remaining pressure. Carefully open the lid.
4. Remove from the pot and serve on a plate.

Nutritional info:
Calories 17, Fat 4g, Carbs 50g, Protein 1g

Cilantro Turkey with Pomegranate Glaze

Prep Time: 10 mins, Cook Time: 30 mins, Servings: 4
Ingredients:
- 1 tbsp. olive oil
- 1 big turkey breast, skinless, boneless and sliced
- 1 cup chicken stock
- 1 cup pomegranate seeds
- 1 tbsp. cilantro, chopped
- 1 tbsp. sweet paprika
- A pinch of salt and black pepper

Instructions:
1. Set your Instant Pot to Sauté and heat the olive oil. Add the turkey slices and brown for 5 minutes, stirring occasionally.
2. Add the remaining ingredients to the Instant Pot and mix well.
3. Lock the lid. Select the Poultry mode and set the cooking time for 25 minutes at High Pressure.
4. Once cooking is complete, do a natural pressure release for 10 minutes, then release any remaining pressure. Carefully open the lid.
5. Remove from the pot to plates and serve.

Nutritional info:
Calories 262, Fat 7g, Carbs 8g, Protein 13g

Thyme Duck and Chives

Prep Time: 10 mins, Cook Time: 20 mins, Servings: 4
Ingredients:
- 1 tbsp. avocado oil
- 2 duck breasts, boneless, skin scored and halved
- 1 cup chicken stock
- 1 yellow onion, chopped
- 2 tsps. thyme, dried
- A pinch of salt and black pepper
- 1 tbsp. chives, chopped

Instructions:
1. Press the Sauté button on the Instant Pot and heat the oil. Add the duck breasts (skin-side down) to the pot and sear for 2 minutes.
2. Add the chicken stock, onion, thyme, salt, and pepper to the pot. Stir well.
3. Lock the lid. Select the Poultry mode and cook for 18 minutes at High Pressure.
4. Once cooking is complete, do a natural pressure release for 10 minutes, then release any remaining pressure. Carefully open the lid.
5. Garnish with the chopped chives and serve.

Nutritional info:
Calories 294, Fat 16g, Carbs 5g, Protein 13g

Cream Turkey Dinner

Prep Time: 12 mins, Cook Time: 15 mins, Servings: 3
Ingredients:
- 8 basil leaves, chopped
- ½ cup coconut cream
- 3 tbsps. olive oil, divided
- 5 garlic cloves, minced
- 1lb. turkey breast, sliced
- Salt and pepper, to taste

Instructions:
1. Season the meat with pepper and salt. Set aside for 10 minutes.
2. Press the Sauté button on the Instant Pot. Heat 2 tablespoons oil and add the meat. Cook for about 5 minutes until evenly browned, stirring occasionally.
3. Remove the meat from the pot to a plate.
4. Add the remaining olive oil and garlic to the pot.
5. Cook for 1 to 2 minutes until
6. Add the cream and let cook for 2 to 3 minutes.
7. Add the turkey and stir gently.
8. Lock the lid. Select the Manual mode and set the cooking time for 8 minutes at High Pressure.
9. Once cooking is complete, do a natural pressure release for 5 minutes, then release any remaining pressure. Carefully open the lid.
10. Top with the basil leaves before serving.

Nutritional info:
Calories 324, Carbs 11 g, Fat 4 g, Protein 35 g

Sautéed Turkey with Cauliflower Purée

Prep Time: 12 mins, Cook Time: 10 mins, Servings: 4
Ingredients:
- 1 tsp. ground dried thyme
- ½ tsp. garlic powder
- 1 tbsp. chopped fresh parsley

- 1 cup chopped cauliflower
- 1 tbsp. olive oil
- 1 lb. turkey breasts
- 1 cup water

Instructions:
1. Purée the cauliflower in a blender, then transfer the cauliflower purée to the Instant Pot.
2. Add the water, garlic powder, and thyme to the pot, and stir well.
3. Lock the lid. Select the Manual mode and cook for 3 minutes at High Pressure.
4. Once cooking is complete, do a quick pressure release. Carefully open the lid. Drain and transfer the cauliflower purée to a bowl and set aside.
5. Set your Instant Pot to Sauté and heat the olive oil.
6. Add the turkey and cook for 3 to 4 on each side until evenly browned.
7. Remove from the pot and serve topped with cauliflower purée and parsley.

Nutritional info:
Calories 298, Fat 4g, Carbs 37g, Protein 31g

Turkey Rice Bowl

Prep Time: 12 mins, Cook Time: 25 mins, Servings: 6

Ingredients:
- 1 tbsp. olive oil
- 8 oz. turkey breasts
- 3 egg whites
- 1 cubed carrot
- 1½ cup brown rice
- 2 cups water
- ¼ cup chopped spring onions

Instructions:
1. Press the Sauté button on the Instant Pot and heat the olive oil.
2. Add the turkey and cook for 4 to 5 minutes until evenly browned. Set aside on a plate.
3. Add the egg whites to the Instant Pot and cook for 2 minutes, then transfer to the plate of turkey.
4. Add 2 cups water, carrot cubes, and rice to the pot.
5. Lock the lid. Select the Rice mode and cook for 20 minutes at Low Pressure.
6. Once cooking is complete, do a natural pressure release for 10 minutes, then release any remaining pressure. Carefully open the lid.
7. Sprinkle with the spring onions and serve the turkey breasts over the rice.

Nutritional info:
Calories 167, Fat 3g, Carbs 16g, Protein 11g

Chapter 6 Vegan and Vegetarian Recipe

Corn on Cob

Prep Time: 6 mins, Cook Time: 15 mins, Servings: 2

Ingredients:
- 2 cups water
- 2 ears corn
- 1 tbsp. vegan butter
- Garlic salt, to taste

Instructions:
1. Add the water to the Instant Pot.
2. Put the steamer basket inside the pot.
3. Place the corn on top of the basket,
4. Lock the lid. Set the Instant Pot to Meat/Stew mode, then set the timer for 2 minutes at High Pressure.
5. Once cooking is complete, do a quick pressure release. Carefully open the lid.
6. Brush corn with vegan butter.
7. Sprinkle with a little garlic salt.
8. Serve as an appetizer or a side dish.

Nutritional info:
Calories 77, Fat 1.1g, Carbs 17.1g, Protein: 2.9g

Roasted Brussels Sprouts

Prep Time: 6 mins, Cook Time: 16 mins, Servings: 4

Ingredients:
- 2 tbsps. olive oil
- 1 onion, chopped
- 1 lb. Brussels sprouts
- Salt and pepper, to taste
- ½ cup vegetable broth

Instructions:
1. Set the Instant Pot to Sauté mode. Add the olive oil and sauté the onion for 2 minutes.
2. Sauté the Brussels sprouts for 1 minute.
3. Sprinkle salt and pepper on top.
4. Pour in the vegetable broth.
5. Lock the lid. Set the Instant Pot to Manual mode, then set the timer for 3 minutes at High Pressure.
6. Once cooking is complete, do a quick pressure release. Carefully open the lid.
7. Serve warm.

Nutritional info:
Calories 136, Fat 7.2g, Carbs 16.3g, Protein: 4.6g

Steamed Lemon Artichokes

Prep Time: 6 mins, Cook Time: 20 mins, Servings: 4

Ingredients:
- 1 cup water
- 2 garlic cloves, minced
- Salt, to taste
- 1 bay leaf
- 4 artichokes, trimmed
- 2 tbsps. freshly squeezed lemon juice

Instructions:
1. Mix the water, garlic, salt and bay leaf inside the Instant Pot.
2. Place steamer basket in the pot.
3. Add the artichokes.
4. Drizzle each one with lemon juice.
5. Lock the lid. Set the Instant Pot to Steam mode, then set the timer for 10 minutes at High Pressure.
6. Once cooking is complete, do a quick pressure release. Carefully open the lid.
7. Remove outer petals and discard.
8. Discard the bay leaf, slice the artichokes into pieces and serve.

Nutritional info:
Calories 64, Fat 0.2g, Carbs 14.6g, Protein: 4.3g

Chickpea and Lentil Salad

Prep Time: 50 mins, Cook Time: 3 hours, Servings: 4

Ingredients:
- 1 tbsp. olive oil
- 12 oz. halved cherry tomatoes
- 1 ½ cups chickpeas, soaked in water overnight, drained
- 1 tsp. Herbes de Provence
- 2 cups vegetable broth
- 1 cup green lentils
- 1 cup water

Instructions:
1. In the Instant Pot, mix the olive oil, water and chickpeas.
2. Choose Manual mode and cook at High Pressure
3. Drain the chickpeas and set aside.
4. Add the lentils, vegetable broth and seasoning.
5. Lock the lid. Set the Instant Pot to Slow Cook mode, then set the timer for 3 hours at High Pressure.
6. Once cooking is complete, do a quick pressure release. Carefully open the lid.
7. Use a salad bowl to toss together chickpeas, tomatoes and lentils.

Nutritional info:
Calories 508, Fat 8.4g, Carbs 78.3g, Protein 31.9g

Chickpea Avocado Salad

Prep Time: 12 mins, Cook Time: 12 mins, Servings: 2

Ingredients:
- 1 cup soaked and rinsed chickpeas
- 1½ cup water
- ¼ cup chopped avocado
- 2 tbsps. pomegranate seeds
- ½ cup quinoa

- 1 tsp. rice vinegar

Instructions:
1. Add the chickpea and 1 cup of water to the Instant Pot. Stir to combine well.
2. Lock the lid. Set the Instant Pot to Manual mode, then set the timer for 10 minutes at High Pressure.
3. Once cooking is complete, do a quick pressure release. Carefully open the lid.
4. Drain water and set aside chickpea.
5. Add the quinoa and ½ cup of water to the Instant Pot. Stir to combine well.
6. Lock the lid, then set the timer for 1 minutes at High Pressure.
7. Once cooking is complete, do a natural pressure release. Carefully open the lid.
8. Drain and add quinoa with the chickpea.
9. Add the vinegar, pomegranate and avocado on top. Serve.

Nutritional info:
Calories 566, Fat 12g, Carbs 26g, Protein 25g

Mediterranean Couscous Salad

Prep Time: 50 mins, Cook time: 20 mins, Servings: 6

Ingredients:
- 2 tbsps. olive oil
- 2 cups couscous
- 4 cups water
- Salt, to taste
- 1 tbsp. lemon juice
- 2 tomatoes, diced
- 1 cucumber, diced

Instructions:
1. Select the Sauté function in the Instant Pot.
2. Add the olive oil.
3. Add the couscous.
4. Cook for 2 minutes.
5. Pour in the water.
6. Add the salt.
7. Lock the lid. Set the Instant Pot to Manual mode, then set the timer for 20 minutes at High Pressure.
8. Once cooking is complete, do a natural pressure release for 10 minutes, then release any remaining pressure. Carefully open the lid.
9. Fluff the couscous using a fork.
10. Toss in lemon juice, tomatoes and cucumber.

Nutritional info:
Calories 349, Fat 0.8g, Carbs 72.2g, Protein 12.1g

Summer Beet Salad

Prep Time: 12 mins, Cook time: 6 mins, Servings: 6

Ingredients:
- 1 cup baby arugula
- 2 tbsps. extra virgin olive oil
- Salt and pepper, to taste
- 1 large tomatoes, chopped
- 4 medium-sized red beets, washed, peeled and cubed
- 1 cup water

Instructions:
1. Place a trivet or the steamer rack in the Instant Pot and pour in the water.
2. Place the beets on the trivet.
3. Lock the lid. Set the Instant Pot to Steam mode, then set the timer for 6 minutes at High Pressure.
4. Once cooking is complete, do a quick pressure release. Carefully open the lid.
5. Take the beets out and allow to cool for a few minutes.
6. Assemble the salad by combining the steamed beets with the rest of the ingredients.
7. Serve chilled.

Nutritional info:
Calories 51, Fat 2.2g, Carbs 7.2g, Protein 1.4g

Zucchini Bulgur Meal

Prep Time: 12 mins, Cook Time: 30 mins, Servings: 3

Ingredients:
- 1 cup bulgur
- 1 tbsp. chopped fresh parsley
- 3 medium zucchinis, wedged
- 2 tsps. olive oil
- 1 small onion, chopped
- 1½ cup water

Instructions:
1. Take the Instant Pot and place over dry kitchen surface; open its top lid and switch it on.
2. Add the bulgur and water to the Instant Pot.
3. Stir to combine well.
4. Lock the lid. Set the Instant Pot to Manual mode, then set the timer for 18 minutes at High Pressure.
5. Once cooking is complete, do a natural pressure release for 10 minutes, then release any remaining pressure. Carefully open the lid.
6. Drain water and set aside bulgur.
7. Press Sauté. Grease the pot with olive oil.
8. Add the onions; cook for 4 minutes until turn translucent and softened.
9. Add the zucchini and cook for 4 to 5 mins, stirring occasionally.
10. Add the bulgur to the pot and give it a good stir. Cook for 2 more minutes.
11. Serve warm with the parsley on top.

Nutritional info:
Calories 146, Fat 5g, Carbs 26g, Protein 4g

Broccoli Cream Pasta
Prep Time: 12 mins, Cook Time: 15 mins, Servings: 7
Ingredients:
- 10 oz. rigatoni
- ½ cup heavy cream
- 1 tsp. butter
- 8 oz. broccoli, chopped
- 1 cup grated Cheddar cheese

Instructions:
1. In the Instant Pot; add the pasta and enough water to cover.
2. Lock the lid. Set the Instant Pot to Manual mode, then set the timer for 7 minutes at High Pressure.
3. Once cooking is complete, do a quick pressure release. Carefully open the lid.
4. Drain water and transfer the cooked pasta in a container.
5. Take the Instant Pot and place over dry kitchen surface; open its top lid and switch it on.
6. Press Sauté.
7. Add and heat the butter in the Instant Pot.
8. Add the broccoli and cream; sauté for 3 to 4 minutes.
9. Add the cheese; cook for 7 minutes.
10. Mix in the pasta and serve.

Nutritional info:
Calories 263, Fat 17g, Carbs 23g, Protein 9g

Cauliflower Pasta
Prep Time: 12 mins, Cook Time: 20 mins, Servings: 6
Ingredients:
- 1 cup chopped cauliflower
- 2 tbsps. chopped green onions
- 12 oz. vermicelli pasta
- 1 tsp. olive oil
- 1 small green chili pepper, chopped

Instructions:
1. In the Instant Pot; add the pasta and enough water to cover.
2. Lock the lid. Set the Instant Pot to Manual mode, then set the timer for 7 minutes at High Pressure.
3. Once cooking is complete, do a quick pressure release. Carefully open the lid.
4. Drain water and transfer the cooked pasta in a container.
5. Take the Instant Pot and place over dry kitchen surface; open its top lid and switch it on.
6. Press Sauté. Grease the pot with olive oil.
7. Add the cauliflower; cook for 7 to 8 minutes until turn softened.
8. Mix in the pasta and serve warm. Top with the green onions.

Nutritional info:
Calories 316, Fat 2g, Carbs 38g, Protein 4g

Onion Penne Pasta
Prep Time: 12 mins, Cook Time: 10 mins, Servings: 6
Ingredients:
- 3 cups water
- 12 oz. penne pasta
- 1 small onion, chopped
- 1 cup skim milk
- 1 tsp. olive oil

Instructions:
1. In the Instant Pot; add the water and pasta.
2. Lock the lid. Set the Instant Pot to Manual mode, then set the timer for 6 minutes at High Pressure.
3. Once cooking is complete, do a natural pressure release for 5 minutes. Carefully open the lid.
4. Drain water and transfer the cooked pasta in a container.
5. Press Sauté. Grease the pot with olive oil.
6. Add the onions and let cook for about 2 minutes until turn translucent and softened.
7. Add the milk and cook for 2 to 3 minutes.
8. Mix in the pasta and serve.

Nutritional info:
Calories 264, Fat 2g, Carbs 46g, Protein 11g

Tangy Spinach Pasta
Prep Time: 12 mins, Cook Time: 16 mins, Servings: 5
Ingredients:
- 1 cup water
- 12 oz. fusilli pasta
- 1 tsp. olive oil
- 1 small onion, chopped
- 1 cup chopped spinach
- 12 oz. diced tomatoes

Instructions:
1. In the Instant Pot; add the water and pasta.
2. Lock the lid. Set the Instant Pot to Manual mode, then set the timer for 7 minutes at High Pressure.
3. Once cooking is complete, do a natural pressure release for 5 minutes. Carefully open the lid.
4. Drain water and transfer the cooked pasta in a container.
5. Press Sauté. Grease the pot with olive oil.
6. Add the onions and sauté for 4 minutes until turn translucent and softened.

7. Mix in the spinach and tomatoes; cook for 4 to 5 minutes.
8. Mix in the pasta and serve warm.

Nutritional info:
Calories 234, Fat 3g, Carbs 37g, Protein 9g

Mushroom Rice Meal
Prep Time: 12 mins, Cook Time: 35 mins, Servings: 3
Ingredients:
- 2 tsps. olive oil
- 1 tbsp. white wine vinegar
- 1 small onion, chopped
- 1 cup wild rice
- 1 cup sliced button mushrooms
- 2 cups water

Instructions:
1. Take the Instant Pot and place over dry kitchen surface; open its top lid and switch it on.
2. Press Sauté. Grease the pot with olive oil.
3. Add the onions and let cook for 4 minutes until turn translucent and softened.
4. Add the mushrooms and cook for 8 to 10 minutes.
5. Pour in the vinegar; stir and cook for 1 minute more, then set aside the mixture in a bowl.
6. Add the water and rice.
7. Lock the lid. Set the Instant Pot to Manual mode, then set the timer for 20 minutes at Low Pressure.
8. Once cooking is complete, do a natural pressure release for 10 minutes, then release any remaining pressure. Carefully open the lid.
9. Transfer the cooked rice in a mushroom bowl.
10. Mix well and serve.

Nutritional info:
Calories 117, Fat 3g, Carbs 13g, Protein 3g

Pure Basmati Rice Meal
Prep Time: 12 mins, Cook Time: 10 mins, Servings: 4
Ingredients:
- 1 cup chopped cauliflower
- ¼ cup chopped green onions
- 1 small onion, sliced
- 1 cup basmati rice
- 1 tsp. olive oil

Instructions:
1. Purée the cauliflower until smooth in a blender and set aside.
2. Press the Sauté bottom on the Instant Pot. Grease the pot with olive oil.
3. Add the onions and sauté for 3 minutes until translucent and softened.
4. Add the cauliflower purée, rice and green onions.
5. Lock the lid. Set the Instant Pot to Manual mode, then set the timer for 4 minutes at Low Pressure.
6. Once cooking is complete, do a natural pressure release. Carefully open the lid.
7. Transfer the cooked recipe on serving plates.
8. Serve warm.

Nutritional info:
Calories 183, Fat 4g, Carbs 34g, Protein 5g

Mushroom Spinach Casserole
Prep Time: 12 mins, Cook Time: 20 mins, Servings: 3
Ingredients:
- 2 cups sliced button mushrooms
- 4 large eggs
- 1 small onion, chopped
- 1 cup water
- 7 oz. fresh spinach
- ¼ cup grated Parmesan cheese

Instructions:
1. In a mixing bowl, thoroughly mix the eggs and cheese.
2. Mix in the spinach, mushrooms, onion, and garlic.
3. Grease a baking pan and line with a parchment; add the mixture in the bowl.
4. Put the Instant Pot over dry kitchen surface; open its top lid and switch it on.
5. Pour the water in the Instant Pot. Arrange the trivet or steamer basket inside it; arrange the pan over the trivet/basket.
6. Lock the lid. Set the Instant Pot to Manual mode, then set the timer for 20 minutes at High Pressure.
7. Once cooking is complete, do a quick pressure release. Carefully open the lid.
8. Transfer the cooked recipe on serving plates.
9. Serve warm.

Nutritional info:
Calories 563, Fat 24g, Carbs 8g, Protein 43g

Coconut Cauliflower Rice
Prep Time: 6 mins, Cook time: 10 mins, Servings: 3
Ingredients:
- 1 onion, chopped
- Salt and pepper, to taste
- 3 garlic cloves, minced
- 1 cauliflower head, grated
- 1 cup freshly squeezed coconut milk

Instructions:

1. Put the cauliflower florets in a food processor and pulse to rice the cauliflower.
2. Place the riced cauliflower and remaining ingredients in the Instant Pot.
3. Lock the lid. Set the Instant Pot to Manual mode, then set the timer for 10 minutes at High Pressure.
4. Once cooking is complete, do a quick pressure release. Carefully open the lid.
5. Serve warm.

Nutritional info:
Calories 231, Fat 19.4g, Carbs 14.6g, Protein 4.4g

Coconut Milk Rice

Prep Time: 12 mins, Cook Time: 10 mins, Servings: 5
Ingredients:
- 1 cup jasmine rice
- 1 tsp. freshly grated ginger
- 1 tbsp. olive oil
- 1 cup water
- 1 onion, chopped
- 1 cup coconut milk

Instructions:
1. Take the Instant Pot and place over dry kitchen surface; open its top lid and switch it on.
2. Press Sauté and grease the pot with olive oil.
3. Add the onions and let cook for 2 to 3 minutes until turn translucent and softened.
4. Pour in the milk and stir the mix. Add the water and stir again; cook for 1 to 2 minutes.
5. Add the rice, ginger, and stir.
6. Lock the lid. Set the Instant Pot to Manual mode, then set the timer for 3 minutes at Low Pressure.
7. Once cooking is complete, do a natural pressure release. Carefully open the lid.
8. Transfer the cooked recipe on serving plates.
9. Serve the recipe warm.

Nutritional info:
Calories 134, Fat 8g, Carbs 9g, Protein 2g

Tomato Onion Rice

Prep Time: 12 mins, Cook Time: 12 mins, Servings: 4
Ingredients:
- 1 cup soaked and drained rice
- 2 tbsps. chopped parsley
- 1 tbsp. olive oil
- 1 red onion, chopped
- 2 cups water
- 1 tbsp. tomato paste

Instructions:

1. Take the Instant Pot and place over dry kitchen surface; open its top lid and switch it on.
2. Press Sauté. Grease the pot with olive oil.
3. Add the onions and sauté for 4 minutes until turn translucent and softened.
4. Add the rice and cook for another 3 to 4 minutes.
5. Add the water and tomato sauce.
6. Lock the lid. Set the Instant Pot to Manual mode, then set the timer for 4 minutes at Low Pressure.
7. Once cooking is complete, do a natural pressure release. Carefully open the lid.
8. Transfer the cooked recipe on serving plates.
9. Serve the recipe warm with some parsley on top.

Nutritional info:
Calories 146, Fat 4g, Carbs 14g, Protein 2g

Chickpea Egg Bowl

Prep Time: 12 mins, Cook Time: 25 mins, Servings: 3
Ingredients:
- 2 tbsps. freshly chopped parsley
- 2 boiled eggs, chopped
- 1 tbsp. lemon juice
- 1 cup rinsed and drained chickpeas
- 1 green onion, chopped

Instructions:
1. Add the chickpea and 1½ cups to the Instant Pot. Stir the ingredients to combine well.
2. Lock the lid. Set the Instant Pot to Manual mode, then set the timer for 12 minutes at High Pressure.
3. Once cooking is complete, do a quick pressure release. Carefully open the lid.
4. Mix in the remaining ingredients and serve.

Nutritional info:
Calories 267, Fat 6g, Carbs 34g, Protein 14g

Asparagus and Mushrooms

Prep Time: 4 mins, Cook time: 5 mins, Servings: 4
Ingredients:
- 1 lb. asparagus spears, trimmed
- 2 garlic cloves, minced
- Salt and pepper, to taste
- ¼ cup water
- ½ cup fresh mushrooms
- 1 tbsp. coconut oil

Instructions:
1. Press the Sauté button on the Instant Pot and heat the oil.

2. Add the garlic and sauté for 2 or 3 minutes until fragrant.
3. Add the asparagus spears and mushrooms.
4. Add salt and pepper and add the water.
5. Lock the lid. Set the Instant Pot to Manual mode, then set the timer for 5 minutes at High Pressure.
6. Once cooking is complete, do a quick pressure release. Carefully open the lid.
7. Serve warm.

Nutritional info:
Calories 61, Fat 3.6g, Carbs 6.5g, Protein 3.1g

Broccoli and Mushrooms

Prep Time: 15 mins, Cook Time: 8 mins, Servings: 4

Ingredients:
- 2 tbsps. coconut oil
- 1 cup sliced mushrooms
- 2 cups broccoli florets
- 1 tbsp. soy sauce
- 1 cup vegetable broth
- Salt and pepper, to taste

Instructions:
1. Set the Instant Pot to Sauté mode and add the coconut oil to melt.
2. Add the mushrooms and sauté for 4 to 5 minutes.
3. Add broccoli and soy sauce and sauté for 1 more minute.
4. Pour the broth over. Sprinkle with salt and pepper.
5. Lock the lid. Set the Instant Pot to Manual mode, then set the timer for 2 minutes at High Pressure.
6. Once cooking is complete, do a quick pressure release. Carefully open the lid.
7. Serve the veggies drizzled with the cooking liquid.
8. Serve immediately!

Nutritional info:
Calories 81, Fat 7g, Carbs 3.9g, Protein 2.1g

Instant Pot Mushrooms

Prep Time: 12 mins, Cook Time: 10 mins, Servings: 1

Ingredients:
- ½ cup water
- 4 oz. mushrooms, sliced
- 2 garlic cloves, minced
- 1 tbsp. olive oil
- Salt and pepper, to taste

Instructions:
1. Pour water along with mushrooms in an Instant Pot.
2. Lock the lid. Set the Instant Pot to Manual mode, then set the timer for 5 minutes at High Pressure.
3. Once cooking is complete, do a quick pressure release. Carefully open the lid.
4. Drain the mushroom and then return back to the Instant Pot.
5. Now add olive oil to the pot and mix.
6. Press the Sauté function of the pot and let it cook for 3 minutes.
7. Sauté every 30 seconds.
8. Add the garlic and sauté for 2 minutes or until fragrant. Sprinkle with salt and pepper, then serve the dish.

Nutritional info:
Calories 153, Fat 14.4g, Carbs 5.7g, Protein 3.9g

Instant Pot Steamed Asparagus

Prep Time: 5mins, Cook time: 5 mins, Servings: 1

Ingredients:
- 7 asparagus spears, washed and trimmed
- ¼ tsp. pepper
- 1 tbsp. extra virgin olive oil
- Juice from freshly squeezed ¼ lemon
- ¼ tsp. salt
- 1 cup water

Instructions:
1. Place a trivet or the steamer rack in the Instant Pot and pour in the water.
2. In a mixing bowl, combine the asparagus spears, salt, pepper, and lemon juice.
3. Place on top of the trivet.
4. Lock the lid. Set the Instant Pot to Steam mode, then set the timer for 5 minutes at High Pressure.
5. Once cooking is complete, do a quick pressure release. Carefully open the lid.
6. Drizzle the asparagus with olive oil.

Nutritional info:
Calories 80, Fat 6.2g, Carbs 6.4g, Protein 1.5g

Steamed Paprika Broccoli

Prep Time: 6 mins, Cook time: 6 mins, Servings: 2

Ingredients:
- ¼ tsp. ground black pepper
- 1 tbsp. freshly squeezed lemon juice
- ¼ tsp. salt
- 1 head broccoli, cut into florets
- 1 tbsp. paprika
- 1 cup water

Instructions:
1. Place a trivet or the steamer rack in the Instant Pot and pour in the water.
2. Place the broccoli florets on the trivet and sprinkle salt, pepper, paprika, and lemon juice.
3. Lock the lid. Set the Instant Pot to Steam mode, then set the timer for 6 minutes at High Pressure.

4. Once cooking is complete, do a quick pressure release. Carefully open the lid.
5. Serve immediately.

Nutritional info:
Calories 22, Fat 0.5g, Carbs 4.7g, Protein 1.3g

Sautéed Brussels Sprouts And Pecans

Prep Time: 4 mins, Cook time: 6 mins, Servings: 4
Ingredients:
- ¼ cup chopped pecans
- 2 garlic cloves, minced
- Salt and pepper, to taste
- 2 tbsps. water
- 2 cups baby Brussels sprouts
- 1 tbsp. coconut oil

Instructions:
1. Press the Sauté button on the Instant Pot and heat the oil.
2. Sauté the garlic for 1 minute or until fragrant.
3. Add the Brussels sprouts. Sprinkle salt and pepper for seasoning.
4. Add the water.
5. Lock the lid. Set the Instant Pot to Manual mode, then set the timer for 3 minutes at High Pressure.
6. Once cooking is complete, do a quick pressure release. Carefully open the lid.
7. Add the pecans and set to the Sauté mode and sauté for 3 minutes or until the pecans are roasted.
8. Serve immediately.

Nutritional info:
Calories 98, Fat 8.1g, Carbs 6.3g, Protein 2.3g

Coconut Cabbage

Prep Time: 6 mins, Cook time: 20 mins, Servings: 4
Ingredients:
- 2 cups freshly squeezed coconut milk
- 1 halved onion
- 1 thumb-size ginger, sliced
- 1 garlic bulb, crushed
- 1 cabbage head, shredded
- Salt and pepper, to taste

Instructions:
1. In the Instant Pot, add all the ingredients. Stir to mix well.
2. Lock the lid. Set the Instant Pot to Manual mode, then set the timer for 20 minutes at High Pressure.
3. Once cooking is complete, do a quick pressure release. Carefully open the lid.
4. Serve warm.

Nutritional info:
Calories 331, Fat 28.9g, Carbs 19.7g, Protein 5.1g

Cauliflower Mushroom Risotto

Prep Time: 7 mins, Cook time: 10 mins, Servings: 3
Ingredients:
- 1 cup freshly squeezed coconut milk
- 1 tbsp. coconut oil
- 1 cauliflower head, cut into florets
- 1 onion, chopped
- 1 lb. shiitake mushrooms, sliced
- Salt and pepper, to taste

Instructions:
1. Press the Sauté button and heat the coconut oil.
2. Sauté the onions for 3 minutes or until fragrant. Add the cauliflower and shiitake mushrooms.
3. Sprinkle salt and pepper for seasoning.
4. Add the coconut milk in three batches.
5. Allow to simmer for 10 minutes.
6. Garnish with chopped parsley if desired.

Nutritional info:
Calories 344, Fat 24.2g, Carbs 34g, Protein 6.3g

Vegetarian Smothered Cajun Greens

Prep Time: 6 mins, Cook time: 3 mins, Servings: 4
Ingredients:
- 2 tsps. crushed garlic
- Salt and pepper, to taste
- 1 onion, chopped
- 6 cups raw greens
- 1 tbsp. coconut oil
- 1 cup water

Instructions:
1. Press the Sauté button on the Instant Pot and heat the coconut oil.
2. Sauté the onion and garlic for 2 minutes or until fragrant.
3. Add the greens and Sprinkle salt and pepper for seasoning.
4. Add the water.
5. Lock the lid. Set the Instant Pot to Manual mode, then set the timer for 3 minutes at High Pressure.
6. Once cooking is complete, do a quick pressure release. Carefully open the lid.
7. Sprinkle with red chili flakes, then serve.

Nutritional info:
Calories 70, Fat 3.8g, Carbs 8.2g, Protein 3.2g

Caramelized Onions

Prep Time: 6 mins, Cook time: 35 mins, Servings: 2
Ingredients:
- 1 tbsp. freshly squeezed lemon juice
- 3 tbsps. coconut oil
- Salt and pepper, to taste
- 3 white onions, sliced

- 1 cup water

Instructions:
1. Press the Sauté button on the Instant Pot and heat the coconut oil.
2. Sauté the onions for 5 minutes and add the remaining ingredients.
3. Add the water and stir.
4. Lock the lid. Set the Instant Pot to Manual mode, then set the timer for 20 minutes at High Pressure.
5. Once cooking is complete, do a quick pressure release. Carefully open the lid.
6. Press the Sauté button and continue cooking for another 10 minutes.
7. Serve warm.

Nutritional info:
Calories 277, Fat 20.7g, Carbs 23.8g, Protein 2.8g

Zucchini and Tomato Melange
Prep Time: 13 mins, Cook time: 10 mins, Servings: 4
Ingredients:
- 5 garlic cloves, minced
- 3 medium zucchinis, chopped
- 1 lb. puréed tomatoes
- 1 onion, chopped
- 1 tbsp. coconut oil
- Salt and pepper, to taste
- 1 cup water

Instructions:
1. Place the tomatoes in a food processor and blend until smooth.
2. Press the Sauté button on the Instant Pot and heat the oil.
3. Sauté the garlic and onions for 2 minutes or until fragrant.
4. Add the zucchini and tomato purée.
5. Sprinkle salt and pepper for seasoning.
6. Add the water to add more moisture.
7. Lock the lid. Set the Instant Pot to Manual mode, then set the timer for 10 minutes at High Pressure.
8. Once cooking is complete, do a quick pressure release. Carefully open the lid.
9. Serve warm.

Nutritional info:
Calories 66, Fat 3.8g, Carbs 7.5g, Protein 2.1g

Instant Pot Veggie Stew
Prep Time: 6 mins, Cook time: 10 mins, Servings: 5
Ingredients:
- ½ cup chopped tomatoes
- 1 stalk celery, minced
- 2 zucchinis, chopped
- 1 lb. mushrooms, sliced
- 1 onion, chopped
- Salt and pepper, to taste

Instructions:
1. Place all ingredients in the Instant Pot.
2. Pour in enough water until half of the vegetables are submerged.
3. Lock the lid. Set the Instant Pot to Manual mode, then set the timer for 10 minutes at High Pressure.
4. Once cooking is complete, do a quick pressure release. Carefully open the lid.
5. Serve warm.

Nutritional info:
Calories 281, Fat 0.9g, Carbs 71.2g, Protein 9.2g

Zucchini and Bell Pepper Stir Fry
Prep Time: 6 mins, Cook time: 5 mins, Servings: 6
Ingredients:
- 2 large zucchinis, sliced
- 1 tbsp. coconut oil
- 4 garlic cloves, minced
- 2 red sweet bell peppers, julienned
- 1 onion, chopped
- Salt and pepper, to taste
- ¼ cup water

Instructions:
1. Press the Sauté button on the Instant Pot.
2. Heat the coconut oil and sauté the onion and garlic for 2 minutes or until fragrant.
3. Add the zucchini and red bell peppers.
4. Sprinkle salt and pepper for seasoning.
5. Pour in the water.
6. Lock the lid. Set the Instant Pot to Manual mode, then set the timer for 5 minutes at High Pressure.
7. Once cooking is complete, do a quick pressure release. Carefully open the lid.
8. Serve warm.

Nutritional info:
Calories 54, Fat 2.7g, Carbs 7.2g, Protein 1.8g

Eggplant, Zucchini, And Tomatoes
Prep Time: 6 mins, Cook time: 8 mins, Servings: 6
Ingredients:
- 3 zucchinis, sliced
- 1 eggplant, chopped
- 3 tbsps. olive oil
- 3 tomatoes, sliced
- 1 onion, diced
- Salt and pepper, to taste
- ¼ cup water

Instructions:
1. Press the Sauté button on the Instant Pot and heat the olive oil.
2. Sauté the onions for 3 minutes or until translucent, then add the eggplants. Sauté for another 2 minutes.
3. Add the tomatoes and zucchini.
4. Sprinkle salt and pepper for seasoning.
5. Add the water.

6. Lock the lid. Set the Instant Pot to Manual mode, then set the timer for 6 minutes at High Pressure.
7. Once cooking is complete, do a quick pressure release. Carefully open the lid.
8. Serve warm.

Nutritional info:
Calories 92, Fat 6.8g, Carbs 7.9g, Protein 1.3g

Instant Pot Baby Bok Choy

Prep Time: 9 mins, Cook time: 4 mins, Servings: 6

Ingredients:
- 1 tsp. peanut oil
- 1 lb. baby Bok choy, trimmed and washed
- Salt and pepper, to taste
- 4 garlic cloves, minced
- 1 tsp. red pepper flakes
- 1 cup water

Instructions:
1. Press the Sauté button on the Instant Pot.
2. Heat the oil and sauté the garlic for 1 minute until fragrant.
3. Add the Bok choy and sprinkle salt and pepper for seasoning.
4. Pour in the water.
5. Lock the lid. Set the Instant Pot to Manual mode, then set the timer for 4 minutes at High Pressure.
6. Once cooking is complete, do a quick pressure release. Carefully open the lid.
7. Sprinkle with red pepper flakes, then serve.

Nutritional info:
Calories 273, Fat 4.7g, Carbs 53.2g, Protein 4.3g

Sesame Bok Choy

Prep Time: 6 mins, Cook Time: 4 mins, Servings: 4

Ingredients:
- 1 tsp. soy sauce
- ½ tsp. sesame oil
- 1½ cups water
- 1 medium Bok choy
- 2 tsps. sesame seeds

Instructions:
1. Pour the water into the Instant Pot.
2. Place the Bok choy inside the steamer basket.
3. Lower the basket.
4. Lock the lid. Set the Instant Pot to Manual mode, then set the timer for 4 minutes at High Pressure.
5. Once cooking is complete, do a quick pressure release. Carefully open the lid.
6. In a serving bowl, set in the Bok choy. Toss with the remaining ingredients to coat.
7. Serve immediately!

Nutritional info:
Calories 54, Fats 2g, Carbs 5g, Protein 3g

Instant Pot Artichokes

Prep Time: 6 mins, Cook time: 30 mins, Servings: 8

Ingredients:
- ½ cup organic chicken broth
- Salt and pepper, to taste
- 4 large artichokes, trimmed and cleaned
- 1 onion, chopped
- 1 garlic clove, crushed

Instructions:
1. Place all ingredients in the Instant Pot.
2. Lock the lid. Set the Instant Pot to Manual mode, then set the timer for 30 minutes at High Pressure.
3. Once cooking is complete, do a quick pressure release. Carefully open the lid.
4. Serve the artichokes with lemon juice.

Nutritional info:
Calories 47, Fat 0.2g, Carbs 10.5g, Protein 3.1g

Cauliflower Mash

Prep Time: 12 mins, Cook time: 10 mins, Servings: 4

Ingredients:
- 1 cup water
- 1 cauliflower head, cut into florets
- ¼ tsp. salt
- ¼ tsp. ground black pepper
- ¼ tsp. garlic powder
- 1 handful chopped chives

Instructions:
1. Set a trivet in the Instant Pot and pour in the water.
2. Place the cauliflower.
3. Lock the lid. Set the Instant Pot to Steam mode, then set the timer for 10 minutes at High Pressure.
4. Once cooking is complete, do a quick pressure release. Carefully open the lid.
5. Using a food processor, pulse the cauliflower.
6. Add the garlic powder, salt, and pepper.
7. Garnish with chives, then serve.

Nutritional info:
Calories 18, Fat 0.2g, Carbs 3.7g, Protein 1.3g

Vegetarian Mac and Cheese

Prep Time: 30 mins, Cook time: 4 mins, Servings: 10

Ingredients:
- 4 cups water
- 1 tsp. garlic powder

- 16 oz. elbow macaroni pasta
- Salt and pepper, to taste
- 2 cups frozen mixed vegetables
- 1 cup shredded Cheddar
- 1 cup milk
- Fresh parsley, for garnish

Instructions:
1. To the Instant Pot, add the water, garlic powder and pasta. Sprinkle with salt and pepper.
2. Lock the lid. Set the Instant Pot to Manual mode, then set the timer for 4 minutes at High Pressure.
3. Once cooking is complete, do a quick pressure release. Carefully open the lid.
4. Add the vegetables, Cheddar and milk, then cover the pot and press Sauté.
5. Simmer until the vegetables have softened.
6. Garnish with fresh parsley and serve.

Nutritional Info:
Calories 456, Fat 4.9g, Carbs 77.5g, Protein 22.1g

Couscous with Vegetables

Prep Time: 30 mins, Cook time: 10 mins, Servings: 3

Ingredients:
- 2 tsps. olive oil
- 1 onion, chopped
- 1 red bell pepper, chopped
- 1 cup grated carrot
- 2 cups couscous
- 2 cups water
- Salt, to taste
- ½ tbsp. lemon juice

Instructions:
1. Grese the Instant Pot with olive oil. Add the onion.
2. Set to the Sauté mode and sauté the onion for 2 minutes.
3. Add the red bell pepper and carrot.
4. Cook for 3 minutes.
5. Add the couscous and water.
6. Season with salt.
7. Lock the lid. Set the Instant Pot to Manual mode, then set the timer for 2 minutes at High Pressure.
8. Once cooking is complete, do a natural pressure release. Carefully open the lid.
9. Fluff the couscous with a fork.
10. Drizzle with the lemon juice before serving.

Nutritional info:
Calories 477, Fat 0.9g, Carbs 99.4g, Protein 15.8g

Quinoa and Veggies

Prep Time: 15 mins, Cook Time: 5 mins, Servings: 4

Ingredients:
- 1½ cups water
- 1 cup rinsed and drained uncooked quinoa
- ¼ cup crumbled feta cheese
- Greek seasoning and olive oil mixture
- ¼ cup sliced cucumber
- ¼ cup diced black olives

Instructions:
1. Pour the water into the Instant Pot.
2. Add the quinoa.
3. Lock the lid. Set the Instant Pot to Manual mode, then set the timer for 1 minute at High Pressure.
4. Once cooking is complete, do a natural pressure release. Carefully open the lid.
5. In a bowl, mix cucumber and black olives.
6. Top with the quinoa and feta cheese.
7. Drizzle with the dressing, then serve.

Nutritional info:
Calories 233, Fat 10.9g, Carbs 28.1g, Protein 6.5g

Greek Style Beans

Prep Time: 10 hours, Cook time: 15 mins, Servings: 8

Ingredients:
- 8 cups water
- 3 cups navy beans
- Salt and pepper, to taste
- 28 oz. canned crushed tomatoes
- 1 garlic clove, peeled
- ¼ cup olive oil
- 1 onion, diced

Instructions:
1. In the Instant Pot, add the water and navy beans.
2. Season with a pinch of salt.
3. Soak for 10 hours.
4. Lock the lid. Set the Instant Pot to Bean/Chili mode, then set the timer for 3 minutes at High Pressure.
5. Once cooking is complete, do a natural pressure release. Carefully open the lid.
6. Set the beans in a bowl.
7. Set aside a cup of the cooking liquid. Drain the rest.
8. Select the Sauté mode and heat the olive oil. Add the tomatoes, garlic and onion to sauté for about 5 minutes.
9. Mix in the reserved cooking liquid.
10. Add the beans back.
11. Lock the lid. Set the Instant Pot to Bean/Chili mode, then set the timer for 5 minutes at High Pressure.
12. Once cooking is complete, do a natural pressure release. Carefully open the lid.
13. Add salt and pepper for seasoning.

Nutritional info:
Calories 352, Fat 7g, Carbs 55g, Protein 20.3g

Stuffed Peppers

Prep Time: 20 mins, Cook Time: 8 mins, Servings: 4

Ingredients:
- ¼ cup tomato sauce
- 4 large bell peppers, trimmed
- 2 cup chopped tomatoes
- Salt and pepper, to taste
- 4 basil leaves, chopped
- ½ cup chopped olives
- 1 cup water

Instructions:
1. Using a bowl, mix basil leaves, olives and tomatoes.
2. Season with salt and pepper.
3. Stuff bell peppers with the mixture. Top with a drizzle of tomato sauce.
4. In the Instant Pot, add the water.
5. Add the steamer rack inside. Carefully lay the bell peppers.
6. Lock the lid. Set the Instant Pot to Manual mode, then set the timer for 8 minutes at High Pressure.
7. Once cooking is complete, do a quick pressure release. Carefully open the lid.
8. Serve warm.

Nutritional info:
Calories 77, Fat 2.3g, Carbs 14.4g, Protein 2.4g

Garlic Baby Potatoes

Prep Time: 30 mins, Cook Time: 11 mins, Servings: 4

Ingredients:
- 1 tbsp. olive oil
- 3 garlic cloves
- 2 lbs. baby potatoes
- 1 sprig rosemary
- 1 cup vegetable stock
- Salt and pepper, to taste

Instructions:
1. Hit the Sauté button in the Instant Pot.
2. Add the olive oil.
3. Add the garlic, baby potatoes and rosemary.
4. Brown the outside of the potatoes.
5. Pierce each potato with a fork.
6. Add the vegetable stock.
7. Lock the lid. Set the Instant Pot to Manual mode, then set the timer for 11 minutes at High Pressure.
8. Once cooking is complete, do a quick pressure release. Carefully open the lid.
9. Season with salt and pepper and serve.

Nutritional info:
Calories 135, Fat 0.2g, Carbs 29g, Protein 6g

Stuffed Sweet Potatoes

Prep Time: 42 mins, Cook Time: 17 mins, Servings: 2

Ingredients:
- 1 cup cooked couscous
- 2 sweet potatoes
- 1 tbsp. olive oil
- 1 tsp. paprika
- Salt and pepper, to taste
- 1 cup cooked chickpeas
- 2 spring onions, chopped

Instructions:
1. Use a fork to pierce sweet potatoes.
2. To the Instant Pot, add enough water to cover.
3. Add the steamer rack inside and set the potatoes on top.
4. Lock the lid. Set the Instant Pot to Manual mode, then set the timer for 8 minutes on High Pressure.
5. Once cooking is complete, do a natural pressure release for 5 minutes. Carefully open the lid.
6. Set the sweet potato aside on a plate. Drain the pot.
7. While the Instant Pot is on Sauté mode, heat the olive oil. Set in chickpeas and paprika with salt and pepper.
8. Half the potatoes and mash the inside.
9. Add the chickpeas and couscous.
10. Top with the chopped spring onion and serve.

Nutritional info:
Calories 437, Fat 3.5g, Carbs 85.6g, Protein 16.5g

Italian Vegetable Medley

Prep Time: 50 mins, Cook Time: 8 mins, Servings: 4

Ingredients:
- 1 cup water
- 1 tbsp. raisins
- 1 zucchini, sliced
- 1 eggplant, cubed
- 3 tbsps. olive oil
- 10 halved cherry tomatoes
- 2 potatoes, cubed
- 2 tbsps. raisins

Instructions:
1. In the Instant Pot, add the water. Add the potatoes and zucchini.
2. Lock the lid. Set the Instant Pot to Manual mode, then set the timer for 8 minutes on High Pressure.
3. Once cooking is complete, do a quick pressure release. Carefully open the lid.
4. Drain water and add olive oil.
5. Mix in the tomatoes and eggplant. Let cook for 2 minutes.
6. Top with the raisins before serving.

Nutritional info:
Calories 172, Fat 1g, Carbs 38.9g, Protein 6.3g

Instant Ratatouille

<u>Prep Time: 20 mins, Cook Time: 10 mins, Servings: 4</u>
Ingredients:
- 2 cups water
- 2 medium zucchini, sliced
- 3 tomatoes, sliced
- 2 eggplants, sliced
- 1 tbsp. olive oil
- Salt and pepper, to taste

Instructions:
1. Pour the water into the Instant Pot.
2. In a baking dish, arrange a layer of the zucchini.
3. Top with a layer of the tomatoes.
4. Place a layer of eggplant slices on top.
5. Continue layering until you use all the ingredients.
6. Drizzle with olive oil.
7. Place the baking dish on the trivet and lower it.
8. Lock the lid. Set the Instant Pot to Manual mode, then set the timer for 10 minutes at High Pressure.
9. Once cooking is complete, do a quick pressure release. Carefully open the lid.
10. Sprinkle with salt and pepper and serve warm!

Nutritional info:
Calories 180, Fat 10g, Carbs 9.5g, Protein 2.5g

Kale and Sweet Potatoes with Tofu

<u>Prep Time: 45 mins, Cook time: 6 mins, Servings: 4</u>
Ingredients:
- 1 tbsp. tamari sauce
- ⅔ cup vegetable broth
- 1 sweet potato, cubed
- 2 cups chopped kale
- 8 oz. cubed tofu
- Salt and pepper, to taste

Instructions:
1. Add tofu in the Instant Pot.
2. Drizzle with half of the tamari and the broth.
3. Cook for about 3 minutes on Sauté function.
4. Add the rest of the ingredients.
5. Lock the lid. Set the Instant Pot to Manual mode, then set the timer for about 3 minutes at High Pressure.
6. Once cooking is complete, do a quick pressure release. Carefully open the lid.
7. Serve immediately!

Nutritional info:
Calories 130, Fat 2.5g, Carbs 13g, Protein 11g

Puréed Chili Carrots

<u>Prep Time: 25 mins, Cook time: 5 mins, Servings: 4</u>
Ingredients:
- 1½ cups water
- 1 tbsp. maple syrup
- 1 tbsp. coconut oil
- 1½ lbs. carrots, chopped
- 1 tsp. chili powder

Instructions:
1. Pour the water into the Instant Pot.
2. Place the chopped carrots inside the steamer basket.
3. Arrange the basket in the Instant Pot.
4. Lock the lid. Set the Instant Pot to Manual mode, then set the timer for 4 minutes on High Pressure.
5. Once cooking is complete, do a quick pressure release. Carefully open the lid.
6. Transfer the carrots along with the remaining ingredients to a food processor.
7. Process until puréed and smooth.
8. Serve immediately!

Nutritional info:
Calories 45, Fat 1g, Carbs 11g, Protein 1g

Lemon Artichokes

<u>Prep Time: 40 mins, Cook Time: 20 mins, Servings: 4</u>
Ingredients:
- 1½ cups water
- 2 artichokes, rinsed and trimmed
- Juice of 1 lemon
- 2 tbsps. Dijon mustard

Instructions:
1. Pour the water into the Instant Pot.
2. Place the artichokes inside the steamer basket, then drizzle the lemon juice over.
3. Arrange the basket in the Instant Pot.
4. Lock the lid. Set the Instant Pot to Manual mode, then set the timer for 20 minutes at High Pressure.
5. Once cooking is complete, do a quick pressure release. Carefully open the lid.
6. Serve immediately!

Nutritional info:
Calories 77, Fat 0.2g, Carbs 17g, Protein 5.3g

Tomato and Tofu Bake

<u>Prep Time: 12 mins, Cook Time: 4 mins, Servings: 4</u>
Ingredients:
- 2 tbsps. jarred banana pepper rings
- 1 tofu block, crumbled
- ½ cup vegetable broth
- 1 tbsp. Italian seasoning
- 1 can undrained and diced tomatoes

Instructions:
1. In the Instant Pot, set in all ingredients.
2. Give the mixture a good stir to incorporate everything well.

3. Lock the lid. Set the Instant Pot to Manual mode, then set the timer for 4 minutes on High Pressure.
4. Once cooking is complete, do a quick pressure release. Carefully open the lid.
5. Serve immediately!

Nutritional info:
Calories 140, Fat 6g, Carbs 9g, Protein 11g

Potato Mash

Prep Time: 15 mins, Cook Time: 8 mins, Servings: 4
Ingredients:
- 2 tbsps. coconut oil
- 4 medium potatoes
- 1 tsp. ground nutmeg
- ¼ cup coconut milk

Instructions:
1. Peel the potatoes and place them in the Instant Pot.
2. Add enough water to cover them.
3. Lock the lid. Set the Instant Pot to Manual mode, then set the timer for 8 minutes at High Pressure.
4. Once cooking is complete, do a quick pressure release. Carefully open the lid.
5. Drain any water present. Mash the potatoes.
6. Add the remaining ingredients.
7. Serve immediately!

Nutritional info:
Calories 210, Fat 7.2g, Carbs 34g, Protein 3.7g

Mango Tofu Curry

Prep Time: 15 mins, Cook Time: 35 mins, Servings: 2
Ingredients:
- 1 cup vegetable broth
- 1lb. vegetables, chopped
- 2 tbsps. curry paste
- 1lb. cubed extra firm tofu
- 1 cup mango sauce
- Salt and pepper, to taste

Instructions:
1. Mix all the ingredients in the Instant Pot.
2. Lock the lid. Set the Instant Pot to Manual mode, then set the timer for 35 minutes at High Pressure.
3. Once cooking is complete, do a quick pressure release. Carefully open the lid.
4. Serve warm.

Nutritional info:
Calories 310, Carbs 20g, Fat 4g, Protein 37g

Graceful Vegetarian Recipe

Prep Time: 12 mins, Cook Time: 12 mins, Servings: 2
Ingredients:
- 2 tsps. olive oil
- 1 cup shredded Cheddar cheese
- 2 cups broccoli florets
- 1½ cups vegetable broth
- Salt and pepper, to taste
- 1 cup long grain uncooked white rice

Instructions:
1. Grease an Instant Pot with olive oil and then add broth, rice, salt, and pepper.
2. Now add the broccoli.
3. Lock the lid. Set the Instant Pot to Manual mode, then set the timer for 12 minutes on High Pressure.
4. Once cooking is complete, do a quick pressure release. Carefully open the lid.
5. Add the cheese and stir twice.
6. Serve hot.

Nutritional info:
Calories 616, Fat 20.3g, Carbs 15g, Protein 3g

Zucchini and Tomato

Prep Time: 12 mins, Cook Time: 10 Mins, Servings: 1
Ingredients:
- ¼ cup crumbled feta cheese
- 1 cup vegetable broth
- Salt and pepper, to taste
- ½ cup fresh cherry tomatoes
- 1 fresh zucchini, chopped

Instructions:
1. Combine all the listed ingredients in the pot.
2. Lock the lid. Set the Instant Pot to Manual mode, then set the timer for 10 minutes at High Pressure.
3. Once cooking is complete, do a quick pressure release. Carefully open the lid.
4. Serve the chunky soup warm.

Nutritional info:
Calories 125, Fat 3.9g, Carbs 14.6g, Protein: 5g

Dump Cake

Prep Time: 12 mins, Cook Time: 25 mins, Servings: 2
Ingredients:
- ½ can apple pie filling
- 1 cup cake mix
- 1 tbsp. butter
- 1 cup water

Instructions:
1. Set butter in an oven to melt and then add to the cake mix.
2. Mix the ingredients well until lumpy.
3. Now pour the pie filling in it and mix well.
4. Now pour the water in the Instant Pot and adjust trivet on top.
5. Place the batter into a heatproof cake pan and adjust on top of the trivet.

6. Lock the lid. Set the Instant Pot to Manual mode, then set the timer for 25 minutes.
7. Once cooking is complete, do a natural pressure release for 10 minutes, then release any remaining pressure. Carefully open the lid.

Nutritional info:
Calories 635, Fat 18.7g, Carbs 114.5g, Protein 5.2g

Chapter 7 Beef, Lamb and Pork Recipe

Beef and Cauliflower

Prep Time: 12 mins, Cook Time: 30 mins, Servings: 4

Ingredients:
- 1 tbsp. extra virgin olive oil
- 1½ lbs. ground beef
- 1 tsp salt
- 1 cup puréed tomato
- 6 cups cauliflower, cut into florets
- 1 cup water

Instructions:
1. Set the Instant Pot to Sauté setting, then add the olive oil and heat until shimmering.
2. Add the beef and sauté for 4 or 5 minutes or until browned.
3. Add the rest of the ingredients.
4. Lock the lid. Select the Manual setting and set the timer at 30 minutes on High Pressure.
5. When the timer beeps, press Cancel, then use a quick pressure release.
6. Carefully open the lid and allow to cool for a few minutes. Serve warm.

Nutritional info:
Calories 418, Carbs 13g, Fat 19g, Protein 47g

Beef and Corn Chili

Prep Time: 12 mins, Cook Time: 30 mins, Servings: 4

Ingredients:
- 1 tbsp. olive oil
- 2 small onions, chopped
- 2 small chili peppers, diced
- ¼ cup canned corn
- 10 oz. lean ground beef
- 3 cups water
- Salt and pepper, to taste

Instructions:
1. Press Sauté on the Instant Pot. Heat the olive oil in the pot.
2. Add the onions, chili peppers, corn, and beef. Sauté for 2 to 3 minutes or until the onions are translucent and the peppers are softened.
3. Add the water to the Instant Pot, and sprinkle with salt and pepper. Mix to combine well.
4. Lock the lid. Press Meat/Stew. Set the timer to 20 minutes at High Pressure.
5. Once cooking is complete, press Cancel, then use a quick pressure release.
6. Open the lid, transfer them on 4 plates and serve.

Nutritional info:
Calories 94, Fat 5g, Carbs 2g, Protein 7g

Beef Meatballs with Tomato

Prep Time: 12 mins, Cook Time: 10 mins, Servings: 4

Ingredients:
- 1 lb. lean ground beef
- 2 large eggs
- 3 tbsps. all-purpose flour
- Salt and pepper, to taste
- 1 tbsp. olive oil
- 2 cups diced tomatoes
- 1 cup water

Instructions:
1. In a large bowl, thoroughly mix the beef, eggs, and flour, then sprinkle with salt and pepper. Mix well and make 6 meatballs of 1½ inch.
2. Grease a baking dish with olive oil and add the meatballs. Add the tomatoes and tightly wrap with a foil.
3. Pour the water in the Instant pot. Arrange the trivet or steamer basket inside, then place the dish on the trivet/basket.
4. Lock the lid. Press Manual. Set the timer to 10 minutes at High Pressure.
5. When the timer goes off, press Cancel, then use a quick pressure release.
6. Carefully open the lid. Allow to cool for a few minutes, then serve warm.

Nutritional info:
Calories 214, Fat 13g, Carbs 4g, Protein 18g

Beef Tenderloin with Cauliflower

Prep Time: 20 mins, Cook Time: 25 mins, Servings: 4

Ingredients:
- 1½ lbs. beef tenderloin
- 1 tsp. sea salt
- 1 tbsp. extra virgin olive oil
- 4 garlic cloves, finely chopped
- 4 cups cauliflower florets

Instructions:
1. On a clean work surface, slice the beef tenderloin into 1-inch thick slices and rub with salt.
2. Put the olive oil in the Instant Pot, set the Sauté setting.
3. Add and brown the beef for 4 to 5 minutes, then add the garlic and sauté for a minute.
4. Add the cauliflower.
5. Lock the lid. Set the Instant Pot to Manual mode and set the cooking time for 20 minutes at High Pressure.
6. Once cooking is complete, use a quick pressure release.
7. Carefully open the lid. Allow to cool for a few minutes. Transfer them on a large plate and serve immediately.

Nutritional info:
Calories 492, Carbs 13g, Fat 25g, Protein 52g

Bell Pepper and Beef

Prep Time: 12 mins, Cook time: 30 mins, Servings: 4

Ingredients:
- 1½ lbs. beef tenderloin
- 1 tsp. sea salt
- 4 green bell peppers, deseeded and stems removed
- 1 tbsp. extra virgin olive oil
- 1 red onion, peeled and diced
- 1 cup water

Instructions:
1. On a clean work surface, cut the beef into 1-inch thick slices, sprinkle with salt
2. Cut the bell peppers into ¼-inch slices.
3. Set Instant Pot to Sauté setting, then add extra virgin olive oil and heat until hot.
4. Add the beef and cook for 4 to 5 minutes or until browned.
5. Add peppers and onion, and sauté for 2 minutes. Pour in the water.
6. Lock the lid. Set the Instant Pot to the Manual setting and set the timer at 30 minutes at High Pressure.
7. When the timer beeps, press Cancel, then use a quick pressure release.
8. Carefully open the lid and allow to cool for a few minutes. Serve warm.

Nutritional info:
Calories 355, Carbs 24g, Fat 10g, Protein 39g

Big Papa's Roast

Prep Time: 12 mins, Coo Time: 1 hour, Servings: 6

Ingredients:
- 3 lbs. beef chuck roast
- 2 tsps. salt
- 6 peppercorns, crushed
- 2 tbsps. extra virgin olive oil
- 2 cups beef stock

Instructions:
1. On a clean work surface, rub the beef with salt and peppercorns.
2. Coat the Instant Pot with olive oil and set the Sauté setting. Heat the oil until shimmering.
3. Add and brown the beef roast for 4 to 5 minutes.
4. Pour in the beef stock.
5. Lock the lid. Set to Manual mode, set the cooking time for 60 minutes at High Pressure.
6. Once cooking is complete, use a natural pressure release for 10 minutes, then release any remaining pressure.
7. Carefully open the lid. Allow to cool for a few minutes. Transfer them on a large plate and serve immediately.

Nutritional info:
Calories 389, Carbs 11g, Fat 21g, Protein 34g

Corned Beef

Prep Time: 6 mins, Cook Time: 1 hour 30 mins, Servings: 4

Ingredients:
- 12 oz. beer
- 1 cup water
- 3 garlic cloves, minced
- 3 lbs. corned beef brisket
- Salt and pepper, to taste

Instructions:
1. Pour the beer and water into the Instant Pot. Add the garlic and mix to combine well.
2. Put the steamer basket inside.
3. Add the beef to the basket and season with salt and pepper.
4. Cover the pot. Select the Meat/Stew mode and cook at High Pressure for 90 minutes.
5. Once cooking is complete, do a quick pressure release for 10 minutes, and then release any remaining pressure. Carefully open the lid.
6. Transfer the beef to a baking pan and cover it with foil.
7. Let it rest for 15 minutes before slicing to serve.

Nutritional info:
Calories 417, Fat 28.3g, Carbs 4.9g, Protein 27.7g

Garlic Prime Rib

Prep Time: 12 mins, Cook Time: 1 hour, Servings: 10

Ingredients:
- 2 tbsps. olive oil
- 10 garlic cloves, minced
- 4 lbs. prime rib roast
- 2 tsps. dried thyme
- Salt and pepper, to taste
- 1 cup water

Instructions:
1. Press the Sauté button on the Instant Pot and heat the oil.
2. Add and sauté the garlic for 1 to 2 minutes until fragrant.
3. Add the prime rib roast and sear on all sides for 3 minutes until lightly browned.
4. Sprinkle with thyme, salt and pepper.
5. Pour in the water and remove the browning at the bottom.
6. Lock the lid. Set the pot to Meat/Stew mode and set the timer to 1 hour at High Pressure.
7. Once cooking is complete, use a natural pressure release for 10 minutes, then release any remaining pressure.

8. Carefully open the lid. Allow to cool for a few minutes. Transfer them on a large plate and serve immediately.

Nutritional info:
Calories 776, Fat 66.5g, Carbs 1.4g, Protein 40.6g

Garlicky Beef
Prep Time: 12 mins, Cook time: 10 mins, Servings: 4

Ingredients:
- 1½ lbs. beef sirloin
- 1 tbsp. sea salt
- 1 tbsp. extra virgin olive oil
- 5 garlic cloves, chopped
- 1 cup heavy cream

Instructions:
1. On a clean work surface, rub the beef with salt.
2. Set the Instant Pot to Sauté mode. Add the olive oil and heat until shimmering.
3. Add the beef and sear for 3 minutes until lightly browned.
4. Add garlic and sauté for 30 seconds or until fragrant.
5. Mix in the heavy cream.
6. Lock the lid. Set the pot to Manual setting and set the timer for 10 minutes at High Pressure.
7. When the timer beeps, press Cancel, then use a natural pressure release for 10 minutes, and then release any remaining pressure.
8. Carefully open the lid. Allow to cool for a few minutes. Transfer them on a large plate and serve immediately.

Nutritional info:
Calories 402, Carbs 14g, Fat 6g, Protein 29g

Ginger Short Ribs
Prep Time: 12 mins, Cook Time: 25 mins, Servings: 6

Ingredients:
- 4 beef short ribs
- 1 tsp. salt
- 3 tbsps. extra virgin olive oil, plus 1 tbsp. for coating
- 1 large onion, diced
- 2-inch knob of ginger, grated
- ¾ cup water

Instructions:
1. On a clean work surface, rub the ribs with salt.
2. Lightly coat the Instant Pot with olive oil and set the setting to Sauté.
3. Add the onion and ginger, then sauté for a minute.
4. Add the ribs and brown for 4 to 5 minutes. Pour in the water.
5. Lock the lid. Set to Manual mode and set the cooking time for 25 minutes at High Pressure.

6. Once cooking is complete, use a natural pressure release for 10 minutes, then release any remaining pressure.
7. Carefully open the lid. Allow to cool for a few minutes. Transfer them on a large plate and serve immediately.

Nutritional info:
Calories 454, Carbs 28g, Fat 18g, Protein 29g

Gingered Beef Tenderloin
Prep Time: 12 mins, Cook Time: 1 hour, Servings: 8

Ingredients:
- 2 tbsps. olive oil
- 2 tbsps. minced garlic
- 2 tbsps. thinly sliced ginger
- 4 fillet mignon steaks
- ¼ cup soy sauce
- Salt and pepper, to taste
- 1 cup water

Instructions:
1. Press the Sauté button on the Instant Pot and heat the olive oil.
2. Sauté the garlic for 1 minute until fragrant.
3. Add the ginger and fillet mignon and allow to sear for 4 minutes or until lightly browned.
4. Drizzle with the soy sauce. Add salt and pepper to taste. Pour in a cup of water.
5. Lock the lid and select the Meat/Stew mode and set the timer to 1 hour at High Pressure.
6. Once cooking is complete, use a natural pressure release for 10 minutes, then release any remaining pressure.
7. Carefully open the lid. Allow to cool for a few minutes. Transfer them on a large plate and discard the bay leaf, then serve.

Nutritional info:
Calories 199, Fat 9.8g, Carbs 1.3g, Protein 24.8g

Herbed Sirloin Tip Roast
Prep Time: 5 mins, Cook Time: 1 hour 30 mins, Servings: 6

Ingredients:
- 2 tbsps. mixed herbs
- 1 tsp. garlic powder
- 3 lbs. sirloin tip roast
- 1¼ tsps. paprika
- 1 cup water
- Salt and pepper, to taste

Instructions:
1. In the Instant Pot, combine all the ingredients. Stir to mix well.

2. Lock the lid. Set the pot to Meat/Stew mode and set the timer to 1 hour 30 minutes at High Pressure.
3. Once cooking is complete, use a natural pressure release for 10 minutes, then release any remaining pressure.
4. Carefully open the lid. Allow to cool for a few minutes. Transfer them on a large plate and discard the bay leaf, then serve.

Nutritional info:
Calories 394, Fat 25.4g, Carbs 1.6g, Protein 37.7g

Instant Pot Rib Roast
Prep Time: 6 mins, Cook Time: 2 hours 30 mins, Servings: 12

Ingredients:
- 5 lbs. beef rib roast
- 1 tsp. garlic powder
- 1 bay leaf
- 1 tbsp. olive oil
- Salt and pepper, to taste
- 1 cup water

Instructions:
1. Put all the ingredients in the Instant Pot. Stir to mix well.
2. Lock the lid. Set the pot to Meat/Stew mode and set the timer to 2 hours 30 minutes at High Pressure.
3. Once cooking is complete, use a natural pressure release for 10 to 20 minutes, then release any remaining pressure.
4. Carefully open the lid. Allow to cool for a few minutes. Transfer them on a large plate and discard the bay leaf, then serve.

Nutritional info:
Calories 601, Fat 52.2g, Carbs 0.5g, Protein 32.3g

Lemon Beef Meal
Prep Time: 12 mins, Cook Time: 10 mins, Servings: 2

Ingredients:
- 1 tbsp. olive oil
- 2 beef steaks
- ½ tsp. garlic salt
- 1 garlic clove, crushed
- 2 tbsps. lemon juice

Instructions:
1. Press Sauté on the Instant Pot. Heat the olive oil in the pot until shimmering.
2. Add the beef and garlic salt and sauté for 4 to 5 minutes to evenly brown.
3. Add the garlic and sauté for 1 minute until fragrant.
4. Serve with lemon juice on top.

Nutritional info:
Calories 86, Fat 7g, Carbs 2g, Protein 2g

Mushroom and Beef Meal
Prep Time: 12 mins, Cook Time: 40 mins, Servings: 4

Ingredients:
- 1 lb. fat removed beef ribs
- Salt, to taste
- 3 cups low-sodium beef stock
- 1 bacon slice, chopped
- 2 cups button mushrooms slices

Instructions:
1. On a clean work surface, rub the beef ribs with salt.
2. Add the ribs and stock to the Instant Pot. Stir to combine well.
3. Lock the lid. Press Manual. Set the timer to 30 minutes at High Pressure.
4. When the timer goes off, press Cancel, then use a natural pressure release for 10 minutes, and then release any remaining pressure.
5. Take out the beef and shred with a knife.
6. Put the shredded beef back to the pot, add the bacon and mushrooms; gently stir to combine.
7. Lock the lid. Press Manual. Set the timer to 7 minutes at High Pressure.
8. Once the timer goes off, press Cancel, then use a quick pressure release.
9. Open the lid, transfer them on 4 plates and serve.

Nutritional info:
Calories 318, Fat 27g, Carbs 3g, Protein 15g

Sautéed Beef and Green Beans
Prep Time: 12 mins, Cook Time: 5 mins, Servings: 4

Ingredients:
- 1 tbsp. olive oil
- 10 oz. fat removed beef sirloin
- 2 spring onions, chopped
- 7 oz. canned green beans
- 2 tbsps. soy sauce
- Salt and pepper, to taste

Instructions:
1. Press Sauté on the Instant Pot. Grease the pot with the olive oil.
2. Add the beef and sauté for 2 to 3 minutes to evenly brown.
3. Add the onions, green beans, and soy sauce, then sauté for another 2 to 3 minutes until the beans are soft. Sprinkle with salt and pepper.
4. Serve warm.

Nutritional info:
Calories 176, Fat 9g, Carbs 2g, Protein 14g

Super Beef Chili
Prep Time: 12 mins, Cook Time: 8 mins, Servings: 4

Ingredients:
- 1 lb. ground beef

- 1½ tsps. sea salt
- 1 medium onion, chopped
- 2 cups tomato purée
- 2 cups zucchini, peeled and rinsed, cut into 1-inch bites
- 1 cup water
- 1 tsp. chili spice powder

Instructions:
1. Select the Instant Pot to Sauté setting. Coat the pot with olive oil and heat until shimmering.
2. Add the beef, salt and onion, then sauté for 4 minutes or until the beef is lightly browned.
3. Add the tomato purée, zucchini, water and chili spice powder. Stir to mix well.
4. Lock the lid. Set the Instant Pot to Manual setting and set the timer for 8 minutes at High Pressure.
5. Once cooking is complete, use a quick pressure release.
6. Carefully open the lid. Allow to cool for a few minutes. Transfer them on a large plate and serve immediately.

Nutritional info:
Calories 399, Carbs 6g, Fat 18g, Protein 51g

Sweet Apricot Beef
Prep Time: 12 mins, Cook Time: 30 mins, Servings: 4
Ingredients:
- 1½ lbs. beef tenderloin
- 1 tsp. sea salt
- 1 tbsp. coconut oil
- 4 apricots, pitted and sliced thinly
- ½ cup chopped almonds
- 1 cup water

Instructions:
1. On a clean work surface, sprinkle the beef with salt and cut into 1-inch thick slices.
2. Set the Instant Pot to Sauté setting, then add coconut oil and heat until melted.
3. Add the beef and sauté for 4 to 5 minutes or until browned.
4. Add the apricot and sauté for a minute. Add the chopped almonds. Pour in the water.
5. Lock the lid. Press the Manual setting and set the timer at 30 minutes at High Pressure.
6. When the timer beeps, press Cancel, then use a quick pressure release.
7. Carefully open the lid and allow to cool for a few minutes. Serve warm.

Nutritional info:
Calories 254, Carbs 7g, Fat 10g, Protein 33g

Sweet Potato Beef
Prep Time: 12 mins, Cook Time: 40 mins, Servings: 4
Ingredients:
- 1 tbsp. olive oil
- 1 lb. lean beef stew meat
- 4 cups low-sodium beef stock
- 1 small sweet potato, diced
- 1 tomato, roughly chopped
- 2 bell peppers, sliced
- Salt and pepper, to taste

Instructions:
1. Press Sauté on Instant Pot. Grease the pot with the olive oil.
2. Add the beef and sauté for 4 to 5 minutes to evenly brown.
3. Mix in the remaining ingredients.
4. Lock the lid. Press Manual. Set the timer to 35 minutes at High Pressure.
5. When the timer beeps, press Cancel, then use a quick pressure release.
6. Open the lid, transfer them in 4 plates and serve warm.

Nutritional info:
Calories 257, Fat 7g, Carbs 18g, Protein 29g

Cheesy Veal Steaks
Prep Time: 12 mins, Cook Time: 35 mins, Servings: 2
Ingredients:
- 1 tbsp. olive oil
- 2 fat removed veal steaks
- 1¼ cup water
- 2 cups cherry tomatoes
- 3 tbsps. grated Cheddar cheese
- ¼ cup reduced fat coconut milk

Instructions:
1. Press Sauté on the Instant Pot. Grease the pot with the olive oil.
2. Add the steaks and sauté for 3 to 4 minutes to evenly brown.
3. Add 1 cup of water and mix well.
4. Lock the lid. Press Manual. Set the timer to 25 minutes at High Pressure.
5. When the timer beeps, press Cancel, then use a natural pressure release for 10 minutes, and then release any remaining pressure.
6. Open the lid, drain the liquid, transfer the steaks to a serving plate.
7. Clean the pot.
8. Press Sauté and add the tomatoes and ¼ cup of water and sauté for 3 to 4 minutes or until lightly wilted.
9. Stir in the cheese and milk, then cook until the cheese melts.
10. Pour them over the steaks and serve.

Nutritional info:
Calories 248, Fat 11g, Carbs 1g, Protein 27g

Rosemary Lamb

Prep Time: 12 mins, Cook Time: 30 mins, Servings: 4
Ingredients:
- 1 tbsp. olive oil
- 2 lamb shanks
- 2 bay leaves
- 2 onions, chopped
- 3 cups low-sodium beef broth
- 2 rosemary sprigs
- Salt and pepper, to taste

Instructions:
1. Press Sauté on the Instant Pot. Grease the pot with the olive oil.
2. Add the lamb and sauté for 4 to 5 minutes to evenly brown.
3. Add the onions and sauté for 4 minutes until translucent and softened.
4. Add the remaining ingredients and stir well.
5. Lock the lid. Press Manual. Set the timer to 20 minutes at High Pressure.
6. When the timer beeps, press Cancel, then use a natural pressure release for 10 minutes, and then release any remaining pressure.
7. Carefully open the top lid, transfer them on 4 serving plates.
8. Remove the rosemary sprigs and bay leaves. Serve warm.

Nutritional info:
Calories 318, Fat 17g, Carbs 3g, Protein 37g

Adobo Pork Chops

Prep Time: 6 mins, Cook Time: 15 mins, Servings: 5
Ingredients:
- 3 tbsps. olive oil
- 1 lb. pork chops
- ¼ cup freshly squeezed lemon juice
- 3 garlic cloves, minced
- ½ cup soy sauce
- Salt and pepper, to taste
- ¼ cup water

Instructions:
1. Coat the Instant pot with olive oil. Arrange the pork chops in the Instant Pot, then add the remaining ingredients.
2. Lock the lid. Press the Meat/Stew button and set the cooking time to 15 minutes at High Pressure.
3. Once cooking is complete, do a natural pressure release for 10 minutes, and then release any remaining pressure. Carefully open the lid.
4. Serve the pork chops on a large platter.

Nutritional info:
Calories 271, Carbs 2.3g, Protein, 18.2g, Fat 23.3g

Asian Lemongrass Pork

Prep Time: 10 mins, Cook Time: 35 min, Servings: 6
Ingredients:
- 4 tbsps. coconut oil
- 6 garlic cloves
- 2 tbsps. lemongrass
- 2 lbs. pork shoulder
- ¼ cup fish sauce
- Salt and pepper, to taste
- 1 cup water

Instructions:
1. Press the Sauté button on the Instant pot and heat the coconut oil until melted.
2. Add and sauté the garlic and lemongrass for 1 minutes or until fragrant.
3. Add and sauté the pork chunks for 3 minutes, or until all sides are seared.
4. Pour in the fish sauce. Sprinkle with salt and pepper, and pour in the water.
5. Lock the lid. Press the Meat/Stew button and set the cooking time to 30 minutes at High Pressure.
6. Once cooking is complete, perform a natural pressure release for 10 minutes, and then release any remaining pressure. Carefully open the lid.
7. Remove the pork from the pot and serve warm.

Nutritional info:
Calories 249, Carbs 0.8g, Protein 21.5g, Fat 23.3g

Asian Striped Pork

Prep Time: 6 mins, Cook Time: 20 mins, Servings: 2
Ingredients:
- 1 tbsp. avocado oil
- 2 garlic cloves
- ½ lb. pork sirloin, sliced
- 1 tbsp. soy sauce
- ½ cup water
- Salt and pepper, to taste
- 2 tbsps. sesame oil

Instructions:
1. Press the Sauté button on the Instant pot and heat the avocado oil.
2. Add and sauté the garlic for 1 minute or until fragrant.
3. Add the pork sirloin and sear on all sides for 3 minutes or until lightly browned.
4. Pour in the soy sauce and water, then sprinkle salt and pepper for seasoning.
5. Lock the lid. Press the Meat/Stew button and set the cooking time to 15 minutes at High Pressure.
6. Once cooking is complete, perform a natural pressure release for 10

minutes, and then release any remaining pressure. Carefully open the lid.
7. Allow to cool for a few minutes. Drizzle with sesame oil. Remove the pork from the pot and baste with the juice remains in the pot before serving.

Nutritional info:
Calories 251, Carbs 0.6g, Protein 12.1g, Fat 23.8g

Balsamic Pulled Pork Casserole
Prep Time: 6 mins, Cook Time: 8 hours, Servings: 4
Ingredients:
- ¼ tsp. balsamic vinegar
- 4 cups leftover pulled pork
- ¼ cup olive oil
- Salt and pepper, to taste
- 4 eggs, beaten

Instructions:
1. In a mixing bowl, combine all ingredients until well incorporated.
2. Pour into the Instant Pot.
3. Lock the lid. Press the Slow Cook button and set the cooking time to 8 hours at High Pressure.
4. Once cooking is complete, perform a natural pressure release for 10 minutes, and then release any remaining pressure. Carefully open the lid.
5. Remove the pork from the pot and serve warm.

Nutritional info:
Calories 372, Carbs 2.1g, Protein 21.7g, Fat 32.2g

Basic Pork Chops
Prep Time: 6 mins, Cook Time: 30 mins, Servings: 6
Ingredients:
- 3 tbsps. butter
- 3 garlic cloves, minced
- 6 boneless pork chops
- ½ cup heavy cream
- ½ cup chicken broth
- Salt and pepper, to taste

Instructions:
1. Press the Sauté button on the Instant Pot.
2. Heat the butter until melted and add and sauté the garlic for 1 minute or until fragrant.
3. Add the pork chops and sear for 3 minutes on each side until lightly browned.
4. Add the heavy cream and broth. Sprinkle salt and pepper for seasoning.
5. Lock the lid. Press the Meat/Stew button and set the cooking time to 30 minutes at High Pressure.
6. Once cooking is complete, perform a natural pressure release for 10 minutes, and then release any remaining pressure. Carefully open the lid.
7. Allow to cool for a few minutes. Remove the pork from the pot and baste with the juice remains in the pot before serving.

Nutritional info:
Calories 439, Carbs 0.9g, Protein 26.7g, Fat 46.2g

Blueberry Pork Yum
Prep Time: 12 mins, Cook time: 7 mins, Servings: 6
Ingredients:
- 1½ lbs. boneless pork chops
- 1 tbsp. sea salt
- 2 tbsps. extra virgin olive oil
- 2 cups fresh blueberries
- 1 cup chicken stock

Instructions:
1. On a clean work surface, rub the chops with salt.
2. Set the Instant Pot to Sauté mode.
3. Add the olive oil to Instant Pot and heat until shimmering.
4. Add the pork and sear for 3 minutes until lightly browned.
5. Add the berries and chicken stock.
6. Lock the lid. Set the pot to Manual and set the timer for 7 minutes at High Pressure.
1. When the timer beeps, press Cancel, then use a quick pressure release.
2. Carefully open the lid. Allow to cool for a few minutes. Transfer them on a large plate and serve immediately.

Nutritional info:
Calories 364, Carbs 7g, Fat 15g, Protein 47g

Coconut Pork
Prep Time: 20 mins, Cook Time: 25 mins, Servings: 4
Ingredients:
- 1 tbsp. extra virgin olive oil
- 4 pork chops
- 1 tbsp. grated ginger
- 1 tsp. sea salt
- 2 cups coconut milk

Instructions:
1. Lightly coat the Instant Pot with olive oil and select the setting to Sauté.
2. Add and brown the pork chops for 3 minutes.
3. Add the remaining ingredients to the pot. Stir to combine well.
4. Lock the lid. Set the Manual mode and set the cooking time to 25 minutes at High Pressure.
5. Once cooking is complete, use a natural pressure release for 10 minutes, then release any remaining pressure.

6. Carefully open the lid. Allow to cool for a few minutes. Transfer them on a large plate and serve immediately.

Nutritional info:
Calories 607, Carbs 13g, Fat 38g, Protein 52g

Creamy Pork Pasta

Prep Time: 12 mins, Cook Time: 5 mins, Servings: 4

Ingredients:
- 1 tbsp. olive oil
- 1 lb. ground pork
- 1½ tsps. salt
- 6 garlic cloves, finely sliced
- 4 eggplant, stem removed, rinsed, cut into 1-inch slices
- 1 cup heavy cream

Instructions:
1. Set the Instant Pot to Sauté setting. Grease with olive oil and heat until shimmering.
2. Add the pork, salt and garlic. Sauté for 3 minutes or until the meat has browned.
3. Add the eggplant and heavy cream. Stir to mix well.
4. Lock the lid. Set the Instant Pot to Manual setting and set the timer for 5 minutes at High Pressure.
5. Once cooking is complete, use a quick pressure release.
6. Carefully open the lid. Allow to cool for a few minutes. Transfer them on a large plate and serve immediately.

Nutritional info:
Calories 399, Carbs 6g, Fat 18g, Protein 51g

Easy Chinese Pork

Prep Time: 10 mins, Cook Time: 25 mins, Servings: 4

Ingredients:
- 4 tbsps. coconut oil
- 4 garlic cloves, minced
- 1 tbsp. fresh ginger
- 4 boneless pork chops
- 2 tbsps. soy sauce
- Salt and pepper, to taste
- 1 cup water

Instructions:
1. Press the Sauté button on the Instant Pot and heat the coconut oil until melted.
2. Add and sauté the garlic and ginger for 1 minutes or until fragrant.
3. Add the pork and sauté for 3 minutes or until lightly browned.
4. Pour in the soy sauce and water, then sprinkle salt and pepper for seasoning.
5. Lock the lid. Press the Meat/Stew button and set the cooking time to 20 minutes at High Pressure.
6. Once cooking is complete, perform a natural pressure release for 10 minutes, and then release any remaining pressure. Carefully open the lid.
7. Press the Sauté button and allow to simmer for 3 to 5 minutes or until the sauce has thickened. Keep stirring.
8. Allow to cool for a few minutes. Remove them from the pot and serve warm.

Nutritional info:
Calories 359, Carbs 1.5g, Protein 19.7g, Fat 41.6g

Eggplant Lasagna

Prep Time: 15 mins, Coo Time: 45 mins, Servings: 7

Ingredients:
- 4 English eggplants, rinsed and stem removed
- 2 tbsps. olive oil
- 1 lb. ground pork
- 1 tsp. salt
- ¾ cup shredded Mozzarella cheese
- 8 cups tomato sauce

Instructions:
1. Slice eggplants into 1-inch slices and douse them in a bowl of water, squeeze slices and set aside.
2. Set the Instant Pot on Sauté setting. Heat the olive oil in the pot until shimmering.
3. Add pork and salt and sauté for 3 minutes or until lightly browned, remove from the pot.
4. Place half of the eggplant on the bottom of pot, pour in half of the tomato sauce, half of the pork and half of the Mozzarella cheese.
5. Top with remaining eggplants, tomato sauce, pork, and cheese.
6. Lock the lid. Set the Instant Pot to the Manual setting and set the time to 45 minutes at High Pressure.
7. Once cooking is complete, use a quick pressure release.
8. Carefully open the lid. Allow to cool for a few minutes. Transfer them on a large plate and serve immediately.

Nutritional info:
Calories 257, Carbs 16g, Fat 16g, Protein 16g

Garlicky Pork Tenderloin

Prep Time: 6 mins, Cook Time: 8 hours, Servings: 10

Ingredients:
- 3 tbsps. extra virgin olive oil
- ¼ cup butter
- 1 tsp. thyme
- 1 garlic clove, minced
- 3 lbs. pork tenderloin
- 1 cup water

- Salt and pepper, to taste

Instructions:
1. Set the Instant Pot on Sauté. Heat the olive oil and butter until the butter is melted.
2. Add and sauté the garlic and thyme for 1 minute or until fragrant.
3. Add the pork tenderloin and sauté for 3 minutes or until lightly browned.
4. Pour in the water and sprinkle salt and pepper for seasoning.
5. Lock the lid. Press the Slow Cook button and set the cooking time to 8 hours at High Pressure.
6. Once cooking is complete, perform a natural pressure release for 10 minutes, and then release any remaining pressure. Carefully open the lid.
7. Allow to cool for a few minutes. Remove the pork from the pot and serve warm.

Nutritional info:
Calories 252, Carbs 0.2g, Protein 11.8g, Fat 35.6g

Indian Roasted Pork
Prep Time: 6 mins, Cook Time: 8 hours, Servings: 3

Ingredients:
- 1 tbsp. olive oil
- 1 lb. pork loin
- 1 tsp. cumin
- 2 garlic cloves, roughly chopped
- 1 onion, sliced
- Salt and pepper, to taste

Instructions:
1. Coat the Instant Pot with olive oil and add the pork loin. Set aside.
2. In a food processor, place the remaining ingredients.
3. Pulse until smooth then pour the mixture over the pork loin.
4. Lock the lid. Press the Slow Cook button and set the cooking time to 8 hours at High Pressure.
5. Once cooking is complete, perform a natural pressure release for 10 minutes, and then release any remaining pressure. Carefully open the lid.
6. Allow to cool for a few minutes. Remove them from the pot and serve warm.

Nutritional info:
Calories 321, Carbs 0.6g, Protein 19.5g, Fat 26.5g

Instant Pot Rib
Prep Time: 6 mins, Cook Time: 8 hours, Servings: 3

Ingredients:
- 1 rack baby back rib
- 1 tbsp. smoked paprika
- 2 tbsps. olive oil
- 1 tbsp. onion powder
- 1 tbsp. garlic powder
- Salt and pepper, to taste
- ½ cup water

Instructions:
1. Prepare a baking sheet. Lay on the ribs. Rub with paprika, olive oil, onion powder, garlic powder, salt, and pepper.
2. Place the well-coated rib in the Instant Pot. Pour in the water.
3. Lock the lid. Press the Slow Cook button and set the cooking time to 8 hours at High Pressure.
4. Once cooking is complete, perform a natural pressure release for 10 minutes, and then release any remaining pressure. Carefully open the lid.
5. Allow to cool for a few minutes. Remove the rib from the pot and serve warm.

Nutritional info:
Calories 1375, Carbs 6.4g, Protein 98.2g, Fat 104.7g

Italian Pork Cutlets
Prep Time: 6 mins, Cook Time: 20 mins, Servings: 6

Ingredients:
- 4 tbsps. olive oil
- 6 pork cutlets
- Salt and pepper, to taste
- 1 tbsp. Italian herb mix
- 1½ cups water

Instructions:
1. In the Instant Pot, add all the ingredients. Stir to combine well.
2. Lock the lid. Press the Meat/Stew button and set the cooking time to 20 minutes at High Pressure.
3. Once cooking is complete, do a natural pressure release for 10 minutes, and then release any remaining pressure. Carefully open the lid.
4. Remove the meat and serve immediately.

Nutritional info:
Calories 322, Carbs 0.9g, Protein 19.4g, Fat 34.6g

Mexican Chili Pork
Prep Time: 6 mins, Cook Time: 35 mins, Servings: 6

Ingredients:
- 3 tbsps. olive oil
- 2 tsps. minced garlic
- 2 lbs. pork sirloin, sliced
- 2 tsps. ground cumin
- 1 tbsp. red chili flakes
- 1 cup water
- Salt and pepper, to taste

Instructions:
1. Press the Sauté button on the Instant pot and heat the olive oil until shimmering.
2. Add and sauté the garlic for 30 seconds or until fragrant.
3. Add the pork sirloin and sauté for 3 minutes or until lightly browned.
4. Add the cumin and chili flakes.
5. Pour in the water and sprinkle salt and pepper for seasoning.
6. Lock the lid. Press the Meat/Stew button and set the cooking time to 30 minutes at High Pressure.
7. Once cooking is complete, perform a natural pressure release for 10 minutes, and then release any remaining pressure. Carefully open the lid.
8. Remove the pork from the pot and serve warm.

Nutritional info:
Calories 159, Carbs 0.8g, Protein 21.1g, Fat 16.8g

Mexican Pulled Pork
Prep Time: 6 mins, Cook Time: 1 hour, Servings: 12
Ingredients:
- 4 lbs. pork shoulder
- 1 tsp. cinnamon
- 2 tsps. garlic powder
- 5 tbsps. coconut oil
- 1 tsp. cumin powder
- 1½ cups water
- Salt and pepper, to taste

Instructions:
1. In the Instant Pot, add all the ingredients. Stir to combine well.
2. Lock the lid. Press the Meat/Stew button and set the cooking time to 1 hour at High Pressure.
3. Once cooking is complete, do a natural pressure release for 10 minutes, and then release any remaining pressure. Carefully open the lid.
4. Remove the meat and shred with two forks to serve.

Nutritional info:
Calories 364, Carbs 0.5g, Protein 20.4g, Fat 35.9g

Mustard Pork and Mushrooms
Prep Time: 6 mins, Cook Time: 35 mins, Servings: 6
Ingredients:
- 3 tbsps. butter
- 2 lbs. pork shoulder
- 3 tbsps. yellow mustard
- 1 cup water
- 1 cup sliced mushrooms
- Salt and pepper, to taste

Instructions:
1. Press the Sauté button on the Instant Pot and heat the butter until melted.
2. Add the pork shoulder and mustard. Sauté for 3 minutes or until the pork is lightly browned.
3. Stir in water and mushrooms. Sprinkle salt and pepper for seasoning.
4. Lock the lid. Press the Meat/Stew button and set the cooking time to 30 minutes at High Pressure.
5. Once cooking is complete, perform a natural pressure release for 10 minutes, and then release any remaining pressure. Carefully open the lid.
6. Remove the pork from the pot and serve warm.

Nutritional info:
Calories 286, Carbs 0.3g, Protein 22.9g, Fat 20.8g

Paprika Pork Loin Roast
Prep Time: 6 mins, Cook Time: 50 mins, Servings: 9
Ingredients:
- 4 tbsps. olive oil
- 4 garlic cloves
- ½ cup chopped paprika
- 3 lbs. pork loin roast
- Salt and pepper, to taste
- 1 cup water

Instructions:
1. Press the Sauté button on the Instant Pot. Coat the pot with olive oil.
2. Add and sauté the garlic and paprika for 1 minute or until fragrant.
3. Add the pork loin roast and sear on all sides for 3 minutes or until lightly browned.
4. Sprinkle salt and pepper for seasoning. Pour in the water.
5. Lock the lid. Press the Meat/Stew button and set the cooking time to 45 minutes at High Pressure.
6. Once cooking is complete, perform a natural pressure release for 10 minutes, and then release any remaining pressure. Carefully open the lid.
7. Allow to cool for a few minutes. Remove the pork from the pot and baste with the juice remains in the pot before serving.

Nutritional info:
Calories 273, Carbs 3.1g, Protein 20.7g, Fat 22.8g

Pear and Pork Butt
Prep Time: 12 mins, Cook time: 50 mins, Servings: 12
Ingredients:
- 4 lbs. pork butt
- 2 tbsps. sea salt
- 3 tbsps. extra virgin olive oil

- 4 pears, peeled, stem removed, deseeded, and cut into ½-inch chunks
- 1½ cups chicken broth

Instructions:
1. On a clean work surface, rub the pork butt with salt.
2. Set the Instant Pot to Sauté setting, then add and heat the olive oil.
3. Place pork in pot and brown for 5 minutes per side.
4. Add pears and chicken broth. Stir to mix well.
5. Lock the lid. Set the pot to Manual setting and set the timer for 45 minutes at High Pressure.
6. When the timer beeps, press Cancel, then use a quick pressure release.
7. Carefully open the lid and allow to cool for a few minutes. Serve warm.

Nutritional info:
Calories 503, Carbs 9g, Fat 31g, Protein 44g

Pine Nut Pork

Prep Time: 20 mins, Cook Time: 25 mins, Servings: 4

Ingredients:
- 1½ lbs. pork tenderloin
- 1 tsp. sea salt
- 1 tbsp. extra virgin olive oil
- 1 medium onion, finely sliced
- ½ cup pine nuts
- 1 cup pesto sauce

Instructions:
1. On a clean work surface, cut the pork tenderloin into 1-inch thick slices and rub with salt.
2. Place the olive oil in Instant Pot, then set to Sauté setting.
3. Add and brown the pork for 3 minutes, then add onion and sauté for a minute or until translucent.
4. Add the pine nuts and pesto sauce.
5. Lock the lid. Set the pot to Manual mode and set the timer to 20 minutes at High Pressure.
6. Once cooking is complete, use a natural pressure release for 10 minutes, then release any remaining pressure.
6. Carefully open the lid. Allow to cool for a few minutes. Transfer them on a large plate and serve immediately.

Nutritional info:
Calories 492, Carbs 13g, Fat 25g, Protein 52g

Pork and Sweet Potato

Prep Time: 20 mins, Cook Time: 25 mins, Servings: 8

Ingredients:
- 2 tbsps. extra virgin olive oil
- 2 lbs. pork tenderloin, slice into 1-inch bites
- 1 tsp. sea salt
- 2 sweet potatoes, peeled and quartered
- 4 cups beef broth

Instructions:
1. Lightly coat the Instant Pot with the olive oil and set the Sauté mode.
2. Add the pork along with salt and brown for 3 minutes on all sides.
3. Add sweet potatoes with beef broth to the pot.
4. Set the setting to Manual mode and set the cooking time for 25 minutes at High Pressure.
5. Once cooking is complete, use a quick pressure release.
6. Carefully open the lid. Allow to cool for a few minutes. Transfer them on a large plate and serve immediately.

Nutritional info:
Calories 492, Carbs 22g, Fat 25g, Protein 52g

Pork Chops and Peas

Prep Time: 12 mins, Cook time: 10 mins, Servings: 4

Ingredients:
- 1 tbsp. olive oil
- 4 pork chops
- 1 medium onion, chopped
- 1 cup peas
- ½ tsp. salt
- 1 tsp. curry powder

Instructions:
1. Coat the Instant Pot with olive oil and set to Sauté setting.
2. Add the pork chops and sear for 3 minutes or until lightly browned.
3. Add the onion and sauté for 1 to 2 minutes or until soft.
4. Add peas, salt and curry powder and sauté for 3 to 5 minutes or until peas are tender.
5. Serve them warm on a large plate.

Nutritional info:
Calories 399, Carbs 6g, Fat 18g, Protein 51g

Pork Chops with Onions

Prep Time: 6 mins, Cook Time: 25 mins, Servings: 4

Ingredients:
- 3 tbsps. butter
- 4 boneless pork chops
- 3 onions, chopped
- ½ cup beef broth
- Salt and pepper, to taste
- ¼ cup heavy cream

Instructions:
1. Press the Sauté button on the Instant Pot.
2. Heat the butter until melted and add the pork chops and onion.

3. Sauté for 3 minutes or until the pork is seared.
4. Stir in the broth and sprinkle salt and pepper for seasoning.
5. Lock the lid. Press the Meat/Stew button and set the cooking time to 20 minutes at High Pressure.
6. Once cooking is complete, perform a natural pressure release for 10 minutes, and then release any remaining pressure. Carefully open the lid.
7. Add the heavy cream. Press the Sauté button and allow to simmer for 5 minutes.
8. Allow to cool for a few minutes. Remove the pork from the pot and serve warm.

Nutritional info:
Calories 468, Carbs 8.4g, Protein 28.1g, Fat 35.2g

Pork Coconut Curry

Prep Time: 6 mins, Cook Time: 35 mins, Servings: 6
Ingredients:
- 3 tbsps. coconut oil
- 3 garlic cloves, minced
- 1 tbsp. garam masala
- 2 lbs. pork shoulders, sliced
- 1 cup freshly squeezed coconut milk
- Salt and pepper, to taste

Instructions:
1. Press the Sauté button on the Instant Pot and heat the coconut oil until melted.
2. Add and sauté the garlic and garam masala until fragrant.
3. Add the pork and allow to sear on all sides for 3 minutes or until lightly browned.
4. Pour in the coconut milk. Sprinkle with salt and pepper.
5. Lock the lid. Press the Meat/Stew button and set the cooking time to 30 minutes at High pressure.
6. Once cooking is complete, perform a natural pressure release for 10 minutes, and then release any remaining pressure. Carefully open the lid.
7. Remove the pork from the pot and serve warm.

Nutritional info:
Calories 371, Carbs 1.8g, Protein 23.4g, Fat 28.7g

Pork Medallions and Mushrooms

Prep Time: 12 mins, Cook time: 8 mins, Servings: 4
Ingredients:
- 2 tsps. extra virgin olive oil
- 4 pork medallions, rinsed and trimmed
- 1 tsp. salt
- 12 oyster mushrooms, quartered
- 1 onion, diced
- 1 cup water

Instructions:
3. Set the Instant Pot to Sauté setting, then add the extra virgin olive oil and heat until the oil is shimmering.
4. Add the pork medallions and brown for 3 to 4 minutes.
5. Add the remaining ingredients.
6. Lock the lid. Select the Manual setting and set the timer to 8 minutes at High Pressure.
7. When the timer beeps, press Cancel, then use a quick pressure release.
8. Carefully open the lid. Allow to cool for a few minutes. Transfer them on a large plate and serve immediately.

Nutritional info:
Calories 624, Carbs 34g, Fat 44g, Protein 31g

Pork Potato Lunch

Prep Time: 12 mins, Cook Time: 25 mins, Servings: 4
Ingredients:
- 1 tbsp. olive oil
- 1 onion, chopped
- 10 oz. fat removed pork neck
- 3 cups low-sodium beef stock
- 1 medium sweet potato, chopped
- Salt and pepper, to taste

Instructions:
1. Press the Sauté bottom on the Instant Pot. Grease the pot with the olive oil.
2. Add the onion and sauté for 2 minutes until translucent and softened.
3. Add the beef and sauté for 4 to 5 minutes to evenly brown.
4. Add the stock and potatoes. Sprinkle with salt and pepper. Stir to mix well.
5. Lock the lid. Press Manual. Set the timer to 20 minutes at High Pressure.
6. When the timer beeps, press Cancel, then use a quick pressure release.
7. Open the lid, transfer them in a large plate and serve warm.

Nutritional info:
Calories 278, Fat 18g, Carbs 12g, Protein 18g

Pork Tenderloin with Celery

Prep Time: 12 mins, Cook Time: 25 mins, Servings: 4
Ingredients:
- 1½ lbs. pork tenderloin
- 2 tsps. sea salt
- ½ tsp. rosemary
- 1 cup heavy cream
- 4 celery stalks, rinsed, sliced into ½-inch pieces
- 1 cup water

Instructions:
1. On a clean work surface, rub the pork with salt and rosemary.
2. Slice the well-coated tenderloin into 1-inch thick slices.
3. Set the Instant Pot to Sauté setting.
4. Add the pork and brown for 3 minutes.
5. Add the celery, heavy cream, and water. Stir to combine well.
6. Lock the lid. Set the Instant Pot to Manual mode and set the timer for 20 minutes at High Pressure.
7. Once cooking is complete, use a natural pressure release for 10 minutes, then release any remaining pressure.
8. Carefully open the lid. Allow to cool for a few minutes. Transfer them on a large plate and serve immediately.

Nutritional info:
Calories 399, Carbs 6g, Fat 18g, Protein 51g

Pork Vindaloo (Curry Pork)
Prep Time: 6 mins, Cook Time: 35 mins, Servings: 6

Ingredients:
- ¼ cup coconut oil
- 2 lbs. pork shoulder, sliced
- 1 tbsp. garam masala
- 3 tbsps. freshly squeezed lemon juice
- 1 cup water
- Salt and pepper, to taste

Instructions:
1. Press the Sauté button on the Instant Pot and heat the coconut oil until melted.
2. Add and sear the pork loin on all sides for 3 minutes or until lightly browned.
3. Add the garam masala and continue sauté for 2 more minutes.
4. Stir in the lemon juice and water. Sprinkle with salt and pepper.
5. Lock the lid. Press the Meat/Stew button and set the cooking time to 30 minutes at High Pressure.
6. Once cooking is complete, perform a natural pressure release for 10 minutes, and then release any remaining pressure. Carefully open the lid.
7. Remove the pork from the pot and serve warm.

Nutritional info:
Calories 322, Carbs 0.4g, Protein 23.9g, Fat 25.2g

Pork with Coconut Meat
Prep Time: 12 mins, Cook Time: 6 mins, Servings: 4

Ingredients:
- 1 tbsp. olive oil
- ½ lb. ground pork
- 1 tsp. salt
- 6 garlic cloves
- 2 cups tomato sauce
- 1 cup water
- 2 cups coconut meat

Instructions:
1. Set the Instant Pot to Sauté function. Coat the pot with olive oil and heat until the oil is shimmering.
2. Add pork to Instant Pot along with salt and garlic, then sauté for 3 minutes until lightly browned.
3. Add the tomato sauce and water.
4. Lock the lid. Set the Instant Port to Manual function and set the cooking time for 6 minutes at High Pressure.
5. Once cooking is complete, use a natural pressure release for 10 minutes, then release any remaining pressure.
6. Carefully open the lid. Allow to cool for a few minutes. Transfer them on a large plate and serve with coconut meat on top.

Nutritional info:
Calories 144, Fat 9g, Protein 5g, Carbs 12g

Pork with Jasmine Rice
Prep Time: 20 mins, Cook Time: 25 mins, Servings: 8

Ingredients:
- 1 tbsp. extra virgin olive oil
- 2 lbs. pork roast, sliced into 1-inch bites
- 1 tsp sea salt
- 1 cup Jasmine rice
- 2 cups crushed tomatoes
- 1 cup water

Instructions:
1. Lightly coat the Instant Pot with olive oil and set the setting to Sauté.
2. Add and brown the pork for 3 minutes.
3. Add the remaining ingredients. Stir to combine well.
4. Lock the lid. Set the Manual mode and set the cooking time for 20 minutes at Low Pressure.
5. Once cooking is complete, use a natural pressure release for 10 minutes, then release any remaining pressure.
6. Carefully open the lid. Allow to cool for a few minutes. Transfer them on a large plate and serve immediately.

Nutritional Info:
Calories 492, Carbs 13g, Fat 25g, Protein 52g

Pork with Paprika and Mushrooms
Prep Time: 6 mins, Cook Time: 8 hours, Servings: 3

Ingredients:
- 4 tbsps. olive oil
- 1 lb. pork loin

- 1 tbsp. thyme
- 2 tbsps. paprika
- 1 cup sliced cremini mushrooms
- Salt and pepper, to taste
- ½ cup water

Instructions:
1. Press the Sauté button on the Instant Pot and heat the olive oil until shimmering.
2. Add and sear the pork loin on all sides for 3 minutes or until lightly browned.
3. Add the thyme, paprika, and mushrooms.
4. Sprinkle with salt and pepper, then add the water.
5. Lock the lid. Press the Slow Cook button and set the time to 8 hours at High Pressure.
6. Once cooking is complete, perform a quick pressure release. Carefully open the lid.
7. Remove the pork from the pot and serve warm.

Nutritional info:
Calories 245, Carbs 1.3g, Protein 17.3g Fat 19.8g

Pork with Turnip
Prep Time: 20 mins, Cook Time: 25 mins, Servings: 4
Ingredients:
- 1 tbsp. extra virgin olive oil
- 2 lbs. pork tenderloin
- 1 tsp sea salt
- 1 turnip, peeled and diced
- 2 carrots, peeled and diced
- 1 cup water

Instructions:
1. Lightly coat the Instant Pot with olive oil and set the setting to Sauté.
2. On a clean work surface, rub the pork with salt, slice into 1-inch slices, then add the pork to the pot and brown for 3 minutes.
3. Add the remaining ingredients.
4. Lock the lid. Set the pot to Manual and set the cooking time for 20 minutes at High Pressure.
5. Once cooking is complete, use a natural pressure release.
6. Carefully open the lid. Allow to cool for a few minutes. Transfer them on a large plate and serve immediately.

Nutritional info:
Calories 492, Carbs 13g, Fat 25g, Protein 52g

Smokey and Spicy Pork Roast
Prep Time: 6 mins, Cook Time: 1 hour, Servings: 12
Ingredients:
- 1 tbsp. cayenne pepper flakes
- 5 tbsps. olive oil
- Salt and pepper, to taste
- 2 tbsps. liquid smoke
- 4 lbs. pork butt
- 1 cup water

Instructions:
1. Place all ingredients in the Instant Pot. Stir to combine well.
2. Lock the lid. Press the Meat/Stew button and set the cooking time to 1 hour at High Pressure.
3. Once cooking is complete, perform a natural pressure release for 10 to 20 minutes, and then release any remaining pressure. Carefully open the lid.
4. Remove the pork from the pot and serve warm.

Nutritional info:
Calories 456, Carbs 0.7g, Protein 32.9g, Fat 39g

Spicy Pulled Pork
Prep Time: 6 mins, Cook Time: 8 hours 5 mins, Servings: 3
Ingredients:
- 1 lb. boneless pork shoulder
- 1 tbsp. cayenne pepper
- 1 tsp. garlic
- 1 tsp. paprika
- Salt and pepper, to taste
- 1 cup water
- 1 cup coconut milk

Instructions:
1. Place the pork shoulder, cayenne pepper, garlic, and paprika in the Instant Pot.
2. Sprinkle with salt and pepper and pour the water.
3. Lock the lid. Press the Slow Cook button and set the time to 8 hours at High Pressure.
4. Once cooking is complete, perform a natural pressure release. Carefully open the lid.
5. Remove the meat from the pot and shred with two forks.
6. Return the meat to the Instant Pot and pour in the coconut milk.
7. Lock the lid. Press the Meat/Stew button and set the cooking time to 5 minutes at High Pressure.
8. Once cooking is complete, perform a natural pressure release for 10 minutes, and then release any remaining pressure. Carefully open the lid.
9. Remove the pork from the pot and serve warm.

Nutritional info:
Calories 298, Carbs 3.1g, Protein 20.1g, Fat 23.6g

Sunday Pork Roast
Prep Time: 12 mins, Cook Time: 15 mins, Servings: 12

Ingredients:
- 4 lbs. pork roast
- 1 tbsp. sea salt
- 4 tbsps. extra virgin olive oil
- 4 Chinese eggplants, rinsed, stem removed, and cut into ¼-inch slices
- 1 cup chicken stock

Instructions:
1. On a clean work surface, rub the pork with salt.
2. Set the Instant Pot to Sauté mode. Add the olive oil to Instant Pot and heat until shimmering.
3. Add pork and brown for 3 minutes on all sides.
4. Add eggplant and stock.
5. Lock the lid. Set the pot to Manual setting and set the timer for 15 minutes at High Pressure.
6. Once cooking is complete, use a quick pressure release.
7. Carefully open the lid. Allow to cool for a few minutes. Transfer them on a large plate and serve immediately.

Nutritional info:
Calories 694, Carbs 66g, Fat 25g, Protein 49g

Super Stew
Prep Time: 20 mins, Cook Time: 30 mins, Servings: 8

Ingredients:
- 1½ lbs. pork tenderloin
- 1 tsp. oregano
- 1 tsp. sea salt
- 2 tbsps. extra virgin olive oil
- 4 cups crushed tomatoes
- 1 cup water

Instructions:
1. On a clean work surface, massage the pork tenderloin with oregano and sea salt.
2. Lightly coat the Instant Pot with olive oil and set to Sauté mode.
3. Add the tomatoes and sauté for 5 minutes.
4. Place the tenderloin in the Instant Pot and sear for 2 minutes on each side.
5. Pour in the water.
6. Lock the lid. Set the setting to Manual and set the cooking time for 25 minutes at High Pressure.
7. Once cooking is complete, use a quick pressure release.
8. Carefully open the lid. Allow to cool for a few minutes. Transfer them on a large plate and serve immediately.

Nutritional info:
Calories 492, Carbs 13g, Fat 25g, Protein 52g

Tomato Chili Pork
Prep Time: 12 mins, Cook Time: 25 mins, Servings: 4

Ingredients:
- 1 tbsps. olive oil
- 2 green chili peppers, diced
- 2 yellow bell peppers, sliced
- 2 cups whole Roma tomatoes
- 1 lb. fat removed and chopped pork neck
- Salt and pepper, to taste
- 2 cups low-sodium beef stock

Instructions:
1. Press Sauté on the Instant Pot. Grease the pot with the olive oil.
2. Add the peppers and sauté for 3 to 4 minutes.
3. Add the tomatoes and sauté for 4 to 5 minutes.
4. Add the pork neck and sauté for 3 minutes or until lightly browned.
5. Season with salt and pepper, then mix in the stock.
6. Lock the lid. Press Manual. Set the timer to 15 minutes at High Pressure.
7. Once the timer goes off, press Cancel, then use a quick pressure release.
8. Carefully open the lid. Allow to cool for a few minutes, then divide them into 4 plates and serve warm.

Nutritional info:
Calories 178, Fat 10g, Carbs 9g, Protein 13g

Bacon and Peas
Prep Time: 12 mins, Cook time: 30 mins, Servings: 4

Ingredients:
- 1 tbsp. extra virgin olive oil
- 1 lb. bacon slices, sliced into quarters
- 1 tsp. sea salt
- 2 cups peas
- 1 tsp. black pepper
- 1 cup water

Instructions:
1. Set the Instant Pot to Sauté setting, then add the olive oil and heat until hot.
2. Add the bacon and sauté for 5 to 6 minutes or until browned on both sides.
3. Add the remaining ingredients.
4. Lock the lid. Select the Manual setting and set the timer at 30 minutes at High Pressure.
5. When the timer beeps, press Cancel, then use a quick pressure release.
6. Carefully open the lid and allow to cool for a few minutes. Serve warm.

Nutritional info:
Calories 226, Carbs 33g, Fat 8g, Protein 6g

Canadian Bacon
Prep Time: 12 mins, Cook Time: 55 mins, Servings: 8
Ingredients:
- ½ lb. peameal bacon, slice into 2-inch bites
- 1 medium onion, minced
- 4 cups zucchini
- 4 tbsps. tomato paste
- 1 tsp. salt
- 4 cups water

Instructions:
1. Set the Instant Pot to Sauté function.
2. Add the bacon and onion, then sauté for 6 minutes until bacon has lightly browned.
3. In the Instant Pot, add the remaining ingredients.
4. Lock the lid. Select the Instant Pot to the Manual setting and set the cooking time to 35 minutes at High Pressure.
5. Once cooking is complete, use a natural pressure release for 20 minutes, and then release any remaining pressure.
6. Carefully open the lid. Allow to cool for a few minutes. Transfer them on a large plate and serve immediately.

Nutritional info:
Calories 485, Fat 11g, Protein 28g, Carbs 7g

Fried Rice with Sausage and Egg
Prep Time: 12 mins, Cook Time: 15 mins, Servings: 2
Ingredients:
- 1 tsp. butter
- 2 oz. chorizo sausage, thinly sliced
- 2 large eggs, beaten
- 2 cups cooked rice
- 1 red bell pepper, chopped
- Salt and pepper, to taste

Instructions:
1. Press Sauté on the Instant Pot. Heat the butter in the pot until melted.
2. Add the sausage and sauté for 2 to 3 minutes per side to evenly brown.
3. Add the beaten eggs and sauté for 2 to 3 minutes to scramble.
4. Add the rice and bell pepper. Sprinkle with salt and pepper. Sauté for 5 minutes; serve warm.

Nutritional info:
Calories 145, Fat 6g, Carbs 17g, Protein 6g

Sausage and Peppers
Prep Time: 12 mins, Cook time: 20 mins, Servings: 4
Ingredients:
- 1 tbsp. olive oil
- 4 links sausage
- 3 red bell peppers, deseeded, stem removed, and julienned
- 1 cup chicken stock
- 1 tsp. Himalayan salt
- 1 onion, chopped
- 1 cup water

Instructions:
1. Set Instant Pot to Sauté setting, Heat the olive oil in the pot until shimmering.
2. Add the sausage and sauté for 8 to 10 minutes or until lightly browned on all sides.
3. Add bell peppers to the Instant Pot and sauté for 2 minutes.
4. Add the remaining ingredients.
5. Lock the lid. Press the Manual setting and set the timer to 20 minutes at High Pressure.
6. When the timer beeps, press Cancel, then use a quick pressure release.
7. Carefully open the lid and allow to cool for a few minutes. Serve warm.

Nutritional info:
Calories 273, Carbs 23g, Fat 12g, Protein 8g

Chapter 8 Soups and Stews Recipe

Asian Egg Drop Soup

Prep Time: 6 mins, Cook Time: 9 mins, Servings: 3

Ingredients:
- 1 tsp. grated ginger
- 3 cups water
- 2 cups chopped kale
- 3 tbsps. coconut oil
- Salt and pepper, to taste
- 2 eggs, beaten

Instructions:
1. Place all ingredients, except for the beaten eggs, in the Instant Pot.
2. Lock the lid. Set the Manual mode and set the timer to 6 minutes at High Pressure.
3. When the timer goes off, perform a natural pressure release for 5 minutes, then release any remaining pressure.
4. Carefully open the lid. Press the Sauté button and bring the soup to a simmer.
5. Gradually pour in the beaten eggs and allow to simmer for 3 more minutes.
6. Pour the soup in a large bowl and serve warm.

Nutritional info:
Calories 209, Carbs 1.7g, Protein 6.5g, Fat 20.3g

Asparagus Soup

Prep Time: 55 mins, Cook Time: 55 mins, Servings: 4

Ingredients:
- 1 tbsp. ghee
- 1 medium onion, chopped
- 1 garlic clove, minced
- 1 cup diced ham
- Salt and pepepr, to taste
- 2 lbs. halved asparagus
- Salt and pepper, to taste

Instructions:
1. Set the Instant Pot to Sauté and melt the ghee.
2. Add the onions and garlic and cook for about 5 minutes
3. Add the diced ham, salt and pepper, and let it simmer for 2 to 3 minutes.
4. Add the asparagus.
5. Lock the lid. Select the Soup mode, then set the timer 45 minutes at High Pressure.
6. Once the timer goes off, do a quick pressure release. Carefully open the lid.
7. Transfer the soup to a food processor and pulse until smooth.
8. Serve warm.

Nutritional info:
Calories 80, Fat 2g, Carbs 0.5g, Protein 6g

Bacon and Potato Soup

Prep Time: 40 mins, Cook Time: 20 mins, Servings: 6

Ingredients:
- 1 tbsp. olive oil
- 2 cups chicken stock
- ½ cup sour cream
- ½ cup chopped onion
- 1½ lbs. potatoes, chopped
- 4 halved bacon slices

Instructions:
1. Set the Instant Pot to Sauté and heat the olive oil.
2. Add the bacon and cook for about 8 minutes until crispy.
3. Drain the bacon in paper towels and then chop. Set aside on a plate.
4. Add the chopped onion and sauté for 2 minutes or until translucent.
5. Add the potatoes and stock. Stir well.
6. Lock the lid. Select the Manual mode, then set the timer for 10 minutes at High Pressure.
7. Once the timer goes off, do a quick pressure release. Carefully open the lid.
8. Transfer the soup to a blender and purée until smooth.
9. Stir in the sour cream. Top with the cooked bacon and serve.

Nutritional info:
Calories 195, Fat 9.6g, Carbs 20g, Protein 7.6g

Beet Soup

Prep Time: 12 mins, Cook Time: 52 mins, Servings: 6

Ingredients:
- 1 cup water
- 8 cups peeled and chopped beets
- 3 cups chopped cabbage
- 1 yellow onion, chopped
- ¼ tsp. salt
- 6 cups chicken stock

Instructions:
1. Add a cup of water to the Instant Pot, then add the beets.
2. Lock the lid and set on Manual mode, then set the timer for 7 minutes at High Pressure.
3. Once the timer goes off, do a quick pressure release. Discard the water, then return the beets to the pot.
4. Add the cabbage, onion, salt and stock. Stir to combine well.
5. Lock the lid. Cook on Manual mode and set the timer for 45 minutes at High Pressure.
6. Once the timer goes off, do a quick pressure release.

7. Carefully open the lid. Ladle soup into bowls and serve.

Nutritional info:
Calories 152, Fat 6g, Carbs 6g, Protein 8g

Black Bean Soup
Prep Time: 12 mins, Cook Time: 20 mins, Servings: 4

Ingredients:
- 2½ cups salsa
- 45 oz. canned black beans and juice
- ½ cup chopped cilantro
- 1 garlic clove
- 2 cups water
- 2 tsps. ground cumin

Instructions:
1. In the Instant Pot, mix the salsa with black beans, cilantro, garlic, water, and cumin, stir to combine well.
2. Lock the lid. Select the Manual mode, then set the timer for 15 minutes at High Pressure.
3. Once the timer goes off, do a quick pressure release.
4. Carefully open the lid. Stir soup one more time, then ladle into bowls and serve.

Nutritional info:
Calories 184, Fat 8g, Carbs 20g, Protein 7g

Broccoli Cheddar Soup
Prep Time: 6 mins, Cook Time: 10 mins, Servings: 4

Ingredients:
- 2 heads fresh broccoli
- 4 cups chicken broth
- 1 cup heavy whipping cream
- Salt and pepper, to taste
- 2 cups shredded Cheddar cheese

Ingredients:
1. Add the trivet to the bottom of the Instant Pot along with broccoli and broth.
2. Lock the lid. Select the Manual mode, then set the timer for 10 minutes at High Pressure.
3. Once the timer goes off, do a quick pressure release. Carefully open the lid.
4. Remove the trivet and add the cream, salt and pepper. Whisk well.
5. Purée the soup with an immersion blender.
6. Add the cheese to the soup and keep stirring until melted.
7. Ladle into bowls and serve.

Nutritional info:
Calories 117, Fat 8g, Carbs 1.5g, Protein 3g

Cabbage Soup
Prep Time: 15 mins, Cook Time: 35 mins, Servings: 2

Ingredients:
- 1 onion, shredded
- 1lb. cabbage, shredded
- 1 tbsp. black pepper
- 2 tbsps. mixed herbs
- 1 cup low-sodium vegetable broth

Instructions:
1. Mix all the ingredients in the Instant Pot.
2. Lock the lid. Select the Soup mode, then set the timer for 35 minutes at High Pressure.
3. Once the timer goes off, do a quick pressure release. Carefully open the lid.
4. Serve warm.

Nutritional info:
Calories 60, Carbs 2g, Fat 2g, Protein 4g

Carrot and Mushroom Soup
Prep Time: 30 mins, Cook Time: 15 mins, Servings: 4

Ingredients:
- 1 tbsp. olive oil
- 4 cups chicken stock
- 1 diced onion
- 2 sliced celery stalks
- 2 sliced carrots
- ¼ cup mushroom
- Zest of 1 lemon, for garnish

Instructions:
1. Set the Instant Pot to Sauté and heat the olive oil.
2. Cook the onion, celery, carrots and mushroom for 5 minutes, stirring occasionally. Pour in the chicken stock and stir well.
3. Lock the lid. Select the Manual mode, then set the timer for 10 minutes at High Pressure.
4. Once the timer goes off, do a quick pressure release. Carefully open the lid.
5. Garnish with lemon zest and serve.

Nutritional info:
Calories 71, Fat 1.2g, Carbs 13.4g, Protein 2.9g

Carrot Soup
Prep Time: 30 mins, Cook Time: 7 mins, Servings: 3

Ingredients:
- 1 tbsp. olive oil
- 1 onion, chopped
- 1 lb. carrots, cubed
- 3 cups vegetable broth
- ¼ tsp. smoked paprika
- ¼ tsp. cumin powder
- Salt and pepper, to taste
- Cilantro, for garnish

Instructions:
1. Select the Sauté setting on the Instant Pot and heat the olive oil.

2. Add the onions and sauté for about 2 minutes until translucent.
3. Add the carrots, vegetable broth, paprika, and cumin powder to the pot and stir well.
4. Lock the lid. Select the Manual mode, then set the timer for 5 minutes at High Pressure.
5. Once the timer goes off, do a quick pressure release. Carefully open the lid.
6. Transfer the soup to a blender and blend until smooth.
7. Season with salt and pepper. Garnish with fresh cilantro and serve.

Nutritional info:
Calories 116, Fat 1.5g, Carbs 19.4g, Protein 6.6g

Cheesy Broccoli Soup
<u>Prep Time: 12 mins, Cook Time: 10 mins, Servings: 8</u>
Ingredients:
- 4 garlic cloves, minced
- 4 cups broccoli florets
- 3½ cups chicken stock
- 1 cup heavy whipping cream
- Salt and pepper, to taste
- 3 cups grated Cheddar cheese

Instructions:
1. Set the Instant Pot to Sauté, then add the garlic and sauté it for 1 minute until fragrant.
2. Add the broccoli, stock and cream. Sprinkle with salt and pepper. Stir to combine well.
3. Lock the lid. Select the Manual mode, then set the timer for 8 to 9 minutes at Low Pressure.
4. Once the timer goes off, do a quick pressure release.
5. Carefully open the lid. Add the cheese and stir until it melts, then ladle into bowls and serve.

Nutritional info:
Calories 291, Fat 20g, Carbs 8g, Protein 13g

Chicken and Tomato Soup
<u>Prep Time: 30 mins, Cook Time: 17 mins, Servings: 6</u>
Ingredients:
- 1 tbsp. olive oil
- 3 garlic cloves, minced
- 1 lb. chicken breasts, cubed
- 6 cups chicken broth
- 1 tsp. mixed garlic and onion powder
- 1 (28 oz) can crushed tomatoes
- ½ cup shredded Parmesan cheese, for garnish
- ½ cup plain Greek yogurt, for serving

Instructions:
1. Set the Instant Pot to Sauté and heat the olive oil.
2. Cook the garlic until fragrant, about 2 minutes.
3. Add the chicken breast cubes and sauté for 5 minutes until browned on both sides.
4. Pour in the remaining ingredients.
5. Lock the lid. Select the Manual mode, then set the timer for 10 minutes at High Pressure.
6. Once the timer goes off, do a natural pressure release for 10 minutes, then release any remaining pressure. Carefully open the lid.
7. Sprinkle the Parmesan cheese on top of the soup and serve with yogurt.

Nutritional info:
Calories 237, Fat 7g, Carbs 12g, Protein 30g

Chicken Soup
<u>Prep Time: 12 mins, Cook Time: 10 mins, Servings: 2</u>
Ingredients:
- 1 cup heavy whipping cream
- ¼ cup onions
- 1 garlic cloves, minced
- 2 packets skinned and deboned chicken breasts
- 1 tbsp. ghee
- 3 cups water

Instructions:
1. Combine all the ingredients, except for the heavy whipping cream, in the Instant Pot.
2. Lock the lid. Select the Manual mode, then set the timer for 6 minutes at High Pressure.
3. Once the timer goes off, do a natural pressure release for 5 minutes, then release any remaining pressure. Carefully open the lid.
4. Remove the chicken from the pot and transfer to a platter to shred it into pieces using forks.
5. Return it to the Instant Pot and add the heavy whipping cream to the soup. Stir to blend ingredients.
6. Serve warm.

Nutritional info:
Calories 150, Fat 4g, Carbs 1g, Protein 19g

Coconut Seafood Soup
<u>Prep Time: 6 mins, Cook Time: 8 mins, Servings: 5</u>
Ingredients:
- 1 cup coconut milk
- 10 shrimps, shelled and deveined
- 1 thumb-size ginger, crushed
- 4 tilapia fillets
- 2 cups water
- Salt and pepper, to taste

Instructions:

1. Place all ingredients in the Instant Pot. Stir to combine well.
2. Lock the lid. Set on the Manual mode, then set the timer to 8 minutes at Low Pressure.
3. When the timer goes off, perform a quick release.
4. Carefully open the lid. Allow to cool before serving.

Nutritional info:
Calories 238, Carbs 2.7, Protein 13.6g, Fat 28.8g

Creamy Broccoli Chicken Bone Soup

Prep Time: 6 mins, Cook Time: 34 mins, Servings: 5
Ingredients:
- ½ lb. chicken bones
- 4 cups water
- Salt and pepper, to taste
- 2 heads broccoli, cut into florets
- 1 small avocado, sliced
- 1 tsp. paprika powder

Instructions:
1. Place the chicken bones and water in the Instant Pot.
2. Sprinkle salt and pepper for seasoning.
3. Lock the lid. Set on the Manual mode, then set the timer to 30 minutes at High Pressure.
4. When the timer goes off, do a natural pressure release for 10 minutes, then release any remaining pressure.
5. Carefully open the lid, then discard the bones with tongs.
6. Add the broccoli.
7. Close the lid again and press the Manual button and cook for 4 minutes at Low Pressure.
8. When the timer goes off, do a quick pressure release.
9. Transfer the soup into a blender, then add avocado slices.
10. Pulse until smooth and set in a bowl.
11. Sprinkle with paprika powder.
12. Serve immediately.

Nutritional info:
Calories 118, Fat 10.3g, Carbs 1.9g, Protein 7.3

Egg Drop Soup with Shredded Chicken

Prep Time: 10 mins, Cook Time: 15 mins, Servings: 6
Ingredients:
- 2 tbsps. coconut oil
- 1 onion, minced
- 1 celery, chopped
- 3 cups shredded chicken
- 4 cups water
- Salt and pepper, to taste
- 4 eggs, beaten

Instructions:
1. Press the Sauté button on the Instant Pot and heat the oil.
2. Sauté the onion and celery for 2 minutes or until fragrant.
3. Add the chicken and water.
4. Sprinkle salt and pepper for seasoning.
5. Lock the lid. Press the Poultry button and set the cooking time to 10 minutes at High Pressure.
6. When the timer goes off, perform a natural pressure release for 5 minutes, then release any remaining pressure.
7. Carefully open the lid. Press the Sauté button and bring the soup to a simmer.
8. Gradually pour in the beaten eggs and allow to simmer for 3 more minutes.
9. Pour the soup in a large bowl and serve warm.

Nutritional info:
Calories 154, Carbs 2.9g, Protein 9.6g, Fat 12.8g

Fish Soup

Prep Time: 12 mins, Cook Time: 8 mins, Servings: 4
Ingredients:
- 1 lb. boneless, skinless and cubed white fish fillets
- 1 carrot, chopped
- 1 cup chopped bacon
- 4 cups chicken stock
- Salt and pepper, to taste
- 2 cups heavy whipping cream

Instructions:
1. In the Instant Pot, mix the fish with carrot, bacon and stock. Sprinkle with salt and pepper. Stir to combine well.
2. Lock the lid. Set to Manual function and set the timer for 5 minutes at Low Pressure.
3. Once the timer goes off, press Cancel. Do a quick pressure release.
4. Carefully open the lid. Add the cream, stir, set the pot to Sauté, cook for 3 minutes more, ladle the soup into bowls and serve.

Nutritional info:
Calories 271, Fat 7g, Carbs 30g, Protein 5g

Ginger Halibut Soup

Prep Time: 6 mins, Cook Time: 12 mins, Servings: 4
Ingredients:
- 1 tbsp. olive oil
- 1 large onion, chopped
- 2 cups water
- 2 tbsps. minced fresh ginger
- 1 lb. halibut, sliced
- Salt and pepper, to taste

Instructions:
1. Press the Sauté button on the Instant Pot and heat the olive oil.

2. Sauté the onion for 3 minutes or until translucent.
3. Add the remaining ingredients. Stir to combine well.
4. Lock the lid. Set on the Manual mode, then set the timer to 10 minutes at Low Pressure.
5. When the timer goes off, perform a quick release.
6. Carefully open the lid. Allow to cool before serving.

Nutritional info:
Calories 259, Carbs 7.9g, Protein 10.9g, Fat 22.8g

Greek Veggie Soup
Prep Time: 30 mins, Cook Time: 17 mins, Servings: 4
Ingredients:
- 1 tbsp. olive oil
- 1 garlic clove, minced
- 3 cups shredded cabbage
- 2 carrots, minced
- 4 cups vegetable broth
- 1 (15 oz) can roasted tomatoes
- Salt and pepper, to taste
- Crumbled feta cheese, for topping

Instructions:
1. Set the Instant Pot to Sauté and heat the olive oil.
2. Add the garlic and cabbage and cook for 5 minutes, stirring occasionally.
3. Add the carrots and cook for 2 more minutes.
4. Pour in the broth and tomatoes. Season with salt and pepper.
5. Lock the lid. Select the Soup mode, then set the timer for 10 minutes at High Pressure.
6. Once the timer goes off, do a quick pressure release. Carefully open the lid.
7. Top with crumbled feta cheese and serve.

Nutritional info:
Calories 94, Fat 1.4g, Carbs 12.9g, Protein 6.8g

Leek and Salmon Soup
Prep Time: 6 mins, Cook Time: 10 mins, Servings: 4
Ingredients:
- 1 lb. salmon, sliced
- 1¾ cup coconut milk
- 2 tbsps. avocado oil
- 3 garlic cloves, minced
- 4 leeks, trimmed and chopped
- Salt and pepper, to taste

Instructions:
1. Place all ingredients in the Instant Pot. Stir to combine well.
2. Lock the lid. Select the Manual mode and cook for 10 minutes at Low Pressure.
3. When the timer goes off, perform a quick release.
4. Carefully open the lid. Allow to cool for a few minutes. Serve immediately.

Nutritional info:
Calories 535, Fat 40.9g, Carbs 19.5g, Protein 27.3g

Leftover Chicken Soup
Prep Time: 6 mins, Cook Time: 12 mins, Servings: 3
Ingredients:
- 1 tbsp. coconut oil
- 1 onion, chopped
- 8 garlic cloves, minced
- 2 cups shredded leftover chicken meat
- Salt and pepper, to taste
- 7 cups water

Instructions:
1. Press the Sauté button on the Instant Pot and heat the coconut oil.
2. Sauté the onions and garlic for 2 to 3 minutes until fragrant.
3. Add the chicken meat and sprinkle salt and pepper for seasoning.
4. Pour in the water. Season with more salt and pepper.
5. Lock the lid. Set on the Manual mode, then set the timer to 10 minutes at High Pressure.
6. When the timer goes off, do a natural pressure release for 10 minutes, then release any remaining pressure.
7. Carefully open the lid and serve warm.

Nutritional info:
Calories 356, Fat 32.1g, Carbs 2.5g, Protein 23.4g

Lemon Chicken Soup
Prep Time: 10 mins, Cook Time: 8 mins, Servings: 4
Ingredients:
- 2 tbsps. lemon juice
- 6 cups chicken stock
- 3 chicken breast fillets
- 1 tsp. garlic powder
- 1 diced onion
- Salt and pepper, to taste

Instructions:
1. Put the chicken stock, chicken breast fillets, garlic powder, and onion in the Instant Pot and mix well.
2. Lock the lid. Select the Manual mode, then set the timer for 6 minutes at High Pressure.
3. Once the timer goes off, do a natural pressure release for 5 minutes, then release any remaining pressure. Carefully open the lid.
4. Remove the chicken and shred.
5. Put it back to the pot and set the Instant Pot to Sauté.

6. Whisk in the lemon juice. Season with salt and pepper. Serve immediately.

Nutritional info:
Calories 238, Fat 9.1g, Carbs 4.3g, Protein 33.2g

Low Carb Chicken Noodle Soup

Prep Time: 30 mins, Cook Time: 27, Servings: 2

Ingredients:
- 2 tsps. coconut oil
- 1 lb. skinless and boneless chicken thighs
- 1 cup celery
- 1 cup diced carrots
- Salt, to taste
- 10½ oz. spiral daikon noodles

Instructions:
1. In the Instant Pot, add the coconut oil and chicken thighs.
2. Set the Instant Pot to Sauté and cook for 10 minutes or until cooked through.
3. Shred the chicken meat with a fork and add the celery and carrots.
4. Continue cooking for 2 minutes more and season with salt.
5. Lock the lid. Change the setting to Soup and set the cooking time for 15 minutes.
6. After the timer stops, add the daikon noodles and serve.

Nutritional info:
Calories 371, Fat: 22g, Carbs 6.5g, Protein 36g

Low Carb Ham and Bean Soup

Prep Time: 12 mins, Cook Time: 40 mins, Servings: 6

Ingredients:
- 2 smoked ham hocks
- 1 cup chopped onion
- 1 cup black beans, soaked in water for at least an hour
- 4 garlic cloves, minced
- 2 cups chopped ham
- 1 tsp. dried oregano
- 1 tsp. Louisiana hot sauce
- 1 cup chopped celery
- ½ tsp. Salt
- 6 cups water

Instructions:
1. Put the ham hocks, onion, black beans, ham, and garlic in the Instant Pot.
2. Add the dried oregano, Louisiana hot sauce, chopped celery, salt, and water. Stir to combine.
3. Lock the lid. Select the Manual mode, then set the timer for 30 minutes at High Pressure.
4. Once the timer goes off, do a quick pressure release. Carefully open the lid.
5. Remove the ham bone and shred the meat remaining on it back to the soup.
6. Use an immersion blender to purée the soup.
7. Serve hot.

Nutritional info:
Calories 111, Fat 1.9g, Carbs 4g, Protein 10g

Minestrone

Prep Time: 12 mins, Cook Time: 6 mins, Servings: 4

Ingredients:
- 27 oz. tomato paste
- 15 oz. drained canned cannellini beans
- 2 cups vegetable soup
- 1 cup cooked orzo pasta
- ¼ cup grated Parmesan cheese

Instructions:
1. In the Instant Pot, mix the tomato paste with beans and vegetable soup, stir to combine well.
2. Lock the lid. Set to the Manual mode and set the timer for 6 minutes at High Pressure.
3. Once the timer goes off, do a natural pressure release for 10 minutes, then release any remaining pressure.
4. Carefully open the lid. Add the orzo pasta and stir, then ladle the soup into bowls and serve with Parmesan sprinkled on top.

Nutritional info:
Calories 254, Fat 2g, Carbs 12g, Protein 4g

Mushroom Chicken Soup

Prep Time: 12 mins, Cook Time: 20 mins, Servings: 4

Ingredients:
- 1 tbsp. olive oil
- 7 oz. chicken breast
- 1 onion, finely chopped
- 2 cups sliced button mushrooms
- 4 cups low-sodium chicken stock
- Salt and pepper, to taste
- ¼ cup heavy whipping cream

Instructions:
1. Press the Sauté bottom on the Instant Pot.
2. Add and heat the olive oil.
3. Add the chicken breast and sauté for 3 to 4 minutes to evenly brown.
4. Add the onions and sauté for 3 minutes or until translucent and softened.
5. Add the mushrooms and stock. Sprinkle with salt and pepper.
6. Lock the lid. Press the Manual bottom in the pot. Set the timer to 15 minutes at High Pressure.
7. Once the timer goes off, press Cancel. Do a quick pressure release.

8. Open the lid, mix in the cream, transfer them in a large bowl and serve.

Nutritional info:
Calories 284, Fat 9g, Carbs 7g, Protein 41g

Onion Soup with Pork Stock

Prep Time: 12 mins, Cook Time: 25 mins, Servings: 4

Ingredients:
- 2 tbsps. olive oil
- 8 cups yellow onions, sliced
- 1 tbsp. balsamic vinegar
- 6 cups pork stock
- 2 bay leaves
- 2 thyme stems
- Salt, to taste

Instructions:
1. Set the Instant Pot to Sauté and heat the olive oil.
2. Stir in the onions and cook until translucent, about 15 minutes.
3. Add the vinegar and stock, bay leaves, thyme, and salt to taste.
4. Lock the lid. Select the Manual mode, then set the timer for about 10 minutes at High Pressure.
5. Once the timer goes off, do a quick pressure release. Carefully open the lid.
6. Discard the thyme stems and bay leaves and then blend the soup using a blender or if you have an immersion blender, then you can blend it directly into the pot.
7. Serve immediately.

Nutritional info:
Calories 55, Fat 1.8g, Carbs 1g, Protein 3.3g

Poached Egg Chicken Bone Soup

Prep Time: 6 mins, Cook Time: 36 mins, Servings: 2

Ingredients:
- 1 lb. chicken bones
- 1 tsp. olive oil
- 2 cups water
- 2 whole eggs
- 1 romaine lettuce head, chopped
- Salt and pepper, to taste

Instructions:
1. Place the chicken bones, olive oil, and water in the Instant Pot.
2. Lock the lid. Set to Poultry mode and the timer to 30 minutes at High Pressure.
3. When the timer goes off, do a natural pressure release for 10 minutes, then release any remaining pressure.
4. Carefully open the lid, then discard the bones with tongs.
5. Press the Sauté button and bring the soup to a simmer.
6. Carefully crack the eggs in the pot and simmer for 3 minutes.
7. Add the lettuce and season with salt and pepper.
8. Allow to simmer for 3 more minutes.
9. Serve warm.

Nutritional info:
Calories 443, Carbs 4.3g, Protein 58.3g, Fat 39.2g

Potato Soup

Prep Time: 12 mins, Cook Time: 15 mins, Servings: 8

Ingredients:
- 3 lbs. potatoes, peeled and cubed
- 2 cups milk
- ¼ tsp. salt
- 12 green onions, chopped
- 1 cup shredded Cheddar cheese

Instructions:
1. In the Instant Pot, mix the potatoes with milk and salt. Stir to combine.
2. Lock the lid. Select the Manual mode and set the timer for 12 minutes at High Pressure.
3. Once the timer goes off, do a quick pressure release. Carefully open the lid.
4. Add the Cheddar cheese and green onions, and stir to mix well.
5. Set the pot to Sauté and cook until the cheese melts, about 3 minutes.
6. Ladle the soup into bowls and serve.

Nutritional info:
Calories 314, Fat 12g, Carbs 17g, Protein 5g

Pumpkin Soup

Prep Time: 30 mins, Cook Time: 8 mins, Servings: 4

Ingredients:
- 1 tsp. garlic powder
- 2 cups chicken stock
- 1 onion, chopped
- 30 oz. pumpkin purée
- 2 cups chopped sweet potato
- Salt and pepper, to taste
- Sour cream, for serving

Instructions:
1. Add all the ingredients, except for the sour cream, in the Instant Pot.
2. Lock the lid. Select the Manual mode, then set the timer for 8 minutes at High Pressure.
3. Once the timer goes off, do a quick pressure release. Carefully open the lid.
4. Transfer the soup into a blender and pulse until smooth.
5. Serve with sour cream on top.

Nutritional info:
Calories 186, Fat 1.4g, Carbs 41.7g, Protein 5.5g

Salmon Meatballs Soup

Prep Time: 2 hours, Cook Time: 10 mins, Servings: 5

Ingredients:
- 2 tbsps. melted butter
- 2 garlic cloves, minced
- 2 large eggs, beaten
- 1 lb. ground salmon
- Salt and pepper, to taste
- 2 cups hot water

Instructions:
1. In a bowl, mix the butter, garlic, eggs and salmon. Sprinkle with salt and pepper.
2. Combine the mixture and use the hands to form the mixture into small balls.
3. Place the fish balls in the freezer to set for 2 hours or until frozen.
4. Pour the hot water in the Instant Pot and drop in the frozen fish balls.
5. Lock the lid. Select the Manual mode and set the timer to 10 minutes at Low Pressure.
6. When the timer goes off, perform a quick release.
7. Carefully open the lid. Allow to cool for a few minutes and remove the fish balls from the pot. Serve immediately.

Nutritional info:
Calories 199, Carbs 0.6g, Protein 13.3g, Fat 19.4g

Swiss Chard and Leek Soup

Prep Time: 12 mins, Cook Time: 6 mins, Servings: 4

Ingredients:
- 8 cups chopped Swiss chard
- 3 leeks, chopped
- Salt, to taste
- 1½ cups chicken stock
- 1 cup coconut milk

Instructions:
1. In the Instant Pot, mix the chard with leeks, salt, stock and coconut milk, stir to combine well.
2. Lock the lid. Select the Manual mode, then set the timer for 6 minutes at High Pressure.
3. Once the timer goes off, do a quick pressure release.
4. Carefully open the lid. Allow to cool for a few minutes, then pour the soup in an immersion blender and process until smooth. Ladle the soup into bowls and serve.

Nutritional info:
Calories 142, Fat 4g, Carbs 6g, Protein 7g

Thai Coconut Shrimp Soup

Prep Time: 6 mins, Cook Time: 6 mins, Servings: 2

Ingredients:
- 6 oz. shrimps, shelled and deveined
- 2 cups water
- Juice of 3 kaffir limes
- 1½ cups coconut milk
- 1 cup fresh cilantro

Instructions:
1. In the Instant Pot, add all the ingredients excluding cilantro.
2. Lock the lid. Set on the Manual mode and set the timer to 6 minutes at Low Pressure.
3. When the timer goes off, perform a quick release.
4. Carefully open the lid. Garnish with the fresh cilantro and serve immediately.

Nutritional info:
Calories 517, Carbs 15.4g, Protein 21.9g, Fat 44.6g

Thai Tom Saap Pork Ribs Soup

Prep Time: 6 mins, Cook Time: 30 mins, Servings: 4

Ingredients:
- 1 lb. pork spare ribs
- 4 lemongrass stalks
- 10 galangal slices
- 10 kaffir lime leaves
- 6 cups water
- Salt and pepper, to taste
- 1 tbsp. sesame oil
- Cilantro, to taste

Instructions:
1. In the Instant Pot, place the spare ribs, lemongrass, galangal, and kaffir lime leaves.
2. Pour in the water and sprinkle salt and pepper for seasoning.
3. Lock the lid. Set on the Manual mode, then set the timer to 30 minutes at High Pressure.
4. When the timer goes off, do a natural pressure release, then release any remaining pressure.
5. Carefully open the lid. Drizzle with sesame oil and garnish with cilantro before serving.

Nutritional info:
Calories 281, Carbs 2.2g, Protein 19.9g, Fat 26.9g

Turkey with Ginger and Turmeric Soup

Prep Time: 6 mins, Cook Time: 17 mins, Servings: 4

Ingredients:
- 1 tbsp. coconut oil
- 2 celery stalks, chopped
- 1 thumb-size ginger, sliced
- 1 tsp. turmeric powder
- 1 lb. turkey meat, chopped
- 3 cups water
- Salt and pepper, to taste

Instructions:
1. Press the Sauté button on the Instant Pot and heat the coconut oil.
2. Add the celery, ginger, and turmeric powder and sauté for 3 minutes or until fragrant and the celery is tender.
3. Add the turkey meat and stir for another 3 minutes until lightly browned.
4. Pour in the water and sprinkle salt and pepper for seasoning.
5. Lock the lid. Set on the Manual mode, then set the timer to 15 minutes at High Pressure.
6. When the timer goes off, do a natural pressure release, then release any remaining pressure.
7. Carefully open the lid. Serve warm.

Nutritional info:
Calories 287, Carbs 0.8g, Protein 22.8g, Fat 24.3g

Turmeric Chicken Soup
Prep Time: 6 mins, Cook Time: 15 mins, Servings: 3
Ingredients:
- 3 boneless chicken breasts
- 1 bay leaf
- ½ cup coconut milk
- 2½ tsps. turmeric powder
- 4 cups water

Instructions:
1. Place all the ingredients in the Instant Pot. Stir to combine well.
2. Lock the lid. Set to Poultry mode and set the timer to 15 minutes at High Pressure.
8. When the timer goes off, perform a natural pressure release for 10 minutes, then release any remaining pressure.
3. Carefully open the lid. Allow to cool for a few minutes, then serve immediately.

Nutritional info:
Calories 599, Carbs 3.8g, Protein 46.8g Fat 61.4g

Salmon Head Soup
Prep Time: 6 mins, Cook Time: 12 mins, Servings: 1
Ingredients:
- 1 tsp. coconut oil
- 1 onion, sliced
- 3 cups water
- 1 salmon head
- 3-inch ginger piece, slivered
- Salt and pepper, to taste

Instructions:
1. Press the Sauté button on the Instant Pot and heat the coconut oil.
2. Sauté the onion for 3 minutes or until translucent.
3. Pour in the water, then add the salmon head and ginger.
4. Sprinkle salt and pepper for seasoning.
5. Lock the lid. Set on the Manual mode, then set the timer to 10 minutes at Low Pressure.
6. When the timer goes off, perform a quick release.
7. Carefully open the lid. Allow to cool before serving.

Nutritional info:
Calories 474, Carbs 1.8g, Protein 15.3g, Fat 54.4g

Simple Chicken and Kale Soup
Prep Time: 6 mins, Cook Time: 20 mins, Servings: 4
Ingredients:
- 1 tbsp. coconut oil
- 1 onion, diced
- 2 celery stalks, chopped
- 1 lb. boneless chicken breasts
- 3 cups water
- Salt and pepper, to taste
- 4 cups chopped kale

Instructions:
1. Press the Sauté button on the Instant Pot and heat the coconut oil.
2. Sauté the onions and celery for 2 minutes until soft.
3. Add the chicken breasts and sear for 2 minutes on each side or until lightly browned.
4. Pour in the water and sprinkle salt and pepper for seasoning.
5. Lock the lid. Set to Poultry mode and set the timer to 15 minutes at High Pressure.
6. When the timer goes off, do a natural pressure release for 10 minutes, then release any remaining pressure.
7. Carefully open the lid. Press the Sauté button and add the kale.
8. Allow to simmer for 3 minutes.
9. Serve warm.

Nutritional info:
Calories 303, Carbs 2.2g, Protein 20.8g, Fat 29.3g

Vegetable and Lentil Soup
Prep Time: 30 mins, Cook Time: 20 mins, Servings: 5
Ingredients:
- 1 tbsp. olive oil
- 6 cups chicken stock
- 1¼ cup green lentils
- 6 garlic cloves, minced
- 5 tbsps. mixed spices
- Salt, to taste
- 4 cups mixed vegetables

Instructions:
1. Set the Instant Pot to Sauté and heat the olive oil. Cook the garlic for 2 minutes or until fragrant.

2. Add the vegetables and spices. Season with salt and cook for 5 minutes more.
3. Add the stock and lentils and stir well.
4. Lock the lid. Select the Manual mode, then set the timer for 12 minutes at High Pressure.
5. Once the timer goes off, do a natural pressure release for 10 minutes, then release any remaining pressure. Carefully open the lid.
6. Serve immediately.

Nutritional info:
Calories 257, Fat 1.7g, Carbs 44.9g, Protein 16.2g

White Bean and Kale Soup

Prep Time: 30 mins, Cook Time: 13 mins, Servings: 10

Ingredients:
- 3 tbsps. olive oil
- 1 (28 oz) can diced tomatoes
- 4 cups kale
- 1 white onion, chopped
- 30 oz. white cannellini beans
- 4 cups vegetable stock

Instructions:
1. Set the Instant Pot to Sauté and heat the olive oil.
2. Sauté the white onion for 3 minutes, stirring occasionally.
3. Add the tomatoes, beans, and vegetable stock, and whisk well.
4. Lock the lid. Select the Manual mode, then set the timer for 10 minutes at High Pressure.
5. Once the timer goes off, do a quick pressure release. Carefully open the lid.
6. Stir in the kale.
7. Cover the pot and let rest for a few minutes until the kale is wilted. Serve warm.

Nutritional info:
Calories 206, Fat 0.5g, Carbs 39.2g, Protein 12.5g

Bean and Tomato Stew

Prep Time: 12 mins, Cook Time: 20 mins, Servings: 4

Ingredients:
- 1 tbsp. olive oil
- 1 large onion, chopped
- 2 large tomatoes, roughly chopped
- 1 lb. green beans
- 2 cups low-sodium chicken stock
- Salt and pepper, to taste
- ¼ cup Parmesan cheese

Instructions:
1. Press the Sauté bottom on the Instant Pot.
2. Add and heat the olive oil.
3. Add the onions and sauté for 2 minutes until translucent and softened.
4. Add the tomatoes and sauté for 3 to 4 minutes or until soft.
5. Add the beans and stock. Sprinkle with salt and pepper.
6. Lock the lid. Press Manual. Set the timer to 15 minutes at High Pressure.
7. Once the timer goes off, press Cancel. Do a quick pressure release.
8. Open the lid, transfer them in a large bowl and serve with Parmesan cheese on top.

Nutritional info:
Calories 112, Fat 5g, Carbs 13g, Protein 5g

Beef Tomato Stew

Prep Time: 12 mins, Cook Time: 30 mins, Servings: 4

Ingredients:
- 2 tsps. olive oil
- 1 lb. lean beef stew meat
- 2 cups diced tomatoes
- 2 spring onions, chopped
- 4 cups low-sodium beef broth
- Salt and pepper, to taste

Instructions:
1. Press the Sauté bottom on the Instant Pot.
2. Add and heat the olive oil.
3. Add the meat and sauté for 3 to 4 minutes to evenly brown.
4. Add the tomatoes and onions, then sauté for 3 to 4 minutes or until soft.
5. Pour in the broth. Sprinkle with salt and pepper.
6. Lock the lid. Press Meat/Stew bottom. Set the timer to 20 minutes at High Pressure.
7. Once the timer goes off, press Cancel. Do a quick pressure release.
8. Open the lid, transfer them in a large bowl and serve.

Nutritional info:
Calories 231, Fat 6g, Carbs 7g, Protein 24g

Calamari Stew

Prep Time: 12 mins, Cook Time: 32 mins, Servings: 3

Ingredients:
- 1 tbsp. olive oil
- 1 lb. separated calamari
- ¼ cup white wine
- ½ bunch parsley, chopped
- 7 oz. tomatoes, chopped

Instructions:
1. Set the Instant Pot to Sauté and add the oil and calamari. Stir to combine well.

2. Lock the lid. Select the Manual mode, then set the timer for 9 minutes at Low Pressure.
3. Once the timer goes off, do a quick pressure release. Carefully open the lid.
4. Add the wine, tomatoes and half of the parsley, and stir well.
5. Lock the lid. Select the Manual mode, then set the timer for 25 minutes at High Pressure.
6. Once the timer goes off, do a quick pressure release. Carefully open the lid.
7. Sprinkle the remaining parsley on top. Divide the soup into bowls and serve.

Nutritional info:
Calories 160, Fat 4g, Carbs 7g, Protein 7g

Chicken and Quinoa Stew
Prep Time: 30 mins, Cook Time: 23 mins, Servings: 6
Ingredients:
- 1¼ lbs. chicken thigh fillets
- 4 cups chicken stock
- 4 cups chopped butternut squash
- 1 cup chopped onion
- ½ cup uncooked quinoa

Instructions:
1. Put the chicken in the Instant Pot. Add the chicken thigh fillets, stock, squash and chopped onion.
2. Lock the lid. Select the Manual mode, then set the timer for 8 minutes at High Pressure.
3. Once the timer goes off, do a quick pressure release. Carefully open the lid.
4. Stir the quinoa into the stew.
5. Set the Instant Pot to Sauté and cook for about 15 minutes, stirring occasionally.
6. Serve the stew in a large serving bowl.

Nutritional info:
Calories 251, Fat 4.2g, Carbs 22.3g, Protein 31g

Chicken Tomato Stew
Prep Time: 12 mins, Cook Time: 30 mins, Servings: 8
Ingredients:
- 4 onions, chopped
- 1 tbsp. olive oil
- 10 oz. chicken breast
- 1 cup diced tomatoes
- 4 cups low-sodium chicken stock
- ¼ cup water

Instructions:
1. Press the Sauté bottom on the Instant Pot.
2. Add and heat the olive oil.
3. Add the onions and sauté for 1 to 2 minutes until turn translucent and softened.
4. Add the chicken and evenly brown for 4 to 5 minutes.
5. Add the tomatoes and sauté for 2 minutes or until soft.
6. Pour in the stock and water.
7. Lock the lid. Press Manual. Set the timer to 20 minutes at High Pressure.
8. Once the timer goes off, press Cancel. Do a quick pressure release.
9. Open the lid, transfer them in a large bowl and serve.

Nutritional info:
Calories 278, Fat 8g, Carbs 6g, Protein 38g

Kale and Veal Stew
Prep Time: 12 mins, Cook Time: 35 mins, Servings: 6
Ingredients:
- 1 tbsp. olive oil
- 2 large onions, finely chopped
- 1 small sweet potato, diced
- 4 cups low-sodium beef stock
- 10 oz. fat removed and chopped veal shoulder
- 1 lb. fresh kale, chopped
- Salt and pepper, to taste

Instructions:
1. Press the Sauté bottom on the Instant Pot.
2. Add and heat the olive oil.
3. Add the onions and sauté for 3 minutes until turn translucent and softened.
4. Add the sweet potato and ¼ cup of stock. Sauté for 5 minutes or until soft.
5. Add the remaining stock, veal shoulder, and kale to the Instant Pot. Sprinkle with salt and pepper. Combine to mix well.
6. Lock the lid. Press Manual. Set the timer to 25 minutes at High pressure.
7. Once the timer goes off, press Cancel. Do a quick pressure release.
8. Open the lid, transfer them in a large bowl and serve

Nutritional info:
Calories 162, Fat 4g, Carbs 8g, Protein 13g

Kidney Bean Stew
Prep Time: 15 mins, Cook Time: 15 mins, Servings: 2
Ingredients:
- 1 cup tomato passata
- 3 tbsps. Italian herbs
- 1lb. cooked kidney beans
- 1 cup low-sodium beef broth

Instructions:
1. Mix all the ingredients in the Instant Pot.

2. Lock the lid. Select the Bean/Chili mode, then set the timer for 15 minutes at High Pressure.
3. Once the timer goes off, do a natural pressure release for 10 minutes, then release any remaining pressure. Carefully open the lid.
4. Serve warm.

Nutritional info:
Calories 270, Carbs 16g, Fat 10g, Protein 23g

Salmon Stew

Prep Time: 6 mins, Cook Time: 13 mins, Servings: 9
Ingredients:
- 2 tbsps. olive oil
- 3 garlic cloves, minced
- 3 cups water
- 3 lbs. salmon fillets
- Salt and pepper, to taste
- 3 cups spinach leaves

Instructions:
1. Press the Sauté button on the Instant Pot and heat the olive oil.
2. Sauté the garlic for a minute until fragrant.
3. Add the water and salmon fillets. Sprinkle salt and pepper for seasoning.
4. Lock the lid. Set on the Manual mode, then set the timer to 10 minutes at Low Pressure.
5. When the timer goes off, perform a quick release.
6. Carefully open the lid. Press the Sauté button and add the spinach.
7. Allow to simmer for 3 minutes.
8. Serve warm.

Nutritional info:
Calories 825, Carbs 2.1g, Protein 46.1g, Fat 94.5g

Slow-Cooked Cabbage and Chuck Roast Stew

Prep Time: 6 mins, Cook Time: 36 mins, Servings: 10
Ingredients:
- 2 tbsps. olive oil
- 2 onions, sliced
- 1 garlic clove, minced
- 3 lbs. chuck roast
- 6 cups water
- Salt and pepper, to taste
- 1 small cabbage head, chopped

Instructions:
1. Press the Sauté button on the Instant Pot and heat the olive oil.
2. Sauté the onions and garlic for 2 minutes until fragrant.
3. Add the chuck roast and sauté for 3 minutes or until lightly browned.
4. Pour in the water and sprinkle salt and pepper for seasoning.
5. Lock the lid. Set on the Manual mode, then set the timer to 30 minutes at High Pressure.
6. When the timer goes off, do a natural pressure release, then release any remaining pressure.
7. Carefully open the lid. Press the Sauté button and add the cabbage.
8. Allow to simmer for 3 minutes.
9. Serve warm.

Nutritional info:
Calories 312, Carbs 6.3g, Protein 20.3g, Fat 15.6g

Veal and Buckwheat Groat Stew

Prep Time: 12 mins, Cook Time: 50 mins, Servings: 4
Ingredients:
- ¼ cup buckwheat groats
- 1 tsp. olive oil
- 1 onion, chopped
- 7 oz. veal shoulder
- 3 cups low-sodium beef stock
- Salt and pepper, to taste

Instructions:
1. Add the buckwheat and pour in enough water to cover the buckwheat in the Instant Pot. Stir the ingredients to combine well.
2. Lock the lid. Press Manual. Set the timer to 12 minutes at Low Pressure.
3. Once the timer goes off, press Cancel. Do a natural pressure release, then release any remaining pressure.
4. Drain water and set the buckwheat aside.
5. Press the Sauté bottom on the Instant Pot.
6. Add and heat the olive oil.
7. Add the onions and cook for 3 minutes until translucent.
8. Add the veal shoulder and sauté for 4 to 5 minutes to evenly brown.
9. Pour in the beef stock. Sprinkle with salt and pepper.
10. Lock the lid. Press Manual. Set the timer to 30 minutes at High Pressure.
11. Once the timer goes off, press Cancel. Do a natural pressure release for 8 to 10 minutes.
12. Open the lid, mix in the buckwheat and transfer them in a large bowl and serve.

Nutritional info:
Calories 134, Fat 4g, Carbs 10g, Protein 14g

Veggie Stew

Prep Time: 40 mins, Cook Time: 20 mins, Servings: 4
Ingredients:
- 1 tbsp. olive oil
- 1 onion, minced
- 1 package mixed frozen vegetables
- 4 cups vegetable broth
- 20 oz. tomato sauce

- 2 tsps. Italian seasoning
- Salt and pepper, to taste

Instructions:
1. Set the Instant Pot to Sauté and heat the olive oil.
2. Cook the onion for 1 minute until translucent. Add the frozen vegetables and cook for 5 minutes, stirring frequently.
3. Add the remaining ingredients and stir to combine.
4. Lock the lid. Select the Manual mode, then set the timer for 15 minutes at High Pressure.
5. Once the timer goes off, do a quick pressure release. Carefully open the lid.
6. Serve immediately.

Nutritional info:
Calories 138, Fat 2.5g, Carbs 22.1g, Protein 8.7g

White Bean and Swiss Chard Stew
Prep Time: 15 mins, Cook Time: 10 mins, Servings: 8
Ingredients:
- 1 tbsp. olive oil
- 1 lb. Great Northern beans, rinsed, soaked and dried
- 2 tsps. dried thyme
- 28 oz. canned roasted tomatoes
- Salt and pepper, to taste
- 4 cups vegetable stock
- 1 bunch Swiss chard, chopped

Instructions:
1. Set the Instant Pot to Sauté and heat the olive oil.
2. Add the beans, thyme and tomatoes. Season with salt and pepper. Stir for 1 minute.
3. Pour in the broth and whisk to combine.
4. Lock the lid. Select the Bean/Chili function, then set the timer for 3 minutes at High Pressure.
5. Once the timer goes off, do a quick pressure release. Carefully open the lid.
6. Select the Sauté button.
7. Add the Swiss chard and cook for 3 minutes until tender. Transfer to a plate and serve.

Nutritional info:
Calories 241, Fat 0.8g, Carbs 44.5g, Protein 15.1g

Chili Con Carne (Chili with Meat)
Prep Time: 15 mins, Cook Time: 35 mins, Servings: 2
Ingredients:
- 2 cups chopped tomatoes
- 3 tbsps. mixed seasoning
- 1lb. ground beef
- 3 squares dark chocolate
- 1 cup mixed beans

Instructions:
1. Mix all the ingredients in the Instant Pot.
2. Lock the lid. Select the Meat/Stew setting. Set the timer for 35 minutes at High Pressure.
3. Once cooking is complete, perform a natural pressure release for 10 minutes, then release any remaining pressure. Carefully open the lid.
4. Serve warm.

Nutritional info:
Calories 340, Carbs 16g, Fat 12g, Protein 46g

Chapter 9 Snacks and Appetizers Recipe

Asian Wings

Prep Time: 10 minutes, Cook Time: 10 minutes, Servings: 4

Ingredients:
- ¼ cup brown sugar
- ¼ cup water
- 4 lbs. chicken wings
- ¼ cup honey
- 2 tbsps. black soy sauce

Instructions:
1. In the Instant Pot, mix the chicken wings with black soy sauce, honey, sugar and water, and stir to combine well.
2. Lock the lid. Select the Manual mode, then set the timer for 5 minutes at High Pressure.
3. Once the timer goes off, do a quick pressure release. Carefully open the lid.
4. Transfer the chicken wings to a baking sheet and broil for about 5 minutes until golden brown.
5. Divide the wings among four plates and serve.

Nutritional info:
Calories 221, Fat 3g, Carbs 10g, Protein 6g

Baby Carrots Snack

Prep Time: 12 mins, Cook Time: 2 mins, Servings: 6

Ingredients:
- ¼ cup Chinese wine
- 1 tbsp. liquid smoke
- 1 lb. baby carrots
- ¼ cup vegetable soup
- ¼ cup soy sauce

Instructions:
1. In the Instant Pot, mix the baby carrots with soy sauce, Chinese wine, soup and liquid smoke. Stir to combine well.
2. Lock the lid. Select the Manual mode, then set the timer for 2 minutes at High Pressure.
3. Once the timer goes off, do a quick pressure release. Carefully open the lid.
4. Drain the carrots and transfer to a platter. You can serve them as a snack with a dip on the side.

Nutritional info:
Calories 176, Fat 3g, Carbs 4g, Protein 4g

BBQ Chicken Wings

Prep Time: 7 mins, Cook Time: 15 mins, Servings: 6

Ingredients:
- ¼ cup red wine
- 2 tbsps. olive oil
- 12 chicken wings
- 1 large onion, chopped
- 18 oz. sweet BBQ sauce

Instructions:
1. Put the oil and onions in the Instant Pot and select the Sauté mode.
2. Sauté for 3 minutes and add chicken wings.
3. Sauté for 2 minutes on each side and add BBQ sauce and red wine. Whisk well.
4. Lock the lid. Select the Manual mode, then set the timer for 10 minutes on High Pressure.
5. Once the timer goes off, do a quick pressure release. Carefully open the lid.
6. Serve immediately.

Nutritional info:
Calories 491, Fat 21.2g, Carbs 19.3g, Protein: 52.9g

BBQ Square Ribs

Prep Time: 12 mins, Cook Time: 20 mins, Servings: 3

Ingredients:
- 1 cup BBQ sauce
- 1 tsp. liquid smoke
- 1 cup apple juice
- 1 rack pork spare ribs
- 1 onion, chopped

Instructions:
1. In the Instant Pot, mix the spare ribs with onion, apple juice, BBQ sauce and liquid smoke, Stir to mix well.
2. Lock the lid. Select the Manual mode, then set the timer for 20 minutes at High Pressure.
3. Once the timer goes off, do a natural pressure release for 10 minutes, then release any remaining pressure. Carefully open the lid.
4. Divide the ribs among three plates and drizzle BBQ sauce all over. Serve immediately.

Nutritional info:
Calories 300, Fat 8g, Carbs 12g, Protein 4g

Black Bean Salsa

Prep Time: 12 mins, Cook Time: 8 mins, Servings: 4

Ingredients:
- 2 red jalapeños, chopped
- 1 small white onion, chopped
- 1 tbsp. olive oil
- 8 oz. canned black beans, drained
- 2 tbsps. lime juice

Instructions:

1. Set the Instant Pot to Sauté and heat the olive oil.
2. Add the onion, stir and cook for 2 to 3 minutes until tender.
3. Add the black beans, lime juice and jalapeños, and stir to combine well.
4. Lock the lid. Select the Manual mode, then set the timer for 3 minutes at High Pressure.
5. Once the timer goes off, do a quick pressure release. Carefully open the lid.
6. Divide the salsa into bowls and serve warm.

Nutritional info:
Calories 172, Fat 3g, Carbs 6g, Protein 3g

Chunky Warm Salsa

Prep Time: 12 mins, Cook Time: 5 mins, Servings: 5

Ingredients:
- 2 tbsps. lime juice
- 2 peaches, roughly chopped
- 1 tbsp. olive oil
- 1 red onion, roughly chopped
- 1 red bell pepper, sliced

Instructions:
1. Set the Instant Pot to Sauté and heat the olive oil.
2. Add the onions, stir, and cook for 2 minutes until translucent.
3. Add the red pepper, peaches and lime juice, and stir to incorporate.
4. Lock the lid. Select the Manual mode, then set the timer for 3 minutes at High Pressure.
5. Once the timer goes off, do a quick pressure release. Carefully open the lid.
6. Remove from the pot to a bowl and serve.

Nutritional info:
Calories 152, Fat 2g, Carbs 4g, Protein 4g

Blue Cheese Dip

Prep Time: 12 mins, Cook Time: 4 mins, Servings: 6

Ingredients:
- 2 tbsps. chopped chives
- 4 tbsps. crumbled blue cheese
- Black pepper, to taste
- 1 cup sour cream
- 1½ tsps. chopped rosemary

Instructions:
1. In the Instant Pot, mix blue cheese with sour cream, rosemary and black pepper, and stir to combine well.
2. Lock the lid. Select the Manual mode, then set the timer for 4 minutes at High Pressure.
3. Once the timer goes off, do a quick pressure release. Carefully open the lid.
4. Scatter the chives all over and stir well. Serve immediately or refrigerate to chill until ready to serve.

Nutritional info:
Calories 200, Fat 7g, Carbs 7g, Protein 4g

Chicken Dip

Prep Time: 12 mins, Cook Time: 15 mins, Servings: 6

Ingredients:
- 1 cup Greek yogurt
- 4 oz. cream cheese
- ½ cup hot sauce
- 3 cups cooked and shredded chicken
- 1 cup shredded Mozzarella cheese

Instructions:
1. In the Instant Pot, mix chicken with cream cheese and hot sauce, and stir to combine well.
2. Lock the lid. Select the Manual mode, then set the timer for 15 minutes at High Pressure.
3. Once the timer goes off, do a natural pressure release for 10 minutes, then release any remaining pressure. Carefully open the lid.
4. Add the yogurt and Mozzarella cheese. Give the mixture a good stir. Let rest for about 8 minutes, then serve.

Nutritional info:
Calories 188, Fat 4g, Carbs 8g, Protein 4g

Cumin Dip

Prep Time: 12 mins, Cook Time: 2 mins, Servings: 4

Ingredients:
- 1 tbsp. hot sauce
- 1 tbsp. lime juice
- 1 cup sour cream
- 1¼ tsps. ground cumin
- ⅓ cup mayonnaise

Instructions:
1. In the Instant Pot, mix sour cream with cumin and hot sauce, and stir to combine well.
2. Lock the lid. Select the Manual mode, then set the timer for 2 minutes at High Pressure.
3. Once the timer goes off, do a quick pressure release. Carefully open the lid.
4. Allow the dip to rest until cooled completely. Add the mayo and lime juice and stir well, then serve.

Nutritional info:
Calories 209, Fat 6g, Carbs 7g, Protein 7g

Ham and Cheese Dip

Prep Time: 12 mins, Cook Time: 12 mins, Servings: 4

Ingredients:
- 8 ham slices, chopped
- 2 tbsps. chopped parsley
- 8 oz. cream cheese
- 1 cup grated Cheddar cheese
- 1 cup Swiss cheese

Instructions:
1. Set the Instant Pot to Sauté and brown the ham for 3 to 4 minutes.
2. Add the Swiss, Cheddar and cream cheese, and stir to combine well.
3. Lock the lid. Select the Manual mode, then set the timer for 6 minutes at High Pressure.
4. Once the timer goes off, do a natural pressure release for 5 minutes, then release any remaining pressure. Carefully open the lid.
5. Scatter the parsley all over and divide into bowls to serve.

Nutritional info:
Calories 243, Fat 4g, Carbs 7g, Protein 4g

Pinto Bean Dip

Prep Time: 12 mins, Cook Time: 8 mins, Servings: 4

Ingredients:
- 2 tbsps. chopped tomatoes
- 1 (8 oz) can pinto beans, drained
- 3 tbsps. lemon juice
- 1¼ cup chopped parsley
- 4 rosemary sprigs, chopped

Instructions:
1. In the Instant Pot, mix pinto beans with rosemary and tomatoes.
2. Lock the lid. Select the Manual mode, then set the timer for 8 minutes at High Pressure.
3. Once the timer goes off, do a quick pressure release. Carefully open the lid.
4. Blend the mixture with an immersion blender. Add the parsley and lemon juice, and pulse until well combined.
5. Store in an airtight container in the fridge until ready to serve.

Nutritional info:
Calories 272, Fat 3g, Carbs 9g, Protein 8g

Steamed Asparagus with Mustard Dip

Prep Time: 7 mins, Cook Time: 8 mins, Servings: 4

Ingredients:
- 1 tsp. Dijon mustard
- 2 tbsps. mayonnaise
- Salt and black pepper, to taste
- 1 cup water
- 12 asparagus stems
- 3 tbsps. lemon juice

Instructions:
1. Mix the Dijon mustard, mayonnaise, salt and black pepper in a bowl. Set aside.
2. Set trivet to the Instant Pot and add the water.
3. Place asparagus stems on the trivet and drizzle with lemon juice.
4. Lock the lid. Select the Manual mode, then set the timer for 8 minutes at High Pressure.
5. Once the timer goes off, do a quick pressure release. Carefully open the lid.
6. Dip the asparagus into mustard mixture.

Nutritional info:
Calories 42, Fat 2.7g, Carbs 3.9g, Protein 1.3g

Brussels Sprouts and Apples Appetizer

Prep Time: 12 mins, Cook Time: 6 mins, Servings: 4

Ingredients:
- 1½ cups water
- 1 lb. halved Brussels sprouts
- 1 cup dried cranberries
- 2 tbsps. canola oil
- 1 green apple, cored and roughly chopped
- 2 tbsps. lemon juice

Instructions:
1. Pour the water into the Instant Pot and arrange the steamer basket in the pot, then add Brussels sprouts.
2. Lock the lid. Select the Manual mode, then set the timer for 4 minutes at High Pressure.
3. Once the timer goes off, do a quick pressure release. Carefully open the lid.
4. Drain the Brussels sprouts and transfer to a bowl.
5. Clean the pot and set it to Sauté. Heat the oil and add Brussels sprouts, stir and cook for 1 minute.
6. Stir in apple, cranberries and lemon juice, and cook for 1 minute. Serve warm.

Nutritional info:
Calories 163, Fat 3g, Carbs 6g, Protein 3g

Creamy Broccoli Appetizer

Prep Time: 12 mins, Cook Time: 3 mins, Servings: 4

Ingredients:
- 1 cup water
- 2 tbsps. mayonnaise
- 1 tbsp. honey
- ½ cup Greek yogurt
- 1 head broccoli, cut into florets
- 1 apple, cored and sliced

Instructions:
1. In the Instant Pot, add the water. Arrange the steamer basket in the pot, then add the broccoli inside.
2. Lock the lid. Select the Manual mode, then set the timer for 3 minutes at Low Pressure.
3. Once the timer goes off, do a quick pressure release. Carefully open the lid.
4. Drain the broccoli florets and transfer to a bowl. Add the apple, mayo, yogurt and honey, and toss well. Serve immediately.

Nutritional info:
Calories 200, Fat 3g, Carbs 7g, Protein 3g

Lemony Endives Appetizer
Prep Time: 12 mins, Cook Time: 13 mins, Servings: 4
Ingredients:
- 3 tbsps. olive oil
- ½ cup chicken stock
- Juice of ½ lemon
- 2 tbsps. chopped parsley
- 8 endives, trimmed

Instructions:
1. Set the Instant Pot to Sauté and heat the olive oil. Add the endives and cook them for 3 minutes.
2. Add lemon juice and stock, and whisk well.
3. Lock the lid. Select the Manual mode, then set the timer for 10 minutes at High Pressure.
4. Once the timer goes off, do a quick pressure release. Carefully open the lid.
5. Transfer the endives to a large bowl. Drizzle some cooking juices all over and sprinkle with the chopped parsley before serving.

Nutritional info:
Calories 120, Fat 2g, Carbs 12g, Protein 4g

Carrot and Beet Spread
Prep Time: 12 mins, Cook Time: 12 mins, Servings: 6
Ingredients:
- 1 bunch basil, chopped
- 8 carrots, chopped
- ¼ cup lemon juice
- 4 beets, peeled and chopped
- 1 cup vegetable stock

Instructions:
1. In the Instant Pot, combine the beets with stock and carrots.
2. Lock the lid. Select the Manual mode and set the cooking time for 12 minutes at High Pressure.
3. Once cooking is complete, do a quick pressure release. Carefully open the lid.
4. Blend the ingredients with an immersion blender, and add the lemon juice and basil, and whisk well. Serve immediately.

Nutritional info:
Calories 100, Fat 1g, Carbs 10g, Protein 3g

Cashew Spread
Prep Time: 12 mins, Cook Time: 6 mins, Servings: 8
Ingredients:
- ¼ cup nutritional yeast
- ¼ tsp. garlic powder
- ½ cup soaked and drained cashews
- 10 oz. hummus
- ½ cup water

Instructions:
1. In the Instant Pot, combine the cashews and water.
2. Lock the lid. Select the Manual mode, then set the timer for 6 minutes at High Pressure.
3. Once the timer goes off, do a quick pressure release. Carefully open the lid.
4. Transfer the cashews to the blender, and add hummus, yeast and garlic powder, and pulse until well combined. Serve immediately.

Nutritional info:
Calories 180, Fat 2g, Carbs 4g, Protein 5g

Crab Spread
Prep Time: 12 mins, Cook Time: 15 mins, Servings: 4
Ingredients:
- 1 tsp. Worcestershire sauce
- ½ bunch scallions, chopped
- ½ cup sour cream
- ¼ cup half-and-half
- 8 oz. crab meat

Instructions:
1. In the Instant Pot, mix the crabmeat with sour cream, half-and-half, scallions and Worcestershire sauce, and stir to combine well.
2. Lock the lid. Select the Manual mode, then set the timer for 15 minutes at Low Pressure.
3. Once the timer goes off, do a quick pressure release. Carefully open the lid.
4. Allow the spread cool for a few minutes and serve.

Nutritional info:
Calories 241, Fat 4g, Carbs 8g, Protein 3g

Creamy Avocado Spread
Prep Time: 12 mins, Cook Time: 2 mins, Servings: 4

Ingredients:
- 1 cup coconut milk
- 2 pitted, peeled and halved avocados
- Juice of 2 limes
- ½ cup chopped cilantro
- ¼ tsp. stevia
- 1 cup water

Instructions:
1. In the Instant Pot, add the water and steamer basket. Place the avocados in the basket.
2. Lock the lid. Select the Manual mode and set the cooking time for 2 minutes at High Pressure.
3. Once cooking is complete, do a quick pressure release. Carefully open the lid.
4. Transfer the avocados to your blender, and add the cilantro, stevia, lime juice, and coconut milk, and blend, or until it reaches your desired consistency. Serve immediately or refrigerate to chill until ready to use.

Nutritional info:
Calories 190, Fat 6g, Carbs 10g, Protein 4g

Scallion and Mayo Spread
Prep Time: 12 mins, Cook Time: 3 mins, Servings: 6

Ingredients:
- 3 tbsps. chopped dill
- 1 cup sour cream
- 1 tbsp. grated lemon zest
- ½ cup chopped scallions
- ¼ cup mayonnaise

Instructions:
1. Set the Instant Pot to Sauté and add the scallions. Stir and cook for 1 minute.
2. Add the sour cream and stir to combine well.
3. Lock the lid. Select the Manual mode, then set the timer for 2 minutes at High Pressure.
4. Once the timer goes off, do a quick pressure release. Carefully open the lid.
5. Leave this mixture to rest until cooled completely. Add the mayo, dill, and lemon zest, and stir well. You can serve this with tortilla chips on the side.

Nutritional info:
Calories 222, Fat 4g, Carbs 8g, Protein 4g

Simple Egg Spread
Prep Time: 12 mins, Cook Time: 5 mins, Servings: 4

Ingredients:
- 1 tbsp. olive oil
- 4 eggs
- 1 cup water
- Salt, to taste
- ½ cup mayonnaise
- 2 green onions, chopped

Instructions:
1. Grease a baking dish with olive oil and crack the eggs in it.
2. Add the water and trivet to the Instant Pot. Place the baking dish on the trivet.
3. Lock the lid. Select the Manual mode, then set the timer for 5 minutes at High Pressure.
4. Once the timer goes off, do a natural pressure release for 3 to 5 minutes. Carefully open the lid.
5. Cool eggs down and mash them with a fork. Sprinkle with salt, mayo, and green onions. Stir well and serve immediately.

Nutritional info:
Calories 222, Fat 3g, Carbs 10g, Protein 4g

Special Ranch Spread
Prep Time: 12 mins, Cook Time: 10 mins, Servings: 12

Ingredients:
- 4 green onions, chopped
- 1 cup sour cream
- 1 lb. bacon, chopped
- 1 cup shredded Monterey Jack cheese
- 1 cup mayonnaise

Instructions:
1. Set the Instant Pot to Sauté and cook the bacon for about 4 minutes on each side until it is crispy.
2. Add the sour cream and green onions, and stir to mix well.
3. Lock the lid. Select the Manual mode, then set the timer for 6 minutes at High Pressure.
4. Once the timer goes off, do a natural pressure release for 5 minutes. Carefully open the lid.
5. Add the cheese and mayo and stir. Allow to cool for a few minutes and serve.

Nutritional info:
Calories 261, Fat 4g, Carbs 7g, Protein 4g

Zucchini Spread
Prep Time: 12 mins, Cook Time: 9 mins, Servings: 6

Ingredients:
- ½ cup water
- 1 tbsp. olive oil
- 1 bunch basil, chopped
- 1½ lbs. zucchinis, chopped
- 2 garlic cloves, minced

Instructions:
1. Set the Instant Pot to Sauté and heat the olive oil. Cook the garlic cloves for 3 minutes, stirring occasionally.

2. Add zucchinis and water, and mix well.
3. Lock the lid. Select the Manual mode, then set the timer for 3 minutes at High Pressure.
4. Once the timer goes off, do a quick pressure release. Carefully open the lid.
5. Add the basil and blend the mixture with an immersion blender until smooth.
6. Select the Simmer mode and cook for 2 minutes more.
7. Transfer to a bowl and serve warm.

Nutritional info:
Calories 120, Fat 2g, Carbs 7g, Protein 2g

Cheesy Shrimp and Tomatoes
Prep Time: 12 mins, Cook Time: 4 mins, Servings: 6
Ingredients:
- 1 lb. shrimp, shelled and deveined
- 2 tbsps. butter
- 1 cup crumbled feta cheese
- 1½ cups chopped onion
- 15 oz. chopped canned tomatoes

Instructions:
1. Set the Instant Pot to Sauté and melt the butter.
2. Add the onion, stir, and cook for 2 minutes.
3. Add the shrimp and tomatoes and mix well.
4. Lock the lid. Select the Manual mode, then set the timer for 2 minutes at Low Pressure.
5. Once the timer goes off, do a quick pressure release. Carefully open the lid.
6. Divide shrimp and tomatoes mixture into small bowls. Top with feta cheese and serve.

Nutritional info:
Calories 201, Fat 3g, Carbs 7g, Protein 4g

Chicken Meatballs in Barbecue Sauce
Prep Time: 6 mins, Cook Time: 15 mins, Servings: 8
Ingredients:
- 24 oz. frozen chicken meatballs
- ½ tsp. crushed red pepper
- 12 oz. barbecue sauce
- ¼ cup water
- 12 oz. apricot preserves

Instructions:
1. Add all the ingredients to the Instant Pot. Stir to mix well.
2. Lock the lid. Select the Manual mode, then set the timer for 5 minutes at High Pressure.
3. Once the timer goes off, do a quick pressure release. Carefully open the lid.
4. Serve the meatballs on a platter.

Nutritional info:
Calories 347, Fat 11.1g, Carbs 47.7g, Protein: 14.6g

Chili Endives Platter
Prep Time: 12 mins, Cook Time: 7 mins, Servings: 4
Ingredients:
- ¼ tsp. chili powder
- 1 tbsp. butter
- 4 trimmed and halved endives
- 1 tbsp. lemon juice
- Salt, to taste

Instructions:
1. Set the Instant Pot to Sauté and melt the butter. Add the endives, salt, chili powder and lemon juice to the pot.
2. Lock the lid. Select the Manual mode, then set the timer for 7 minutes at High Pressure.
3. Once the timer goes off, do a quick pressure release. Carefully open the lid.
4. Divide the endives into bowls. Drizzle some cooking juice over them and serve.

Nutritional info:
Calories 90, Fat 4g, Carbs 12g, Protein 3g

Fish and Carrot Balls
Prep Time: 12 mins, Cook Time: 10 mins, Servings: 16
Ingredients:
- ¼ cup cornstarch
- 1 carrot, grated
- 1½ cups fish stock
- 3 egg whites
- 1½ lbs. skinless, boneless and ground pike fillets

Instructions:
1. In a bowl, mix the fillets with egg whites, cornstarch and carrot. Form the mixture into equal-sized balls with your hands.
2. Put the stock and fish balls into the Instant pot.
3. Lock the lid. Select the Manual function and cook for 10 minutes at Low Pressure.
4. Once cooking is complete, do a quick pressure release. Carefully open the lid.
5. Drain the fish balls and arrange them on a platter and serve.

Nutritional info:
Calories 162, Fat 3g, Carbs 8g, Protein 4g

Greek Meatballs

Prep Time: 12 mins, Cook Time: 12 mins, Servings: 10

Ingredients:
- 1 egg, whisked
- ¼ cup chopped mint
- 1 lb. ground beef
- 3 tbsps. olive oil
- ¼ cup white vinegar

Instructions:
1. In a bowl, mix the beef with mint and egg, and whisk well. Shape the beef mixture into 10 meatballs with your hands.
2. Set the Instant Pot to Sauté and heat the olive oil.
3. Add the beef meatballs and brown them for about 4 minutes on each side.
4. Add the vinegar and stir to mix well.
5. Lock the lid. Select the Manual mode, then set the timer for 4 minutes at High Pressure.
6. Once the timer goes off, do a quick pressure release. Carefully open the lid.
7. Divide the meatballs among plates and serve them with a yogurt dip on the side.

Nutritional info:
Calories 200, Fat 4g, Carbs 8g, Protein 10g

Green Olive Pâté

Prep Time: 12 mins, Cook Time: 2 mins, Servings: 4

Ingredients:
- ½ cup olive oil
- 2 anchovy fillets
- 1 tbsp. chopped capers
- 2 cups pitted green olives
- 2 garlic cloves, minced

Instructions:
1. In a food processor, process the olives with anchovy fillets, garlic, capers and olive oil, then transfer to the Instant Pot.
2. Lock the lid. Select the Manual mode, then set the timer for 2 minutes at Low Pressure.
3. Once the timer goes off, do a quick pressure release. Carefully open the lid.
4. Remove from the pot and serve warm.

Nutritional info:
Calories 118, Fat 2g, Carbs 5g, Protein 4g

Broccoli and Bacon Appetizer Salad

Prep Time: 12 mins, Cook Time: 12 mins, Servings: 4

Ingredients:
- 1½ cups water
- ½ tbsp. apple cider vinegar
- ¼ cup chopped cilantro
- 2 tbsps. olive oil
- 1 head broccoli, cut into florets
- 4 bacon slices, chopped

Instructions:
1. Add the water and steamer basket to the Instant Pot. Arrange the broccoli florets in the basket.
2. Lock the lid. Select the Manual mode, then set the timer for 3 minutes at High Pressure.
3. Once the timer goes off, do a quick pressure release. Carefully open the lid.
4. Drain the broccoli and transfer to a bowl.
5. Clean the pot and set it to Sauté. Add the bacon, stir and cook for 4 minutes per side until it's crispy.
6. Roughly chop broccoli and return it to the Instant Pot. Stir and cook for 1 minute more.
7. Add the oil, cilantro and vinegar, and mix well. Remove from the heat to a plate and serve.

Nutritional info:
Calories 200, Fat 4g, Carbs 6g, Protein 4g

Brussels Sprouts and Broccoli Appetizer Salad

Prep Time: 12 mins, Cook Time: 6 mins, Servings: 6

Ingredients:
- 1½ cups water
- 2 tsps. mustard
- 1 head broccoli, cut into florets
- ½ cup walnut oil
- 1 lb. halved Brussels sprouts
- ¼ cup balsamic vinegar

Instructions:
1. Put the water in the Instant Pot and arrange the steamer basket in the pot, then add broccoli and Brussels sprouts.
2. Lock the lid. Select the Manual mode, then set the timer for 4 minutes at High Pressure.
3. Once the timer goes off, do a quick pressure release. Carefully open the lid.
4. Drain the vegetables and transfer to a bowl.
5. Clean the pot and set it to Sauté. Heat the oil and add broccoli and Brussels sprouts. Stir and cook for 1 minute.
6. Drizzle with the vinegar and cook for 1 minute more, then transfer to a bowl.

7. Add the mustard and toss well. Serve immediately or refrigerate to chill.

Nutritional info:
Calories 200, Fat 6g, Carbs 8g, Protein 5g

Cheesy Broccoli Appetizer Salad
Prep Time: 12 mins, Cook Time: 4 mins, Servings: 4

Ingredients:
- 1½ cups water
- 2 tbsps. balsamic vinegar
- 4 oz. cubed Cheddar cheese
- 1 cup mayonnaise
- 1 head broccoli, cut into florets
- ⅛ cup pumpkin seeds

Instructions:
1. Put the water into the Instant Pot and arrange the steamer basket in the pot, then add the broccoli.
2. Lock the lid. Select the Manual mode, then set the timer for 3 minutes at High Pressure.
3. Once the timer goes off, do a quick pressure release. Carefully open the lid.
4. Drain the broccoli and chop, then transfer to a bowl.
5. Add the cheese, pumpkin seeds, mayo and vinegar, and toss to combine. Serve immediately.

Nutritional info:
Calories 182, Fat 4g, Carbs 7g, Protein 4g

Grated Carrot Appetizer Salad
Prep Time: 12 mins, Cook Time: 3 mins, Servings: 4

Ingredients:
- 1 lb. carrots, grated
- ¼ cup water
- Salt, to taste
- 1 tbsp. lemon juice
- 1 tsp. red pepper flakes
- 1 tbsp. chopped parsley

Instructions:
1. In the Instant Pot, mix the carrots with water and salt.
2. Lock the lid. Select the Manual mode, then set the timer for 3 minutes at High Pressure.
3. Once the timer goes off, do a quick pressure release. Carefully open the lid.
4. Drain the carrots and cool them in a bowl.
5. Add the lemon juice, pepper flakes and parsley to the bowl, and toss well. Serve immediately.

Nutritional info:
Calories 152, Fat 3g, Carbs 4g, Protein 3g

Creamy Endives Appetizer Salad
Prep Time: 12 mins, Cook Time: 18 mins, Servings: 3

Ingredients:
- 1 cup vegetable soup
- 3 big endives, roughly chopped
- 3 tbsps. heavy cream
- 2 tbsps. extra virgin olive oil
- ½ yellow onion, chopped

Instructions:
1. Set the Instant Pot to Sauté and heat the olive oil. Add the onion, stir and cook for 4 minutes until tender.
2. Add the endives, stir and cook for 4 minutes more. Pour in the stock and whisk to combine.
3. Lock the lid. Select the Manual mode, then set the timer for 10 minutes at High Pressure.
4. Once the timer goes off, do a quick pressure release. Carefully open the lid.
5. Stir in the heavy cream and cook for 1 minute. Remove from the pot and serve in bowls.

Nutritional info:
Calories 253, Fat 4g, Carbs 12g, Protein 15g

Green Beans Appetizer Salad
Prep Time: 12 mins, Cook Time: 2 mins, Servings: 4

Ingredients:
- 1 tbsp. red wine vinegar
- 1 lb. green beans
- ½ cup water
- 2 sliced red onions
- 1 tbsp. olive oil
- 1 tbsp. Creole mustard

Instructions:
1. In the Instant Pot, mix green beans with water.
2. Lock the lid. Select the Manual mode, then set the timer for 2 minutes at High Pressure.
3. Once the timer goes off, do a quick pressure release. Carefully open the lid.
4. Drain the green beans and transfer to a bowl. Add the onion slices, mustard, vinegar, and oil, and gently toss to combine. Serve immediately.

Nutritional info:
Calories 121, Fat 4g, Carbs 6g, Protein 4g

Crunchy Brussels Sprouts Salad
Prep Time: 12 mins, Cook Time: 6 mins, Servings: 4

Ingredients:
- 2 tbsps. apple cider vinegar
- 1 lb. halved Brussels sprouts
- 1 tbsp. olive oil
- ½ cup chopped pecans
- 1 tbsp. brown sugar
- 1½ cups water

Instructions:
1. Place the water in the Instant Pot and arrange the steamer basket in the pot, then add Brussels sprouts.
2. Lock the lid. Select the Manual mode, then set the timer for 4 minutes at High Pressure.
3. Once the timer goes off, do a quick pressure release. Carefully open the lid.
4. Drain the Brussels sprouts and transfer to a bowl.
5. Clean the pot and set it to Sauté. Heat the olive oil and add Brussels sprouts and vinegar, stir and cook for 1 minute.
6. Add the sugar and pecans, stir, and cook for 30 seconds more. Remove from the pot to a plate and serve.

Nutritional info:
Calories 186, Fat 4g, Carbs 9g, Protein 3g

Kale and Carrots Salad
Prep Time: 12 mins, Cook Time: 7 mins, Servings: 4
Ingredients:
- 1 tbsp. olive oil
- 3 carrots, sliced
- 1 red onion, chopped
- 10 oz. kale, roughly chopped
- ½ cup chicken stock

Instructions:
1. Set the Instant Pot to Sauté and heat the olive oil.
2. Add the onion and carrots, stir, and cook for 1 to 2 minutes.
3. Stir in stock and kale.
4. Lock the lid. Select the Manual mode, then set the timer for 5 minutes at High Pressure.
5. Once the timer goes off, do a quick pressure release. Carefully open the lid.
6. Divide the vegetables among four bowls and serve.

Nutritional info:
Calories 128, Fat 2g, Carbs 8g, Protein 4g

Kale and Wild Rice Appetizer Salad
Prep Time: 12 mins, Cook Time: 25 mins, Servings: 4
Ingredients:
- 1 tsp. olive oil
- 1 avocado, peeled, pitted and chopped
- 3 oz. goat cheese, crumbled
- 1 cup cooked wild rice
- 1 bunch kale, roughly chopped

Instructions:
1. Set the Instant Pot to Sauté and heat the olive oil.
2. Add the rice and toast for 2 to 3 minutes, stirring often.
3. Add kale and stir well.
4. Lock the lid. Select the Manual mode, then set the timer for 20 minutes at Low Pressure.
5. Once the timer goes off, do a natural pressure release for 10 minutes, then release any remaining pressure. Carefully open the lid.
6. Add avocado and toss well. Sprinkle the cheese on top and serve.

Nutritional info:
Calories 182, Fat 3g, Carbs 4g, Protein 3g

Minty Kale Salad with Pineapple
Prep Time: 12 mins, Cook Time: 3 mins, Servings: 4
Ingredients:
- 2 tbsps. lemon juice
- 2 tbsps. chopped mint
- 1 bunch kale, roughly chopped
- 1 tsp. sesame oil
- 1 cup chopped pineapple

Instructions:
1. Set the Instant Pot to Sauté and heat the oil.
2. Add kale, stir, and cook for 1 minute.
3. Add pineapple, lemon juice and mint, and stir well. Divide the salad among plates and serve.

Nutritional info:
Calories 121, Fat 1g, Carbs 4g, Protein 2g

Watercress Appetizer Salad
Prep Time: 12 mins, Cook Time: 2 mins, Servings: 4
Ingredients:
- 1 bunch watercress, roughly torn
- ½ cup water
- 1 tbsp. lemon juice
- 1 cubed watermelon
- 1 tbsp. olive oil
- 2 peaches, pitted and sliced

Instructions:
1. In the Instant Pot, mix watercress with water.
2. Lock the lid. Select the Manual mode, then set the timer for 2 minutes at High Pressure.
3. Once the timer goes off, do a quick pressure release. Carefully open the lid.
4. Drain the watercress and transfer to a bowl. Add peaches, watermelon, oil, and lemon juice, and toss well. Divide the salad into salad bowls and serve.

Nutritional info:
Calories 111, Fat 3g, Carbs 5g, Protein 3g

Goat Cheese Mushrooms
Prep Time: 12 mins, Cook Time: 10 mins, Servings: 8
Ingredients:
- 1½ cups water

- ½ cup chopped, drained and roasted sweet red peppers
- ½ cup crumbled goat cheese
- 4 tsps. olive oil
- 24 baby Portobello mushrooms
- White pepper, to taste

Instructions:
1. Add the trivet and water to the Instant Pot.
2. Place mushroom caps in a greased baking pan and top with cheese and red pepper.
3. Sprinkle with white pepper and drizzle with olive oil.
4. Place the baking pan on the trivet.
5. Lock the lid. Select the Manual mode, then set the timer for 10 minutes at High Pressure.
6. Once the timer goes off, do a quick pressure release. Carefully open the lid.
7. Allow to cool before serving.

Nutritional info:
Calories 90, Fat 3g, Carbs 9.6g, Protein 9.6g

Hummus
Prep Time: 20 mins, Cook Time: 30 mins, Servings: 6
Ingredients:
- 1 (15 oz.) can chickpeas
- 1 cup water
- 3 garlic cloves, minced
- 2 oz. sliced fresh jalapeño pepper
- 2 tbsps. lemon juice
- ½ tsp. ground cumin

Instructions:
1. Drain the chickpeas but reserve the liquid in a bowl.
2. Pour the water and chickpeas into the Instant Pot.
3. Lock the lid. Select the Manual mode, then set the timer for 35 minutes at High Pressure.
4. Once the timer goes off, do a quick pressure release. Carefully open the lid.
5. Transfer the chickpeas to a food processor.
6. Add the remaining ingredients to the food processor and pulse until smooth.
7. Serve with crackers, bread or vegetable strips.

Nutritional info:
Calories 23, Fat 0.2g, Carbs 4.5g, Protein 1g

Simple Red Pepper Hummus
Prep Time: 12 mins, Cook Time: 1 hour 30 mins, Servings: 4
Ingredients:
- ½ cup lemon juice
- 2 tbsps. sesame oil
- 1 tbsp. tahini paste
- 3 roasted red peppers
- 1 lb. chickpeas, soaked in water overnight

Instructions:
1. In the Instant Pot, mix chickpeas with water.
2. Lock the lid. Select the Manual mode, then set the timer for 1 hour and 30 minutes at High Pressure.
3. Once the timer goes off, do a quick pressure release. Carefully open the lid.
4. Drain the chickpeas and transfer to a food processor. Add the roasted peppers, sesame oil, lemon juice, and tahini paste to the chickpeas, and pulse until it reaches your preferred consistency.
5. Serve immediately or refrigerate to chill until ready to use.

Nutritional info:
Calories 162, Fat 4g, Carbs 7g, Protein 8g

Lettuce Wrapped Tofu
Prep Time: 12 mins, Cook Time: 5 mins, Servings: 4
Ingredients:
- 1 cup water
- 2 tbsps. tomato ketchup
- 4 lettuce leaves
- 1 tbsp. BBQ sauce
- ½ cup shredded Mozzarella cheese
- 2 blocks firmly pressed tofu

Instructions:
1. Add the trivet and water to the Instant Pot.
2. Wrap the tofu well in lettuce leaves along with a little rubbing of BBQ sauce and tomato ketchup.
3. Transfer the wrapped tofu on the trivet and top with Mozzarella cheese.
4. Lock the lid. Select the Manual mode, then set the timer for 5 minutes at High Pressure.
5. Once the timer goes off, do a quick pressure release. Carefully open the lid.
6. Serve hot.

Nutritional info:
Calories 68, Fat 3.3g, Carbs 4.7g, Protein 6.3g

Maple Brussels Sprouts with Orange Juice
Prep Time: 12 mins, Cook Time: 6 mins, Servings: 4
Ingredients:
- 2 tbsps. maple syrup
- ¼ cup orange juice
- 1 tbsp. butter
- 2 lbs. halved Brussels sprouts

- 1 tsp. orange zest

Instructions:
1. Set the Instant Pot to Sauté and melt the butter.
2. Add orange juice, orange zest and maple syrup, stir and cook for 1 to 2 minutes.
3. Add Brussels sprouts and stir well.
4. Lock the lid. Select the Manual mode, then set the timer for 4 minutes at High Pressure.
5. Once the timer goes off, do a quick pressure release. Carefully open the lid.
6. Serve the Brussels sprouts on a plate.

Nutritional info:
Calories 90, Fat 2g, Carbs 12g, Protein 3g

Mexican Corn on the Cob
Prep Time: 12 mins, Cook Time: 15 mins, Servings: 4

Ingredients:
- 4 ears of corn
- ¼ cup mayonnaise
- 1 tbsp. butter
- ¼ tsp. cayenne pepper
- 1 cup water
- ¾ cup crumbled feta cheese

Instructions:
1. On a clean work surface, brush the corn generously with mayo and butter. Season with cayenne pepper.
2. Add the water and steamer basket to the Instant Pot. Arrange the corn in the steamer basket.
3. Lock the lid. Select the Manual mode, then set the timer for 15 minutes at High Pressure.
4. Once the timer goes off, do a quick pressure release. Carefully open the lid.
5. Transfer the corn to a large platter. Sprinkle the feta cheese all over and serve hot.

Nutritional info:
Calories 172, Fat 4g, Carbs 5g, Protein 3g

Mushroom Bacon Skewers
Prep Time: 12 mins, Cook Time: 20 mins, Servings: 12

Ingredients:
- 24 medium fresh mushrooms
- 12 bacon strips
- ½ cup BBQ sauce
- ¼ cup chilli sauce
- ¼ cup vinegar
- 1 cup water

Instructions:
1. Wrap each mushroom with a piece of bacon and secure with a toothpick.
2. Thread onto wooden skewers and brush with BBQ sauce, chilli sauce and vinegar.
3. Add the trivet and water to the Instant Pot. Place the skewers on the trivet.
4. Lock the lid. Select the Manual mode, then set the timer for 20 minutes at High Pressure.
5. Once the timer goes off, do a quick pressure release. Carefully open the lid.
6. Serve hot.

Nutritional info:
Calories 126, Fat 9.1g, Carbs 5.2g, Protein 5.2g

Prosciutto Wrapped Asparagus
Prep Time: 6 mins, Cook Time: 4 mins, Servings: 4

Ingredients:
- 1 cup water
- 2 tbsps. honey
- 1 lb. thick asparagus
- 1 cup shredded Cheddar cheese
- 3 tbsps. mustard sauce
- 9 oz. prosciutto, thinly sliced

Instructions:
1. In the Instant Pot, add the water and trivet.
2. Wrap the asparagus well in thin slices of prosciutto and rub with mustard sauce.
3. Place the wrapped asparagus on the trivet and top with honey and cheese.
4. Lock the lid. Select the Manual mode, then set the timer for 4 minutes at High Pressure.
5. Once the timer goes off, do a quick pressure release. Carefully open the lid.
6. Serve hot.

Nutritional info:
Calories 275, Fat 14.2g, Carbs 15.3g, Protein 22.9g

Southern Peanuts
Prep Time: 12 mins, Cook Time: 1 hour 15 mins, Servings: 4

Ingredients:
- 1 lb. peanuts
- ¼ cup sea salt
- 1 tbsp. Cajun seasoning
- 2 garlic cloves, minced
- 1 jalapeño pepper, chopped

Instructions:
1. In the Instant Pot mix peanuts with sea salt, Cajun seasoning, garlic and jalapeño.
2. Add enough water to cover.
3. Lock the lid. Select the Manual mode, then set the timer for 1 hour and 15 minutes at High Pressure.

4. Once the timer goes off, do a quick pressure release. Carefully open the lid.
5. Drain the peanuts and transfer to bowls, then serve.

Nutritional info:
Calories 100, Fat 4g, Carbs 7g, Protein 2g

Chapter 10 Broths and Sauces Recipe

Béarnaise Sauce

Prep Time: 6 mins, Cook Time: 3 mins, Servings: 4
Ingredients:
- 2 tsps. freshly squeezed lemon juice
- 2 tbsps. fresh tarragon
- 4 beaten egg yolks
- ¼ tsp. onion powder
- ⅔ lb. butter

Instructions:
1. Press the Sauté button on the Instant Pot and melt the butter.
2. Transfer the melted butter to a mixing bowl.
3. Slowly add the egg yolks to the bowl while whisking.
4. Continue stirring so that no lumps form.
5. Add the lemon juice, onion powder, and fresh tarragon, and whisk well.
6. Béarnaise sauce is suitable for many dishes, you can serve it with roasted beef chops, grilled pork chops, or chicken tenderloin.

Nutritional info:
Calories 603, Carbs 1.4g, Protein 3.5g, Fat 66.2g

Chimichurri Sauce

Prep Time: 6 mins, Cook Time: 3 hours, Servings: 6
Ingredients:
- 2 garlic cloves, minced
- 1 green chili pepper, chopped
- 1 lemon, juice and zest
- 2 tbsps. olive oil
- ½ yellow bell pepper, chopped
- 1 tbsp. white wine vinegar

Instructions:
1. Place all ingredients in the Instant Pot and stir to combine.
2. Lock the lid. Select the Slow Cook mode, then set the timer for 3 hours at High Pressure.
3. Once the timer goes off, do a quick pressure release. Carefully open the lid.
4. Allow to cool for 30 minutes and serve with grilled meats, steaks, or sausages.

Nutritional info:
Calories 326, Carbs 1.9g, Protein 0.3g, Fat 36.5g

Creamy Cheese Sauce

Prep Time: 6 mins, Cook Time: 4 hours, Servings: 4
Ingredients:
- ¼ cup cream cheese
- ¼ cup heavy whipping cream
- 2 tbsps. melted butter
- Salt and pepper, to taste
- ½ cup grated Cheddar cheese

Instructions:
1. Put all the ingredients in the Instant Pot and stir to combine.
2. Lock the lid. Select the Slow Cook mode, then set the timer for 4 hours at High Pressure.
3. Once the timer goes off, do a quick pressure release. Carefully open the lid.
4. You can serve this cheese sauce with French fries, Nachos, chicken nuggets, or pretzels.

Nutritional info:
Calories 250, Carbs 5.3g, Protein 10.9g, Fat 20.3g

Hollandaise Sauce

Prep Time: 6 mins, Cook Time: 5 mins, Servings: 4
Ingredients:
- ⅔ lb. butter
- 4 egg yolks, beaten
- 2 tbsps. lemon juice
- Salt and pepper, to taste

Instructions:
1. Press the Sauté button on the Instant Pot.
2. Add the butter and heat to melt.
3. Whisk vigorously while adding the yolks. Cook for 1 minute.
4. Continue stirring and add the lemon juice, salt, and pepper.
5. You can serve the hollandaise sauce with poached or grilled fish or chicken.

Nutritional info:
Calories 606, Fat 66.8g, Carbs 2.2g, Protein 3.5g

Satay Sauce

Prep Time: 6 mins, Cook Time: 3 hours, Servings: 6
Ingredients:
- ⅓ cup peanut butter
- 1 red chili pepper, finely chopped
- 4 tbsps. soy sauce
- 1 cup coconut milk
- 1 garlic clove, minced

Instructions:
1. Place all ingredients in the Instant Pot and stir until everything is well combined.
2. Lock the lid. Select the Slow Cook mode, then set the timer for 3 hours at High Pressure.
3. Once the timer goes off, do a quick pressure release. Carefully open the lid.
4. Serve the satay sauce with beef kebabs or chicken skewers, or you can serve it as dipping sauce.

Nutritional info:
Calories 138, Carbs 6.9g, Protein 2.1g, Fat 12.3g

Caesar Salad Dressing
Prep Time: 6 mins, Cook Time: 3 hours, Servings: 6
Ingredients:
- ½ cup olive oil
- 1 tbsp. Dijon mustard
- ½ cup grated Parmesan cheese
- ⅔ oz. chopped anchovies
- ½ freshly squeezed lemon juice
- ¼ cup water
- Salt and pepper, to taste

Instructions:
1. Place all the ingredients in the Instant Pot and stir to incorporate.
2. Lock the lid. Select the Slow Cook mode, then set the timer for 3 hours at High Pressure.
3. Once the timer goes off, do a quick pressure release. Carefully open the lid.
4. You can use the Caesar dressing to marinate the meat or dress the salad, or you can use it as a dipping sauce for crudités.

Nutritional info:
Calories 203, Carbs 1.5g, Protein 3.4g, Fat 20.7g

Spicy Thousand Island Dressing
Prep Time: 10 mins, Cook Time: 2 hours, Servings: 4
Ingredients:
- 1 tsp. tabasco
- 1 shallot, finely chopped
- 1 cup mayonnaise
- 4 tbsps. chopped dill pickles
- 1 tbsp. freshly squeezed lemon juice
- ¼ cup water
- Salt and pepper, to taste

Instructions:
1. Place all the ingredients in the Instant Pot and whisk to combine.
2. Lock the lid. Select the Slow Cook mode, then set the timer for 2 hours at High Pressure.
3. Once the timer goes off, do a quick pressure release. Carefully open the lid.
4. You can use this dressing to serve the burgers, sandwiches, or salads.

Nutritional info:
Calories 85, Carbs 2.3g, Protein 1.7g, Fat 7.8g

Chicken Bone Broth
Prep Time: 12 mins, Cook time: 2 to 3 hours, Servings: 4
Ingredients:
- 1 lb. bones of one whole chicken
- 2 tbsps. apple cider vinegar
- 2 cloves garlic, minced
- 8 cups water
- 1 tsp. sea salt

Instructions:
1. Add all the ingredients to the Instant Pot.
2. Lock the lid. Select the Soup mode, then set the timer for 2 to 3 hours at High Pressure.
3. Once the timer goes off, do a natural pressure release for 10 to 20 minutes, then release any remaining pressure. Carefully open the lid.
4. Strain the liquid and transfer the broth to an airtight container to store in the refrigerator for up to 5 days. Bone soup is healthy and recommended for those with a leaky gut.

Nutritional info:
Calories: 100, Fat: 1g, Carbs: 0g, Protein: 20g

Chili Aioli
Prep Time: 6 mins, Cook Time: 2 mins, Servings: 6
Ingredients:
- ½ tsp. chili flakes
- 1 tbsp. lemon juice
- 1 egg yolk
- 2 garlic cloves, minced
- ¾ cup avocado oil

Instructions:
1. Put all ingredients in the Instant Pot and whisk vigorously.
2. Press the Sauté button and allow to heat for 2 minutes while stirring. Do not bring to a boil.
3. You can serve the chili aioli on top of the seafood or salad.

Nutritional info:
Calories 253, Carbs 0.7g, Protein 0.5g, Fat 28.1g

Keto Gravy
Prep Time: 6 mins, Cook Time: 10 mins, Servings: 6
Ingredients:
- 2 tbsps. butter
- 1 white onion, chopped
- 2 cups chicken bone broth
- 1 tbsp. balsamic vinegar
- ¼ cup coconut milk

Instructions:
1. Press the Sauté button on the Instant Pot.
2. Melt the butter and sauté the onions for 2 minutes.
3. Add the remaining ingredients. Stir constantly for 5 minutes or until slightly thickened.
4. You can serve the gravy on top of any roasted steaks, meats, or seafoods. You can even use it as a dressing for your salad.

Nutritional info:
Calories 59, Fat 6.3g, Carbs 1.1g, Protein 0.2g

Ranch Dip

Prep Time: 6 mins, Cook Time: 2 mins, Servings: 8

Ingredients:
- 1 cup olive oil
- Salt and pepper, to taste
- 1 cup beaten egg whites
- 1 tsp. mustard paste
- Juice of 1 lemon

Instructions:
1. In the Instant Pot, add all the ingredients and mix well.
2. Press the Sauté button and heat for 2 minutes while stirring. Do not bring to a simmer.
3. You can serve the ranch dip with chicken nuggets, French fries, or green salad.

Nutritional info:
Calories 258, Carbs 1.2g, Protein 3.4g, Fat 27.1g

Chapter 11 Beans, Grains and Legumes Recipe

Vegan Rice Pudding

Prep Time: 6 mins, Cook Time: 18 mins, Servings: 6

Ingredients:
- ⅔ cup Jasmine rice, rinsed and drained
- ¼ cup granulated sugar
- 3 cups almond milk
- Salt, to taste
- 1½ tsps. vanilla extract

Instructions:
1. Add all the ingredients, except vanilla extract, to the Instant Pot.
2. Lock the lid. Select the Manual mode, then set the timer for 18 minutes at Low Pressure.
3. Once the timer goes off, do a natural pressure release for 10 minutes, then release any remaining pressure. Carefully open the lid.
4. Stir in the vanilla extract and cool for 10 minutes, then serve.

Nutritional info:
Calories 154, Fat 1.3g, Carbs 32.6g, Protein: 2g

Almond Arborio Risotto

Prep Time: 10 mins, Cook Time: 5 mins, Servings: 2

Ingredients:
- ½ cup Arborio rice
- 2 cups vanilla almond milk
- 1 tsp. vanilla extract
- 2 tbsps. agave syrup
- ¼ cup toasted almond flakes, for garnish

Instructions:
1. Add all the ingredients, except for the almond flakes, to the Instant Pot. Stir to mix well.
2. Lock the lid. Set to the Manual mode, then set the timer for 5 minutes at Low Pressure.
3. Once the timer goes off, perform a natural pressure release. Carefully open the lid.
4. Serve the risotto with almond flakes immediately.

Nutritional info:
Calories 116, Carbs 22.5g, Protein 2.0g, Fat 2.1g

Butternut Squash Arborio Risotto

Prep Time: 10 mins, Cook Time: 12 mins, Servings: 4

Ingredients:
- 1 tbsp. olive oil
- 2 garlic cloves, whole
- 1 sprig sage, leaves removed
- ½ butternut squash, diced
- 1 cup Arborio rice
- ½ tsp. freshly ground nutmeg
- 2 tbsps. white wine
- 1 tsp. sea salt
- 2 cups water

Instructions:
1. Grease the Instant Pot with olive oil.
2. Set the pot to Sauté mode, then add the garlic and sage. Sauté for 2 minutes or until fragrant.
3. Add the butternut squash and sauté for 5 minutes.
4. Add the remaining ingredients. Stir to mix well.
5. Lock the lid. Set to the Manual mode, then set the timer for 5 minutes at Low Pressure.
6. Once the timer goes off, perform a natural pressure release. Carefully open the lid.
7. Serve immediately.

Nutritional info:
Calories 323, Carbs 62.4g, Protein 5.3g, Fat 5.2g

Quinoa Risotto

Prep Time: 6 mins, Cook Time: 3 hours, Servings: 4

Ingredients:
- ¾ cup diced onion
- 1 garlic clove, minced
- 1 tbsp. butter
- Salt and pepper, to taste
- 2½ cups chicken broth
- 1 cup rinsed quinoa
- ¼ cup shredded Parmesan cheese

Instructions:
1. Combine the onion, garlic, and butter in a microwave-safe bowl.
2. Microwave for 5 minutes, stirring every 90 seconds.
3. Put the mixture in the Instant Pot.
4. Add the salt, pepper, broth, and quinoa and stir to combine.
5. Lock the lid. Select the Slow Cook mode, then set the timer for 3 hours at High Pressure.
6. Once the timer goes off, perform a natural release for 10 minutes, then release any remaining pressure. Carefully open the lid.
7. Mix the Parmesan into the mixture. Taste and adjust the seasoning, if needed.

Nutritional info:
Calories 282, Fat 8.5g, Carbs 39.7g, Protein 12.1g

Parmesan Risotto

Prep Time: 6 mins, Cook Time: 20 mins, Servings: 4

Ingredients:
- 4 cups chicken broth, divided
- 4 tbsps. butter

- 1 small onion, diced
- 2 garlic cloves, minced
- 1½ cups Arborio rice
- Salt and pepper, to taste
- ¼ cup shredded Parmesan cheese

Instructions:
1. Set the Instant Pot to sauté and melt the butter.
2. Mix the onions in and let them cook for 2 minutes until they have become soft.
3. Add the garlic and rice and stir. Cook for 1 more minute.
4. Add 1 cup of broth and cook about 3 minutes, or until the broth is absorbed.
5. Add 3 cups of broth, salt, and pepper.
6. Sprinkle with Parmesan cheese.
7. Lock the lid. Select the Manual mode, then set the timer for 10 minutes at Low Pressure.
8. Once the timer goes off, perform a natural release for 5 minutes, then release any remaining pressure. Carefully open the lid.
9. Ladle the rice into bowls and serve.

Nutritional info:
Calories 359, Fat 18.4g, Carbs 39.9g, Protein 9.8g

Green Tea Rice Risotto

Prep Time: 6 mins, Cook Time: 20 mins, Servings: 4

Ingredients:
- ¼ cup lentils, rinsed
- Salt, to taste
- 3 green tea bags
- 1 cup brown rice, rinsed
- 7 cups water

Instructions:
1. In the Instant Pot, add all ingredients and stir gently.
2. Lock the lid. Select the Manual mode, then set the timer for 20 minutes at Low Pressure.
3. Once the timer goes off, do a quick pressure release. Carefully open the lid.
4. Serve immediately.

Nutritional info:
Calories 123, Carbs 24.5g, Fat 1g, Protein 3g

Mixed Rice Meal

Prep Time: 6 mins, Cook Time: 20 mins, Servings: 4

Ingredients:
- 3 cups mixture of brown rice and white rice
- 1½ tsps. salt
- 4½ cups water
- 2 tbsps. olive oil

Instructions:
1. Add all the ingredients to the pot.
2. Lock the lid. Select the Multigrain mode, then set the timer for 20 minutes at Low Pressure.
3. Once the timer goes off, do a natural pressure release for 10 minutes, then release any remaining pressure. Carefully open the lid.
4. Check if the grains are soft and cooked well. If not, cook for 5 minutes more.
5. Fluff the mixture with a fork and serve.

Nutritional info:
Calories 126, Carbs 18g, Fat 5g, Protein 0g

Basmati Rice

Prep Time: 2 minutes; Cook Time: 6 mins, Servings: 4

Ingredients:
- 2 cups Indian basmati rice
- 2 cups water

Instructions:
1. Add the rice and water to the Instant Pot.
2. Lock the lid. Select the Rice mode, then set the timer for 6 minutes at Low Pressure.
3. Once the timer goes off, do a natural pressure release for 3 to 5 minutes. Carefully open the lid.
4. Use a fork to fluff the rice, then serve.

Nutritional info:
Calories 130, Fat 0.2g, Carbs 28.7g, Protein 2.4g

Mexican Rice

Prep Time: 6 mins, Cook Time: 10 mins, Servings: 4

Ingredients:
- 2 cups long-grain rice
- 2½ cup water
- ½ cup green salsa
- 1 cup cilantro
- 1 avocado
- Salt and pepper, to taste

Instructions:
1. Add the rice and water to the Instant Pot.
2. Lock the lid. Select the Rice mode, then set the timer for 5 minutes at Low Pressure.
3. Once the timer goes off, do a natural pressure release for 3 to 5 minutes. Carefully open the lid.
4. Fluff rice and let it cool. Put the salsa, cilantro, and avocado in a blender.
5. Pulse the ingredients together until they are creamy and mix into the rice.
6. Mix everything together and season with salt and pepper.
7. Serve immediately.

Nutritional info:
Calories 250, Fat 1.3g, Carbs 25.8g, Protein 2.8g

Multigrain Rice

Prep Time: 2 mins, Cook Time: 20 mins, Servings: 6 to 8

Ingredients:
- 2 tbsps. olive oil
- 3¾ cups water
- 3 cups wild brown rice
- Salt, to taste

Instructions:
1. Combine the oil, water, and brown rice in the pot.
2. Season with salt.
3. Lock the lid. Select the Multigrain mode, then set the timer for 20 minutes on Low Pressure.
4. Once the timer goes off, do a natural pressure release for 5 minutes. Carefully open the lid.
5. Fluff the rice with a fork.
6. Serve immediately.

Nutritional info:
Calories 160, Fat 1.5g, Carbs 33.0g, Protein 5.0g

Raisin Butter Rice

Prep Time: 3 mins, Cook Time: 12 mins, Servings: 4

Ingredients:
- 3 cups wild rice, soaked in water overnight and drained
- 3 cups water
- ½ cup raisins
- ¼ cup salted butter
- 1 tsp. salt

Instructions:
1. Add all the ingredients to the Instant Pot.
2. Lock the lid. Select the Rice mode, then set the timer for 12 minutes at Low Pressure.
3. Once the timer goes off, perform a natural release for 8 to 10 minutes.
4. Carefully open the lid and use a fork to fluff the rice.
5. Serve warm.

Nutritional info:
Calories 271, Fat 3.0g, Carbs 58.1g, Protein 2.4g

Basic Tomato Rice

Prep Time: 6 mins, Cook Time: 5 mins, Servings: 4

Ingredients:
- 1 tbsp. extra virgin olive oil
- 2 cups white rice, rinsed and drained
- 4½ cups water
- 1 large, ripe tomato
- Salt and pepper, to taste

Instructions:
1. Add olive oil, rice, and water to Instant Pot. Gently stir.
2. Place whole tomato, bottom-side up, in the middle.
3. Lock the lid. Select the Rice mode, then set the timer for 5 minutes at Low Pressure.
4. Once the timer goes off, do a natural pressure release for 3 to 5 minutes, then release any remaining pressure. Carefully open the lid.
5. Using a rice paddle, break up tomato while fluffing up rice. Season with salt and pepper.
6. Serve immediately.

Nutritional info:
Calories 183, Carbs 25.4g, Fat 5g, Protein 19g

Black Olives in Tomato Rice

Prep Time: 12 mins, Cook Time: 5 mins, Servings: 4

Ingredients:
- ¼ tsp. balsamic vinegar
- 4½ cups water
- ¼ cup black olives in brine rings
- 1 cup ripe tomato, deseeded and minced
- 2 cups Basmati rice, rinsed and drained
- Salt and pepper, to taste

Instructions:
1. Pour all the ingredients into Instant Pot. Gently stir.
2. Lock the lid. Select the Rice mode, then set the timer for 5 minutes at Low Pressure.
3. Once the timer goes off, do a natural pressure release for 3 to 5 minutes, then release any remaining pressure. Carefully open the lid.
4. Using a rice paddle, fluff up rice.
5. Serve warm.

Nutritional info:
Calories 176, Carbs 23.4g, Fat 3.1g, Protein 13g

Confetti Basmati Rice

Prep Time: 12 mins, Cook Time: 13 mins, Servings: 6

Ingredients:
- 1 tbsp. olive oil
- 1 onion, chopped
- ½ cup frozen peas
- 2 cups basmati rice
- Salt and pepper, to taste
- 3 cups water
- 1 carrot, grated
- 1 medium bell pepper, chopped

Instructions:
1. Set the pot to Sauté and add the olive oil to coat the pot.
2. Add the onion and sauté for 3 minutes or until it becomes soft.
3. Put the peas and rice into the pot. Season with salt and pepper, and mix well.

4. Add the water, carrots, and bell pepper and stir again.
5. Lock the lid. Select the Manual mode, then set the timer for 3 minutes at Low Pressure.
6. Once the timer goes off, perform a natural release for 1 minutes, then release any remaining pressure. Carefully open the lid.
7. Fluff with a fork and enjoy.

Nutritional info:
Calories 271, Fat 2.9g, Carbs 54.8g, Protein 5.5g

Cauliflower and Pineapple Rice
Prep Time: 20 mins, Cook Time: 20 mins, Servings: 4
Ingredients:
- 2 tsps. extra virgin olive oil
- 2 cups jasmine rice
- 1 cauliflower, florets separated and chopped
- ½ pineapple, peeled and chopped
- 4 cups water
- Salt and ground black pepper, to taste

Instructions:
1. Mix all the ingredients in your Instant Pot and stir to incorporate.
2. Lock the lid. Select the Manual mode and cook for 20 minutes at Low Pressure.
3. Once cooking is complete, do a natural pressure release for 10 minutes, then release any remaining pressure. Carefully open the lid.
4. Using a fork to fluff the rice and serve in bowls.

Nutritional info:
Calories 441, Carbs 95.3g, Protein 7.6g, Fat 3.0g

Chickpea and Tomato Rice
Prep Time: 12 mins, Cook Time:25 mins, Servings: 4
Ingredients:
- ½ cup canned chickpeas
- 4½ cups water
- 1 cup deseeded and minced ripe tomato
- Salt and pepper, to taste
- 2 cups rinsed and drained white rice

Instructions:
1. Pour all the ingredients into Instant Pot. Gently stir.
2. Lock the lid. Select the Rice mode, then set the timer for 5 minutes at Low Pressure.
3. Once the timer goes off, do a quick pressure release. Carefully open the lid.
4. Using a rice paddle, fluff up rice.
5. Serve immediately.

Nutritional info:
Calories 154, Carbs 23.5g, Fat 3g, Protein 16g

Chipotle-Style Cilantro Rice
Prep Time: 20 mins, Cook Time: 20 mins, Servings: 4
Ingredients:
- 2 cups brown rice, rinsed
- 4 small bay leaves
- 2¾ cups water
- 1½ tbsps. olive oil
- ½ cup chopped cilantro
- 1 lime, juiced
- 1 tsp. salt

Instructions:
1. Place the brown rice, bay leaves, and water in the Instant Pot.
2. Lock the lid. Select the Rice mode and cook for 20 minutes at High Pressure.
3. Once cooking is complete, do a natural pressure release for 10 minutes, then release any remaining pressure. Carefully open the lid.
4. Add the olive oil, cilantro, lime juice, and salt to the pot and stir until well combined. Serve warm.

Nutritional info:
Calories 394, Carbs 73.8g, Protein 7.3g, Fat 7.7g

Copycat Cilantro Lime Rice
Prep Time: 3 minutes; Cook Time: 10 mins, Servings: 2
Ingredients:
- 1¼ cups water
- 1 cup white rice
- Salt, to taste
- 3 tbsps. fresh chopped cilantro
- 1 tbsp. fresh lime juice
- 2 tbsps. vegetable oil

Instructions:
1. Mix the rice and water together in the Instant Pot and stir to combine. Season with salt.
2. Lock the lid. Select the Rice mode, then set the timer for 5 minutes at Low Pressure.
3. Once the timer goes off, do a natural pressure release for 3 to 5 minutes. Carefully open the lid.
4. Use a quick release to get rid of the remaining pressure. Use a fork to fluff up the rice.
5. Mix the lime juice, cilantro, and oil in a bowl.
6. Whisk well and mix into the rice. Serve immediately.

Nutritional info:
Calories 242, Fat 0.4g, Carbs 53.4g, Protein 4.4g

Khichdi Dal
Prep Time: 4 minutes; Cook Time: 12 mins, Servings: 4
Ingredients:

- 1 tbsp. butter
- 2 cups water
- ¼ tsp. salt
- 1 tsp. Balti seasoning
- 1 cup khichdi mix

Instructions:
1. Set the Instant Pot to Sauté. Add the butter and heat to melt.
2. Mix in the Balti seasoning and cook for 1 minute.
3. Add the Khichdi mix, water, and salt to the pot.
4. Lock the lid. Select the Porridge mode, then set the timer for 10 minutes at High Pressure.
5. Once the timer goes off, do a natural pressure release for 3 to 5 minutes. Carefully open the lid.
6. Fluff the khichdi with a fork and serve warm.

Nutritional info:
Calories 242, Fat 0.4g, Carbs 53.4g, Protein 4.4g

Couscous with Spinach and Tomato

Prep Time: 12 mins, Cook Time: 6 mins, Servings: 4
Ingredients:
- 1 tbsp. butter
- 1 cup couscous
- 1¼ cups vegetable broth
- ½ cup chopped spinach, blanched
- 1½ tomatoes, chopped

Instructions:
1. Set the Instant Pot to Sauté mode, then add and melt the butter.
2. Add the couscous and sauté for 1 minute.
3. Pour in the vegetable broth. Stir to mix well.
4. Lock the lid. Set to the Manual mode, then set the timer for 5 minutes at High Pressure.
5. Once the timer goes off, perform a quick pressure release. Carefully open the lid.
6. Mix in the spinach and tomatoes, then serve warm.

Nutritional info:
Calories 130, Carbs 15.8g, Protein 2.9g, Fat 6.3g

Israeli Couscous

Prep Time: 4 mins, Cook Time: 10 mins, Servings: 10
Ingredients:
- 2 tbsps. butter
- 2 cups couscous
- 2½ cups chicken broth

Instructions:
1. Set the Instant Pot to Sauté and melt the butter.
2. Add the couscous and broth to the pot. Whisk well.
3. Lock the lid. Select the Rice mode, then set the timer for 5 minutes at High Pressure.
4. Once the timer goes off, do a natural pressure release for 3 to 5 minutes. Carefully open the lid.
5. Use a fork to fluff couscous, then serve warm.

Nutritional info:
Calories 380, Fat 1g, Carbs 80g, Protein 12g

Creamy Polenta

Prep Time: 1 mins, Cook Time: 8 mins, Servings: 2
Ingredients:
- 2⅓ cups milk, divided
- ½ tsp. salt
- ½ cup polenta
- 3 tbsps. butter

Instructions:
1. Set the pot to Sauté and add 2 cups of milk and bring it to a boil.
2. Add the salt and polenta into the milk.
3. Lock the lid. Select the Porridge mode, then set the timer for 8 minutes at High Pressure.
4. Once the timer goes off, do a natural pressure release for 5 minutes. Carefully open the lid.
5. Stir in the remaining milk and butter, then serve.

Nutritional info:
Calories 160, Fat 2.6g, Carbs 27.7g, Protein 7.3g

Honey Polenta with Toasted Pine Nuts

Prep Time: 13 mins, Cook Time: 15 mins, Servings: 4
Ingredients:
- ½ cup honey
- 5 cups water
- 1 cup polenta
- ½ cup heavy cream
- Salt, to taste
- ¼ cup pine nuts, toasted

Instructions:
1. Stir together the honey and water in your Instant Pot.
2. Select the Sauté mode and bring the mixture to a boil, stirring occasionally.
3. Stir in the polenta and lock the lid. Select the Manual mode and set the cooking time for 12 minutes at High Pressure.
4. When the timer beeps, do a quick pressure release. Carefully open the lid.

5. Fold in the heavy creamy and stir until well incorporated. Allow the dish to rest for 1 minute.
6. Season with salt and give it a good stir. Serve topped with toasted pine nuts.

Nutritional info:
Calories 294, Carbs 48.5g, Protein 2.7g, Fat 11.6g

Wheat Berries

Prep Time: 6 mins, Cook Time: 30 mins, Servings: 4

Ingredients:
- 1 cup wheat berries
- 3 cups water
- ¼ tsp. salt

Instructions:
1. Add all the ingredients to the Instant Pot.
2. Lock the lid. Select the Manual mode, then set the timer for 30 minutes at High Pressure.
3. Once the timer goes off, perform a natural release for 8 to 10 minutes. Carefully open the lid.
4. Drain the wheat berries and enjoy.

Nutritional info:
Calories 150, Fat 0.5g, Carbs 32g, Protein 6g

Peaches and Steel-Cut Oats

Prep Time: 12 mins, Cook Time: 3 mins, Servings: 2

Ingredients:
- 2 peaches, diced
- 1 cup steel-cut oats
- 1 cup coconut milk
- ½ vanilla bean, scraped, seeds and pod
- 2 cups water

Instructions:
1. Put all the ingredients into the Instant Pot. Stir to mix well.
2. Lock the lid. Set to the Manual mode, then set the timer for 3 minutes at High Pressure.
3. Once the timer goes off, perform a quick pressure release. Carefully open the lid.
4. Serve immediately.

Nutritional info:
Calories 450, Carbs 52.2g, Protein 12.3g, Fat 32.3g

Strawberry and Rolled Oats

Prep Time: 10 mins, Cook Time: 10 mins, Servings: 2

Ingredients:
- 2 cups water
- ⅓ cup rolled oats
- 2 tbsps. frozen dried strawberries
- ⅔ cup whole milk
- Pinch of salt
- ½ tsp. white sugar

Instructions:
1. Arrange the steamer rack in the Instant Pot, then pour in the water.
2. Combine the oats, strawberries, milk, and salt in a bowl. Stir to mix well.
3. Put the bowl on the steamer rack.
4. Lock the lid. Set to the Manual mode, then set the timer for 10 minutes at High Pressure.
5. Once the timer goes off, perform a natural pressure release for 5 minutes, then release any remaining pressure. Carefully open the lid.
6. Remove the bowl from the pot, then sprinkle with sugar and serve.

Nutritional info:
Calories 105, Carbs 18.6g, Protein 5.4g, Fat 3.8g

Coconut Quinoa

Prep Time: 2 mins, Cook Time: 3 hours, Servings: 6

Ingredients:
- 1 tsp. sugar
- 1 cup rinsed quinoa
- 1 tsp coconut oil
- 1 can black beans
- 1 can coconut milk
- 2 tsps. garlic powder
- Salt, to taste

Instructions:
1. Place all the ingredients in the Instant Pot.
2. Lock the lid. Select the Slow Cook mode, then set the timer for 3 hours at High Pressure.
3. Once the timer goes off, perform a quick release. Carefully open the lid.
4. Serve warm.

Nutritional info:
Calories 207, Fat 11.1g, Carbs 22.6g, Protein 5.9g

Quinoa Pilaf

Prep Time: 13 mins, Cook Time: 2 mins, Servings: 4

Ingredients:
- 1 tbsp. extra virgin olive oil
- 2 cloves garlic, minced
- 2 cups quinoa, rinsed
- 2 tsps. turmeric
- 2 tsps. ground cumin
- Salt, to taste
- 3 cups water
- 1 handful parsley, chopped

Instructions:
1. Set the Instant Pot to Sauté mode, then add and heat the olive oil.
2. Add the garlic and sauté for a minute or until fragrant.
3. Add the quinoa, turmeric, cumin, salt, and water. Stir to combine well.

4. Lock the lid. Set to the Manual mode, then set the timer for 1 minutes at High Pressure.
5. Once the timer goes off, perform a natural pressure release. Carefully open the lid.
6. Spread the pilaf with parsley and serve.

Nutritional info:
Calories 389, Carbs 57.5g, Protein 12.9g, Fat 12.3g

Quinoa with Cranberry and Almond
Prep Time: 5 mins, Cook Time: 10 mins, Servings: 2

Ingredients:
- 1 cup quinoa, rinsed
- 2 cups water
- ¼ cup salted sunflower seeds
- ½ cup slivered almonds
- 1 cup dried cranberries

Instructions:
1. Pour the quinoa and water into the Instant Pot.
2. Lock the lid. Set to the Manual mode, then set the timer for 1 minutes at High Pressure.
3. Once the timer goes off, perform a natural pressure release. Carefully open the lid.
4. Mix in the remaining ingredients and serve immediately.

Nutritional info:
Calories 425, Carbs 63.2g, Protein 15.4g, Fat 13.3g

Quinoa with Vegetables
Prep Time: 13 mins, Cook Time: 2 mins, Servings: 4

Ingredients:
- 1½ cups rinsed quinoa
- 4 cups spinach, chopped
- 3 stalks celery, chopped
- 1 bell pepper, chopped
- 1½ cups chicken broth
- ¼ tsp. salt

Instructions:
1. Combine all ingredients in the Instant Pot. Stir to mix well.
2. Lock the lid. Set to the Manual mode, then set the timer for 2 minutes at High Pressure.
3. Once the timer goes off, perform a natural pressure release. Carefully open the lid.
4. Serve immediately.

Nutritional info:
Calories 254, Carbs 43.8g, Protein 10.8g, Fat 4.2g

Brothy Heirloom Beans with Cream
Prep Time: 15 mins, Cook Time: 45 mins, Servings: 4

Ingredients:
- 2 cups mixed dried heirloom beans, soaked overnight
- 8 cups chicken stock
- 4 sprigs thyme
- Salt, to taste
- ½ cup heavy cream

Instructions:
1. Add the beans, chicken stock, thyme, and salt to the Instant Pot. Stir well.
2. Lock the lid. Select the Manual mode and set the cooking time for 45 minutes at High Pressure.
3. Once cooking is complete, do a quick pressure release. Carefully open the lid.
4. Set your Instant Pot to Sauté and stir in the heavy cream.
5. Allow to simmer for 5 minutes, then transfer to four bowls. Serve warm.

Nutritional info:
Calories 261, Carbs 24.6g, Protein 13.8g, Fat 11.5g

Refried Pinto Beans
Prep Time: 5 mins, Cook Time: 1 hour, Servings: 2

Ingredients:
- 1 cup pinto beans, drained and rinsed
- 3 cups water
- 1 tbsp. olive oil
- 1 onion, chopped
- 2 cloves garlic, chopped
- 1 jalapeño pepper, chopped
- 1 bay leaf
- 1 tsp. salt

Instructions:
1. Put the pinto beans in the Instant Pot, then pour in the water.
2. Lock the lid. Set to the Manual mode, then set the timer for 40 minutes at High Pressure.
3. Once the timer goes off, perform a quick pressure release. Carefully open the lid.
4. Pat the beans dry with paper towels, then reserve the bean water.
5. Select the Sauté mode of the pot, then add the olive oil.
6. Add the onion, garlic, and jalapeño to the pot and sauté for 3 minutes or until fragrant.
7. Add the beans, reserved bean water, bay leaf, and salt to the pot. Stir to mix well.
8. Lock the lid. Set to the Manual mode, then set the timer for 20 minutes at High Pressure.
9. Once the timer goes off, perform a quick pressure release. Carefully open the lid. Discard the bay leaf.
10. Serve the beans on a plate immediately.

Nutritional info:
Calories 331, Carbs 29.0g, Protein 8.6g, Fat 21.1g

Simple Pinto Beans with Spices

Prep Time: 10 mins, Cook Time: 25 mins, Servings: 2

Ingredients:
- 1 cup dried Pinto beans
- 2 tbsps. garlic powder
- 1 tbsp. onion powder
- 1 tbsp. chili powder
- 1 tsp. oregano
- ½ tsp. salt
- 5 cups water

Instructions:
1. Add the beans, garlic powder, onion powder, chili powder, oregano, and salt to the Instant Pot. Pour in the water and stir to combine.
2. Lock the lid. Select the Manual mode and cook for 25 minutes at High Pressure.
3. Once cooking is complete, do a natural pressure release for 20 minutes, then release any remaining pressure. Carefully open the lid.
4. Taste and adjust the seasoning, if needed.

Nutritional info:
Calories 391, Carbs 72.5g, Protein 23.2g, Fat 1.9g

Simple Italian Flavor Cannellini Beans

Prep Time: 12 mins, Cook Time: 8 mins, Servings: 4

Ingredients:
- 1 cup cannellini beans, soaked overnight
- 1 clove garlic, smashed
- 1 bay leaf
- 4 cups water
- Dash of vinegar
- 1 tbsp. olive oil
- 1 sprig mint
- Salt and ground black pepper to taste

Instructions:
1. Put the beans, garlic, bay leaf, and water in the Instant Pot. Stir to mix well.
2. Lock the lid. Set to the Manual mode, then set the timer for 8 minutes at High Pressure.
3. Once the timer goes off, perform a natural pressure release for 5 minutes, then release any remaining pressure. Carefully open the lid. Discard the bay leaf.
4. Strain the beans, then drizzle with vinegar and olive oil. Sprinkle with mint, salt, and pepper. Mix and serve.

Nutritional info:
Calories 201, Carbs 31.0g, Protein 11.9g, Fat 3.9g

Black-Eyed Peas with Ham

Prep Time: 25 mins, Cook Time: 30 mins, Servings: 4

Ingredients:
- ½ lb. dried black-eyed peas
- 3 oz. ham, diced
- 3½ cups chicken stock
- Salt and ground black pepper, to taste

Instructions:
1. Place the peas, ham, and chicken stock in the Instant Pot.
2. Lock the lid. Select the Manual mode and cook for 30 minutes at High Pressure.
3. Once cooking is complete, do a natural pressure release for 20 minutes, then release any remaining pressure. Carefully open the lid.
4. Season as needed with salt and pepper, then serve.

Nutritional info:
Calories 160, Carbs 13.2g, Protein 10.6g, Fat 7.1g

Creamy Corn Kernels with Cottage Cheese

Prep Time: 11 mins, Cook Time: 4 mins, Servings: 2

Ingredients:
- 2 ounces Cottage cheese, at room temperature
- 1 cup corn kernels
- ⅓ cup double cream
- ⅓ teaspoon dried parsley flakes
- ¼ teaspoon red pepper flakes
- 1 tablespoon butter, cut into pieces
- 1 cup water
- Kosher salt and ground black pepper, to taste

Instructions:
1. Combine all the ingredients in the Instant Pot. Stir to mix well.
2. Lock the lid. Set to the Manual mode, then set the timer for 4 minutes at High Pressure.
3. Once the timer goes off, perform a natural pressure release. Carefully open the lid.
4. Serve immediately.

Nutritional info:
Calories 279, Carbs 19.8g, Protein 10.0g, Fat 19.3g

Creamy Fig Millet

Prep Time: 15 mins, Cook Time: 10 mins, Servings: 4

Ingredients:
- 1¾ cups millet
- 2 cups water
- 1 cup almond milk
- ⅓ cup chopped dried figs
- 2 tbsps. coconut oil

Instructions:

1. Place all the ingredients in the Instant Pot and mix well.
2. Lock the lid. Select the Rice mode and set the cooking time for 10 minutes at High Pressure.
3. When the timer goes off, do a natural pressure release for 10 minutes, then release any remaining pressure. Carefully open the lid.
4. Using a fork to fluff the dish and serve on plates.

Nutritional info:
Calories 450, Carbs 74.5g, Protein 12.1g, Fat 11.8g

Cheesy Grits with Half-and-Half

Prep Time: 17 mins, Cook Time: 13 mins, Servings: 6
Ingredients:
- 2 tbsps. olive oil
- 2 cup stone-ground grits
- 1 cup half-and-half
- 4 oz. Cheddar cheese
- 2 tbsps. butter
- 1½ tsps. salt
- 3 cups water

Instructions:
1. Set the Instant Pot to Sauté mode, then add and heat the olive oil.
2. Add the grits and sauté for 3 minutes.
3. Add the half-and-half, cheese, butter, salt, and water. Stir to combine well.
4. Lock the lid. Set to the Manual mode, then set the timer for 10 minutes at High Pressure.
5. Once the timer goes off, perform a natural pressure release for 5 minutes, then release any remaining pressure. Carefully open the lid.
6. Serve immediately.

Nutritional info:
Calories 230, Carbs 15.0g, Protein 6.9g, Fat 16.2g

Ritzy Corn, Lentil, and Brown Rice Stew

Prep Time: 10 mins, Cook Time: 20 mins, Servings: 4
Ingredients:
- ½ tbsp. olive oil
- 1 medium carrot, sliced
- ⅓ cup dried lentils
- ½ cup fresh or frozen corn
- 1 medium tomato
- 3½ cups water
- ½ cup cooked brown rice
- 1 tbsp. soy sauce
- Salt and pepper, to taste

Instructions:
1. Grease the Instant Pot with olive oil. Set the Instant Pot to Sauté mode.
2. Add the carrots and sauté for 5 minutes or until soft.
3. Add the lentils, corn, tomatoes, corn, and water to the pot.
4. Lock the lid. Set to the Manual mode, then set the timer for 15 minutes at High Pressure.
5. Once the timer goes off, perform a quick pressure release. Carefully open the lid.
6. Mix in the cooked brown rice and soy sauce. Sprinkle with salt and pepper before serving.

Nutritional info:
Calories 239, Carbs 47.4g, Protein 10.1g, Fat 1.5g

Chapter 12 Pasta and Side Dishes Recipe

Minty Carrots

Prep Time: 12 mins, Cook Time: 5 mins, Servings: 4

Ingredients:
- 16 oz. baby carrots
- 1 cup water
- Salt, to taste
- 1 tbsp. butter
- 1 tsp. sweet paprika
- 1 tbsp. chopped mint

Instructions:
1. In the Instant Pot, mix the carrots with water.
2. Lock the lid. Select the Manual mode, then set the timer for 3 minutes at High Pressure.
3. Once the timer goes off, perform a quick release. Carefully open the lid.
4. Drain and transfer to a bowl.
5. Clean the pot and set it to Sauté. Add the butter and heat to melt.
6. Add the mint, stir and cook for 1 minute.
7. Add the carrots, salt and paprika, toss, divide between plates and serve as a side dish.

Nutritional info:
Calories 172, Fat 3g, Carbs 8g, Protein 4g

Simple Corn Side Dish

Prep Time: 12 mins, Cook Time: 12 mins, Servings: 4

Ingredients:
- 2 tbsps. butter
- 3 garlic cloves, minced
- 2 cups corn kernels
- 6 oz. cream cheese
- 1/3 cup milk

Instructions:
1. Set the Instant Pot to Sauté, add butter, melt it, add garlic, stir and cook for 2 minutes.
2. Stir in the corn and let cook for 2 additional minutes.
3. Add cream cheese and milk, stir.
4. Lock the lid. Select the Manual mode, then set the timer for 7 minutes at High Pressure.
5. Once the timer goes off, perform a quick release. Carefully open the lid.
6. Toss creamy corn one more time, divide between plates and serve as a side dish.

Nutritional info:
Calories 200, Fat 3g, Carbs 10g, Protein 3g

Pearl Onions Side Dish

Prep Time: 12 mins, Cook Time: 10 mins, Servings: 6

Ingredients:
- 1 lb. rainbow carrots, quartered
- 2 cups pearl onions
- ½ cup water
- 3 tbsps. butter
- 2 tbsps. chopped parsley
- 2 tbsps. balsamic vinegar

Instructions:
1. In the Instant Pot, mix carrots with onions and water.
2. Lock the lid. Select the Manual mode, then set the timer for 4 minutes at High Pressure.
3. Once the timer goes off, perform a quick release. Carefully open the lid.
4. Drain and transfer to a bowl.
5. Clean the pot and select the Sauté mode, add butter, melt it, add onions and carrots, vinegar and parsley, stir and sauté for 5 minutes.
6. Toss again, divide between plates and serve as a side dish.

Nutritional info:
Calories 162, Fat 4g, Carbs 12g, Protein 4g

Acorn Squash Side Dish

Prep Time: 12 mins, Cook Time: 15 mins, Servings: 4

Ingredients:
- 1 cup water
- 2 acorn squash, halved and sliced into wedges
- 4 tbsps. butter
- 1 tbsp. brown sugar
- 1 tsp. smoked paprika
- 3 tbsps. roasted pepitas

Instructions:
1. In the Instant Pot, add the water and steamer basket. Add acorn wedges in the basket.
2. Lock the lid. Select the Manual mode, then set the timer for 5 minutes at High Pressure.
3. Once the timer goes off, perform a quick release. Carefully open the lid.
4. Transfer to a bowl.
5. Clean the pot and select the Sauté mode, add butter, melt it, add acorn wedges, sugar, paprika and pepitas, stir and cook for 10 minutes.
6. Enjoy as a side dish.

Nutritional info:
Calories 128, Fat 4g, Carbs 6g, Protein 8g

Simple Spinach Side Dish

Prep Time: 12 mins, Cook Time: 5 mins, Servings: 3

Ingredients:
- ½ tsp. turmeric powder

- 1 tsp. olive oil
- 6 oz. spinach leaves
- ½ cup vegetable soup
- ½ tsp. garam masala

Instructions:
1. Set the Instant Pot to Sauté and heat the olive oil. Add spinach, stir and toss for 1 to 2 minutes.
2. Add garam masala, turmeric and soup, stir.
3. Lock the lid. Select the Manual mode, then set the timer for 3 minutes at High Pressure.
4. Once the timer goes off, perform a quick release. Carefully open the lid.
5. Serve as a side dish!

Nutritional info:
Calories 100, Fat 3g, Carbs 6g, Protein 1g

Tasty Maple Acorn Squash Dish

Prep Time: 12 mins, Cook Time: 10 mins, Servings: 4

Ingredients:
- 2 tsps. sriracha sauce
- ¼ cup maple syrup
- 4 thyme sprigs, chopped
- 3 tbsps. butter
- 2 halved acorn squash

Instructions:
1. Set the Instant Pot to Sauté, add butter, melt it, add acorn squash wedges, stir and cook for 1 to 2 minutes.
2. Add maple syrup, sriracha sauce and thyme, stir.
3. Lock the lid. Select the Manual mode, then set the timer for 8 minutes at High Pressure.
4. Once the timer goes off, perform a quick release. Carefully open the lid.
5. Toss squash wedges gently, divide between plates and serve as a side dish.

Nutritional info:
Calories 200, Fat 2g, Carbs 5g, Protein 4g

Kidney Beans and Corn Side Dish

Prep Time: 12 mins, Cook Time: 10 mins, Servings: 2

Ingredients:
- ½ tsp. chili powder
- 1½ cups chicken stock
- 1 cup cooked kidney beans
- ½ cup corn
- 1 small red onion, chopped

Instructions:
1. In the Instant Pot, mix beans with corn, onion, chili powder and stock, stir.
2. Lock the lid. Select the Manual mode, then set the timer for 10 minutes at High Pressure.
3. Once the timer goes off, perform a quick release. Carefully open the lid.
4. Enjoy the side dish!

Nutritional info:
Calories 203, Fat 7g, Carbs 9g, Protein 2g

Green Beans and Cranberries Side Dish

Prep Time: 12 mins, Cook Time: 6 mins, Servings: 6

Ingredients:
- ¼ cup dried cranberries
- ½ cup water
- 2 lbs. green beans
- ¼ cup chopped almonds
- ¼ tsp. salt
- 3 tbsps. olive oil

Instructions:
1. Put the water and steamer basket in the Instant Pot. Arrange the green beans and cranberries in the basket.
2. Lock the lid. Select the Manual mode, then set the timer for 2 minutes at High Pressure.
3. Once the timer goes off, perform a quick release. Carefully open the lid.
4. Transfer to a bowl.
5. Clean the pot and select the Sauté mode. Heat the olive oil and toss in green beans, almonds, salt, and cranberries. Cook for 4 additional minutes.
6. Serve as a side dish.

Nutritional info:
Calories 130, Fat 3g, Carbs 7g, Protein 4g

Green Cabbage and Tomatoes Side Dish

Prep Time: 12 mins, Cook Time: 5 mins, Servings: 4

Ingredients:
- 15 oz. chopped canned tomatoes
- 3 tbsps. olive oil
- ½ cup chopped yellow onion
- 1 green cabbage head, chopped
- 2 tsps. turmeric powder

Instructions:
1. Set the Instant Pot to Sauté and heat the olive oil. Add onion, stir, and cook for 2 minutes.
2. Add cabbage, tomatoes and turmeric, stir.
3. Lock the lid. Select the Manual mode, then set the timer for 4 minutes at High Pressure.
4. Once the timer goes off, perform a quick release. Carefully open the lid.
5. Divide between plates and serve as a side dish.

Nutritional info:
Calories 152, Fat 5g, Carbs 9g, Protein 7g

Brown Rice Salad

Prep Time: 12 mins, Cook Time: 20 mins, Servings: 2
Ingredients:
- ½ cup mung beans
- 1 tsp. lemon juice
- ½ tsp. cumin seeds
- ½ cup brown rice
- 4 cups water

Instructions:
1. In the Instant Pot, mix mung beans with rice, water, lemon juice and cumin, stir.
2. Lock the lid. Select the Manual mode, then set the timer for 20 minutes at Low Pressure.
3. Once the timer goes off, perform a quick release. Carefully open the lid.
4. Enjoy the side dish!

Nutritional info:
Calories 170, Fat 6, Carbs 12g, Protein 4g

Radishes Side Salad

Prep Time: 12 mins, Cook Time: 8 mins, Servings: 3
Ingredients:
- 2 chopped bacon slices
- ½ cup veggie stock
- 2 tbsps. sour cream
- 1 tbsp. chopped green onions
- 7 oz. halved red radishes

Instructions:
1. Set the Instant Pot to Sauté, add bacon, stir and cook for 6 minutes on both sides.
2. Add radishes and stock, stir.
3. Lock the lid. Select the Manual mode, then set the timer for 4 minutes at High Pressure.
4. Once the timer goes off, perform a quick release. Carefully open the lid.
5. Add sour cream and green onions, stir.
6. Lock the lid, then set the timer for 2 minutes.
7. Divide between plates and serve as a side dish.

Nutritional info:
Calories 187, Fat 6g, Carbs 10g, Protein 8g

Tomatoes Side Salad

Prep Time: 12 mins, Cook Time: 6 mins, Servings: 4
Ingredients:
- ¼ tsp. chopped parsley
- 1 tbsp. sherry vinegar
- 15 oz. drained canned garbanzo beans
- 2 tbsps. olive oil
- 4 cups halved mixed cherry tomatoes

Instructions:
1. Set the Instant Pot to Sauté. Heat the olive oil and add garbanzo beans and tomatoes, stir and cook for 3 minutes.
2. Add parsley and vinegar, stir.
3. Lock the lid. Select the Manual mode, then set the timer for 3 minutes at High Pressure.
4. Once the timer goes off, perform a quick release. Carefully open the lid.
5. Enjoy as side dish!

Nutritional info:
Calories 132, Fat 3g, Carbs 7g, Protein 5g

Arborio Rice Side Salad

Prep Time: 12 mins, Cook Time: 4 mins, Servings: 4
Ingredients:
- 1 bunch basil, chopped
- 4 cups water
- 2 cups Arborio rice
- ¼ tsp. salt
- 1 cup pitted and sliced black olives in oil

Instructions:
1. In the Instant Pot, mix rice with water.
2. Lock the lid. Select the Manual mode, then set the timer for 20 minutes at Low Pressure.
3. Once the timer goes off, perform a natural release for 10 minutes, then release any remaining pressure. Carefully open the lid.
4. Drain and transfer to a salad bowl.
5. Add a pinch of salt, olives and basil, toss well, divide between plates and serve as a side salad.

Nutritional info:
Calories 120, Fat 4g, Carbs 5g, Protein 2g

Haricots Verts Side Salad

Prep Time: 12 mins, Cook Time: 8 mins, Servings: 4
Ingredients:
- 4 oz. pancetta, chopped
- Black pepper, to taste
- ½ cup chicken stock
- ½ cup sliced dates
- 2 lbs. haricot verts

Instructions:
1. Set the Instant Pot to Sauté, add pancetta, stir and cook for 3 minutes.
2. Add haricot verts, dates and black pepper, stir and cook for 2 minutes more.
3. Stir in the stock.
4. Lock the lid. Select the Manual mode, then set the timer for 3 minutes on High Pressure.
5. Once the timer goes off, perform a quick release. Carefully open the lid.
6. Set in serving bowls and enjoy as a side dish.

Nutritional info:
Calories 128, Fat 3g, Carbs 16g, Protein 4g

Sweet and Sour Side Salad
Prep Time: 12 mins, Cook Time: 7 mins, Servings: 8
Ingredients:
- 1 cup water
- 3 lbs. rainbow carrots, chopped
- 3 tbsps. vinegar
- 3 tbsps. honey
- 3 tbsps. butter
- 1 onion, chopped

Instructions:
1. Add the water to the Instant Pot, then add the carrots.
2. Lock the lid. Select the Manual mode, then set the timer for 3 minutes at High Pressure.
3. Once the timer goes off, perform a quick release. Carefully open the lid.
4. Drain and transfer to a bowl.
5. Clean the pot and select the Sauté mode, add butter, melt it, add onion, stir and cook for 2 minutes.
6. Stir in carrots, honey, and vinegar. Cook for 2 more minutes on High while covered.
7. Set in serving plates and enjoy as a side dish.

Nutritional info:
Calories 192, Fat 3g, Carbs 10g, Protein 3g

Brussels Sprouts Side Salad
Prep Time: 12 mins, Cook Time: 5 mins, Servings: 4
Ingredients:
- 2 tbsps. olive oil
- 1 lb. halved Brussels sprouts
- ½ cup chopped pecans
- 3 tbsps. balsamic vinegar
- 2 tsps. Dijon mustard

Instructions:
1. Set the Instant Pot to Sauté. Heat the olive oil and add the Brussels sprouts to sauté for 2 minutes.
2. Add pecans, vinegar and mustard, toss
3. Lock the lid. Select the Manual mode, then set the timer for 3 minutes at High Pressure.
4. Once the timer goes off, perform a quick release. Carefully open the lid.
5. Divide Brussels sprouts mix on plates and serve as a side dish.

Nutritional info:
Calories 167, Fat 4g, Carbs 6g, Protein 4g

Tomatoes and Corn Side Salad
Prep Time: 12 mins, Cook Time: 7 mins, Servings: 6
Ingredients:
- 1½ cups water
- 3 oz. goat cheese, crumbled
- 6 sweet corn ears, shucked
- ¼ cup mint leaves
- 1 tbsp. olive oil
- 4 tomatoes, roughly chopped

Instructions:
1. Place the water in the Instant Pot, then add the corn.
2. Lock the lid. Select the Manual mode, then set the timer for 5 minutes at High Pressure.
3. Once the timer goes off, perform a quick release. Carefully open the lid.
4. Drain and transfer to a bowl.
5. Clean the pot and select the Sauté mode. Heat the olive oil and add corn and tomatoes, stir and cook for 2 minutes.
6. Add mint, stir, cook for 2 minutes more, divide between plates and serve with cheese on top.

Nutritional info:
Calories 122, Fat 3g, Carbs 6g, Protein 4g

Tasty Carrots and Walnuts Salad
Prep Time: 12 mins, Cook Time: 5 mins, Servings: 4
Ingredients:
- 2 lbs. baby carrots
- 1 cup water
- 2 tbsps. butter
- 3 oz. canned walnuts
- 1 tsp. syrup
- Salt, to taste
- 1 tbsp. apple cider vinegar

Instructions:
1. In the Instant Pot, add the carrots and water.
2. Lock the lid. Select the Manual mode, then set the timer for 3 minutes at High Pressure.
3. Once the timer goes off, perform a quick release. Carefully open the lid.
4. Drain and transfer to a bowl.
5. Clean the pot and select the Sauté mode. Melt the butter and add carrots, stir and cook for 1 minute.
6. Add walnuts and syrup, salt and vinegar, toss, cook for 1 minute more, divide between plates and serve as a side dish.

Nutritional info:
Calories 172, Fat 3g, Carbs 10g, Protein 4g

Tomatoes and Burrata Side Salad
Prep Time: 12 mins, Cook Time: 3 mins, Servings: 4
Ingredients:
- 4 tomatoes, diced
- 2 tbsps. olive oil
- ½ tsp. dried oregano
- 1 tbsp. water
- 5 oz. burrata cheese, shredded

Instructions:

1. In the Instant Pot, mix tomatoes with oil, oregano and water, toss a bit.
2. Lock the lid. Select the Manual mode, then set the timer for 3 minutes at High Pressure.
3. Once the timer goes off, perform a quick release. Carefully open the lid.
4. Divide on plates, add burrata on top and serve an as a side dish.

Nutritional info:
Calories 111, Fat 2g, Carbs 3g, Protein 3g

Delicious Green Beans and Blue Cheese

Prep Time: 12 mins, Cook Time: 7 mins, Servings: 4

Ingredients:
- ½ cup water
- 1½ lbs. green beans
- 2 tbsps. lemon juice
- ½ cup chopped almonds
- ¼ cup olive oil
- 2 tbsps. crumbled blue cheese

Instructions:
1. Put the water and steamer basket in the Instant Pot, then add green beans inside.
2. Lock the lid. Select the Manual mode, then set the timer for 2 minutes at High Pressure.
3. Once the timer goes off, perform a quick release. Carefully open the lid.
4. Drain and transfer them to a bowl.
5. Clean the pot and select the Sauté mode. Heat the oil and add green beans, stir and cook for 3 minutes.
6. Add lemon juice and almonds, stir and cook for 2 minutes more.
7. Divide on plates, sprinkle blue cheese all over and serve as a side dish.

Nutritional info:
Calories 200, Fat 4g, Carbs 7g, Protein 4g

Kale Sauté

Prep Time: 12 mins, Cook Time: 7 mins, Servings: 4

Ingredients:
- 1 tbsp. olive oil
- 3 garlic cloves
- ½ cup veggie stock
- Juice of ½ lemon
- 1 lb. kale, trimmed

Instructions:
1. Set the Instant Pot to Sauté. Heat the oil and add garlic, stir and cook for 2 minutes.
2. Add kale, stock and lemon juice, stir a bit.
3. Lock the lid. Select the Manual mode, then set the timer for 5 minutes at High Pressure.
4. Once the timer goes off, perform a quick release. Carefully open the lid.
5. Stir and divide between plates and serve as a side dish.

Nutritional info:
Calories 132, Fat 3g, Carbs 8g, protein 2g

Mixed Veggies

Prep Time: 12 mins, Cook Time: 10 mins, Servings: 4

Ingredients:
- 2 cups roughly chopped butternut squash
- 1 red onion. chopped
- 2 tbsps. balsamic vinegar
- 1 red bell pepper, chopped
- 1 tbsp. olive oil
- 1 cup water

Instructions:
1. In a bowl, mix squash with red onion, oil, bell pepper and vinegar and toss well.
2. In the Instant Pot, add the water and steamer basket, then add mixed veggies inside.
3. Lock the lid. Select the Manual mode, then set the timer for 10 minutes at High Pressure.
4. Once the timer goes off, perform a quick release. Carefully open the lid.
5. Divide mixed veggies between plates and serve as a side dish.

Nutritional info:
Calories 128, Fat 3g, Carbs 9g, Protein 8g

Creamy Spinach

Prep Time: 10 minutes. Cook Time: 6 mins, Servings: 4

Ingredients:
- Ground nutmeg
- 10 oz. spinach, roughly chopped
- 2 shallots, chopped
- 2 cups heavy cream
- 2 tbsps. butter

Instructions:
1. Set the Instant Pot to Sauté, add butter, melt it, add shallots, stir and cook for 2 minutes.
2. Add spinach, stir, and cook for 30 seconds more.
3. Add cream and nutmeg, stir.
4. Lock the lid. Select the Manual mode, then set the timer for 3 minutes at High Pressure.
5. Once the timer goes off, perform a quick release. Carefully open the lid.
6. Divide everything between plates and serve as a side dish.

Nutritional info:
Calories 200, Fat 3g, Carbs 15g, Protein 3g

Garlic Green Beans
Prep Time: 12 mins, Cook Time: 7 mins, Servings: 4
Ingredients:
- 1 cup water
- 1½ lbs. green beans
- 1 tbsp. shaved Parmesan
- 4 garlic cloves, minced
- ½ tsp. red pepper flakes
- 3 tbsps. olive oil

Instructions:
1. Put the water in the Instant Pot, arrange the steamer basket in the pot, add green beans inside.
2. Lock the lid. Select the Manual mode, then set the timer for 2 minutes at High Pressure.
3. Once the timer goes off, perform a quick release. Carefully open the lid.
4. Drain and transfer to a bowl.
5. Clean the pot and select the Sauté mode. Heat the oil and add garlic, stir and cook for 30 seconds.
6. Return green beans, also add pepper flakes, stir and sauté everything or 4 minutes more.
7. Divide green beans on plates, sprinkle shaved Parmesan on top and serve as a side dish.

Nutritional info:
Calories 172, Fat 3g, Carbs 6g, Protein 4g

Tasty Spinach and Salami
Prep Time: 12 mins, Cook Time: 6 mins, Servings: 4
Ingredients:
- 10 oz. baby spinach
- ½ cup chicken stock
- 3 garlic cloves, minced
- 3 tbsps. olive oil
- 3 salami slices, chopped

Instructions:
1. Set the Instant Pot to Sauté. Heat the oil and add garlic, stir and cook for 1 minute.
2. Add salami, stir, and cook for 2 minutes more.
3. Add spinach and stock, stir a bit.
4. Lock the lid. Select the Manual mode, then set the timer for 3 minutes at High Pressure.
5. Once the timer goes off, perform a quick release. Carefully open the lid.
6. Enjoy as a side dish.

Nutritional info:
Calories 172, Fat 3g, Carbs 12g, Protein 3g

Braised Collard Greens
Prep Time: 12 mins, Cook Time: 10 mins, Servings: 4
Ingredients:
- 1 tbsp. balsamic vinegar
- 2 tbsps. chopped tomatoes
- 1 bunch collard greens
- ½ cup chicken stock
- 2 tbsps. olive oil

Instructions:
1. In the Instant Pot, mix collard greens with stock, oil, tomatoes and vinegar, stir.
2. Lock the lid. Select the Manual mode, then set the timer for 10 minutes at High Pressure.
3. Once the timer goes off, perform a quick release. Carefully open the lid.
4. Divide kale mix on plates and serve as a side dish.

Nutritional info:
Calories 122, Fat 7g, Carbs 10g, Protein 4g

Chinese Mustard Greens
Prep Time: 12 mins, Cook Time: 7 mins, Servings: 4
Ingredients:
- 2 lbs. mustard greens, chopped
- 2 tbsps. vegetable oil
- ½ cup veggie stock
- 2 tsps. grated ginger
- 2 Chinese sausages, chopped

Instructions:
1. Set the Instant Pot to Sauté. Heat the oil and add ginger, stir and cook for 30 seconds.
2. Add Chinese sausages, stir and cook for 1 minute more.
3. Add mustard greens and stock, stir.
4. Lock the lid. Select the Manual mode, then set the timer for 4 minutes at High Pressure.
5. Once the timer goes off, perform a quick release. Carefully open the lid.
6. Enjoy as a side dish.

Nutritional info:
Calories 178, Fat 5g, Carbs 8g, Protein 9g

Collard Greens and Peas
Prep Time: 12 mins, Cook Time: 40 mins, Servings: 5
Ingredients:
- 1 smoked ham hock
- 1 lb. collard greens, trimmed and roughly chopped
- 1 onion, chopped
- 1 lb. dried black-eyed peas
- 2 cups chicken stock

Instructions:
1. In the Instant Pot, mix peas with stock, onion and ham hock, stir.
2. Lock the lid. Select the Manual mode, then set the timer for 38 minutes at High Pressure.
3. Once the timer goes off, perform a natural release for 10 minutes, then

release any remaining pressure. Carefully open the lid.
4. Add collard greens, stir.
5. Lock the lid, then set the timer for 2 minutes at High Pressure.
6. Once the timer goes off, perform a quick release. Carefully open the lid.
7. Divide collard greens and peas between plates and serve as a side dish.

Nutritional info:
Calories 271, Fat 4g, Carbs 12g, Protein 4g

Chestnut Mushrooms
Prep Time: 12 mins, Cook Time: 10 mins, Servings: 4
Ingredients:
- 2 lbs. halved mushrooms
- ½ cup vegetable soup
- 1 tsp. Worcestershire sauce
- 1 cup halved jarred chestnuts
- 6 bacon slices, chopped

Instructions:
1. Set the Instant Pot to Sauté, add bacon, stir and cook for 5 minutes on both sides.
2. Stir in the chestnuts and sauté for 1 more minute.
3. Add mushrooms, Worcestershire sauce and soup, stir.
4. Lock the lid. Select the Manual mode, then set the timer for 8 minutes at High Pressure.
5. Once the timer goes off, perform a quick release. Carefully open the lid.
6. Enjoy as a side dish.

Nutritional info:
Calories 180, Fat 2g, Carbs 10g, Protein 2g

Cauliflower and Grapes
Prep Time: 12 mins, Cook Time: 5 mins, Servings: 4
Ingredients:
- 1 cup water
- 3 tbsps. olive oil
- 1 tsp. grated lemon zest
- 2 tbsps. capers
- 1 head cauliflower, cut into florets
- 1½ cups grapes

Instructions:
1. In the Instant Pot, add the water and steamer basket, then add cauliflower florets inside.
2. Lock the lid. Select the Manual mode, then set the timer for 1 minutes at High Pressure.
3. Once the timer goes off, perform a quick release. Carefully open the lid.
4. Drain and transfer to a bowl.
5. Clean the pot and select the Sauté mode. Heat the oil and return the cauliflower to the pot. Stir and cook for 2 minutes.
6. Add grapes, capers and lemon zest, stir, cook for 2 minutes more, divide between plates and serve as a side dish.

Nutritional info:
Calories 114, Fat 3g, Carbs 5g, Protein 2g

Tasty Carrots Mix
Prep Time: 12 mins, Cook Time: 10 mins, Servings: 6
Ingredients:
- 2½ lbs. baby carrots
- 1 tsp. thyme
- 2 tbsps. olive oil
- 1 cup water
- 3 shallots, chopped
- ¼ cup Greek yogurt

Instructions:
1. In a bowl, mix baby carrots with thyme and olive oil and toss.
2. Add the water to the Instant Pot, arrange the steamer basket in the pot, add carrots inside.
3. Lock the lid. Select the Manual mode, then set the timer for 5 minutes.
4. Once the timer goes off, perform a quick release. Carefully open the lid.
5. Transfer them to a bowl.
6. Clean the pot and set it to Sauté, add shallots and brown them for 1 to 2 minutes.
7. Add carrots, toss and heat them up.
8. Add yogurt, toss, divide between plates and serve as a side dish.

Nutritional info:
Calories 162, Fat 4g, Carbs 12g, Protein 5g

Sweet Pearl Onion Mix
Prep Time: 12 mins, Cook Time: 5 mins, Servings: 4
Ingredients:
- 4 tbsps. balsamic vinegar
- 1 tbsp. sugar
- 1 lb. pearl onions
- ½ cup water
- ¼ tsp. salt

Instructions:
1. In the Instant Pot, mix pearl onions with salt, water, vinegar and sugar, stir.
2. Lock the lid. Select the Manual mode, then set the timer for 5 minutes on Low Pressure.
3. Once the timer goes off, perform a quick release. Carefully open the lid.
4. Toss onions again, divide them between plates and serve as a side dish.

Nutritional info:
Calories 130, Fat 2g, Carbs 7g, Protein 1g

Eggplant and Cashews Mix

Prep Time: 12 mins, Cook Time: 15 mins, Servings: 3

Ingredients:
- 1 tsp. lime juice
- 1 tbsp. coriander seeds
- 1 cup vegetable soup
- 2 tbsps. chopped cashews
- 4 baby eggplants, roughly chopped

Instructions:
1. In the Instant Pot, mix eggplants with stock and coriander, stir.
2. Lock the lid. Select the Manual mode, then set the timer for 10 minutes at High Pressure.
3. Once the timer goes off, perform a quick release. Carefully open the lid.
4. Add cashews and lime juice, stir, divide between plates and serve as a side dish.

Nutritional info:
Calories 170, Fat 4g, Carbs 7g, Protein 3g

Red Onions and Apples Mix

Prep Time: 12 mins, Cook Time: 6 mins, Servings: 4

Ingredients:
- 3 tbsps. vegetable oil
- 3 tbsps. maple syrup
- 2 red onions, chopped
- 3 apples, cored and wedged
- ½ cup chicken stock

Instructions:
1. Set the Instant Pot to Sauté. Heat the oil and add onion and apple wedges, stir and cook for 2 to 3 minutes.
2. Add maple syrup and stock, stir a bit.
3. Lock the lid. Select the Manual mode, then set the timer for 4 minutes at High Pressure.
4. Once the timer goes off, perform a quick release. Carefully open the lid.
5. Enjoy as a side dish.

Nutritional info:
Calories 110, Fat 3g, Carbs 4g, Protein 2g

Delicious Shiitake Mushrooms Mix

Prep Time: 12 mins, Cook Time: 10 mins, Servings: 4

Ingredients:
- 2 tsps. ginger
- 1 cup veggie stock
- 1 lb. shiitake mushroom caps, quartered
- 2 tbsps. butter
- 2 cups edamame

Instructions:
1. Set the Instant Pot to Sauté, add butter, melt it, add ginger, stir and cook for 30 seconds.
2. Add mushrooms, stir and cook for 1 to 2 minutes.
3. Add edamame and stock, stir.
4. Lock the lid. Select the Manual mode, then set the timer for 8 minutes at High Pressure.
5. Once the timer goes off, perform a quick release. Carefully open the lid.
6. Serve as a side dish.

Nutritional info:
Calories 164, Fat 3g, Carbs 8g, Protein 3g

Flavored Parmesan Mushrooms

Prep Time: 12 mins, Cook Time: 10 mins, Servings: 4

Ingredients:
- 1½ lbs. cremini mushrooms, sliced
- 3 tbsps. olive oil
- Salt, to taste
- ¼ cup lemon juice
- ¼ cup grated Parmesan cheese
- 1 cup water

Instructions:
1. In a bowl, mix mushrooms with oil, lemon juice, Parmesan and salt and toss well.
2. Add the water and steamer basket to the Instant Pot, then add mushrooms inside.
3. Lock the lid. Select the Manual mode, then set the timer for 10 minutes at High Pressure.
4. Once the timer goes off, perform a quick release. Carefully open the lid.
5. Serve as a side dish.

Nutritional info:
Calories 128, Fat 4g, Carbs 9g, Protein 4g

Tasty Mushrooms and Rosemary

Prep Time: 12 mins, Cook Time: 10 mins, Servings: 6

Ingredients:
- ½ cup white wine
- 3 lbs. mixed mushroom caps
- 3 rosemary sprigs, chopped
- 4 garlic cloves, minced
- ¾ cup olive oil

Instructions:
1. Set the Instant Pot to Sauté, add oil, heat, add garlic and rosemary, stir and cook for 2 to 3 minutes.
2. Add mushroom caps and wine, stir.
3. Lock the lid. Select the Manual mode, then set the timer for 7 to 8 minutes at High Pressure.
4. Once the timer goes off, perform a quick release. Carefully open the lid.
5. Stir mushroom mix again, divide between plates and serve as a side dish.

Nutritional info:
Calories 172, Fat 3g, Carbs 17g, Protein 3g

Brussels Sprouts and Chestnuts
Prep Time: 12 mins, Cook Time: 5 mins, Servings: 5
Ingredients:
- 3 tbsps. olive oil
- ¼ cup vegetable soup
- 1 red vinegar splash
- 2 lbs. halved Brussels sprouts
- 1 cup halved jarred chestnuts

Instructions:
1. Set the Instant Pot to Sauté. Heat the oil and add Brussels sprouts, stir and cook for 2 minutes.
2. Add chestnuts, stock and vinegar, stir.
3. Lock the lid. Select the Manual mode, then set the timer for 3 minutes at High Pressure.
4. Once the timer goes off, perform a quick release. Carefully open the lid.
5. Enjoy the side dish.

Nutritional info:
Calories 182, Fat 3g, Carbs 6g, Protein 4g

Tasty Vidalia Onions Mix
Prep Time: 12 mins, Cook Time: 15 mins, Servings: 4
Ingredients:
- 2 tbsps. butter
- 4 Vidalia onions, sliced
- 1 tbsp. chopped sage
- ¼ cup chicken stock
- ½ cup cornbread stuffing cubes

Instructions:
1. Set the Instant Pot to Sauté, add butter, melt it, add onions and sage, toss a bit and cook for 3 minutes.
2. Add stock, stir.
3. Lock the lid. Select the Manual mode, then set the timer for 7 minutes at High Pressure.
4. Once the timer goes off, perform a quick release. Carefully open the lid.
5. Add cornbread stuffing cubes, set the pot in Sauté mode again, toss and cook everything for 3 to 4 minutes more.
6. Serve as a side dish!

Nutritional info:
Calories 146, Fat 4g, Carbs 8g, Protein 5g

Parmesan Zucchini Fries
Prep Time: 12 mins, Cook Time: 8 mins, Servings: 4
Ingredients:
- ½ cup grated Parmesan cheese
- 2 tbsps. chopped parsley
- ½ tsp. dried oregano
- 4 zucchinis, quartered
- 2 tbsps. olive oil
- 1 cup water

Instructions:
1. In a bowl, mix the Parmesan with parsley and oregano and toss.
2. In another bowl, mix the zucchini with the oil and toss well.
3. Dunk the oiled zucchini in the bowl of Parmesan mixture to coat well.
4. Put the water and steamer basket in the Instant Pot, then add zucchini inside.
5. Lock the lid. Select the Manual mode, then set the timer for 8 minutes at High Pressure.
6. Once the timer goes off, perform a quick release. Carefully open the lid.
7. Arrange on plates and serve as a side dish.

Nutritional info:
Calories 162, Fat 3g, Carbs 5g, Protein 4g

Simple Buttery Potatoes
Prep Time: 12 mins, Cook Time: 6 mins, Servings: 4
Ingredients:
- 1 cup water
- 3 lbs. red potatoes, halved
- ¼ cup grated Parmesan cheese
- ½ tsp. basil
- Salt, to taste
- 2 tbsps. butter

Instructions:
1. Place the water in the Instant Pot, add potatoes.
2. Lock the lid. Select the Manual mode, then set the timer for 1 minutes at High Pressure.
3. Once the timer goes off, perform a quick release. Carefully open the lid.
4. Drain the potatoes and transfer to a bowl.
5. Clean the pot and select the Sauté mode, add butter, melt it, add potatoes, basil, salt and Parmesan, toss, cook for 5 minutes, divide between plates and serve as a side dish.

Nutritional info:
Calories 137, Fat 3g, Carbs 10g, Protein 3g

Green Beans Fries
Prep Time: 12 mins, Cook Time: 9 mins, Servings: 4
Ingredients:
- 1 cup water
- 2 eggs, whisked
- 1½ lbs. green beans, trimmed
- 1 cup panko
- Salt, to taste
- ½ cup grated Parmesan cheese

Instructions:
1. Place the water in the Instant Pot and arrange the steamer basket in the pot, then add green beans.

2. Lock the lid. Select the Manual mode, then set the timer for 5 minutes at High Pressure.
3. Once the timer goes off, perform a quick release. Carefully open the lid.
4. Transfer to a bowl.
5. In a bowl, mix panko with Parmesan and salt and stir.
6. Put the eggs in a separate bowl.
7. Dredge green beans in panko and then in eggs mix.
8. Set the pot to Sauté. Add green beans fries and cook them for 2 to 3 minutes on each side. Transfer them to plates and serve as a side dish.

Nutritional info:
Calories 174, Fat 3g, Carbs 7g, Protein 7g

Appendix: Recipes Index

A

Apple Cinnamon Oatmeal 25
Acorn Squash Side Dish 143
Adobo Pork Chops 95
Allspice Turkey Drumsticks with Beer 73
Almond Arborio Risotto 134
Apple Bread 39
Apples and Wine Sauce 46
Arborio Rice Side Salad 145
Asian Egg Drop Soup 106
Asian Lemongrass Pork 95
Asian Striped Pork 95
Asian Wings 119
Asparagus and Mushrooms 80
Asparagus Soup 106

B

Baby Carrots Snack 119
Bacon and Potato Soup 106
Bacon and Peas 104
Baked Custard 45
Balsamic Pulled Pork Casserole 96
Balsamic Turkey and Onions 73
Banana and Raisin Porridge 28
Banana Quinoa 31
Basic Pork Chops 96
Basic Tomato Rice 136
Basil and Tomatoes Chicken Soup 68

Basmati Rice 135
BBQ Chicken 69
BBQ Chicken Wings 119
BBQ Square Ribs 119
Béarnaise Sauce 131
Big Papa's Roast 91
Black Bean Salsa 119
Black Bean Soup 107
Black Olives in Tomato Rice 136
Blackberry Egg Cake 32
Black-Eyed Peas with Ham 141
Blue Cheese Dip 120
Blueberry and Coconut Sweet Bowls 48
Blueberry Breakfast Bowl 26
Blueberry Pork Yum 96
Boiled Garlic Clams 62
Braised Collard Greens 148
Broccoli and Bacon Appetizer Salad 125
Broccoli and Egg Casserole 32
Broccoli and Mushrooms 81
Broccoli Chicken with Black Beans 70
Broccoli Chicken with Parmesan 69
Broccoli Cheddar Soup 107
Broccoli Cream Pasta 78
Brothy Heirloom Beans with Cream 140

Brown Rice and Chickpeas Medley 34

Brown Rice Salad 145

Brussels Sprouts and Apples Appetizer 121

Brussels Sprouts and Broccoli Appetizer Salad 125

Brussels Sprouts and Chestnuts 151

Brussels Sprouts Side Salad 146

Bread Pudding 31

Breakfast Arugula Salad 34

Breakfast Banana Bread 27

Breakfast Cobbler 33

Breakfast Coconut Yogurt 35

Breakfast Rice Pudding 31

Bulletproof Hot Choco 40

Butternut Squash Arborio Risotto 134

Buttery Smoked Cod with Scallions 56

Buttery Steamed Lobster Tails 61

Bean and Tomato Stew 115

Bell Pepper and Beef 91

Beef and Cauliflower 90

Beef and Corn Chili 90

Beef Meatballs with Tomato 90

Beef Tomato Stew 115

Beef Tenderloin with Cauliflower 90

Beet Soup 106

C

Cabbage Soup 107

Cajun Chicken with Zucchini 63

Calamari Stew 115

Canadian Bacon 105

Caramelized Onions 82

Carrot and Beet Spread 122

Carrot and Mushroom Soup 107

Carrot Soup 107

Cashew and Mango Oatmeal 25

Cashew Chicken with Sautéed Vegetables 65

Cashew Spread 122

Cauliflower and Barley Bowls 26

Cauliflower and Grapes 149

Cauliflower and Pineapple Rice 137

Cauliflower Breakfast Hash 27

Cauliflower Mash 84

Cauliflower Mushroom Risotto 82

Cauliflower Pasta 78

Caesar Salad Dressing 132

Chickpea and Lentil Salad 76

Chickpea and Tomato Rice 137

Chickpea Avocado Salad 76

Chickpea Egg Bowl 80

Chicken and Quinoa Stew 116

Chicken and Tomato Soup 108

Chicken Bone Broth 132

Chicken Cacciatore 65

Chicken Coconut Curry 63

Chicken Curry 66

Chicken Dip 120

Chicken Meatballs in Barbecue Sauce 124

Chicken Peas Rice 63

Chicken Soup 108

Chicken Stew with Tomatoes and Spinach 68

Chicken Tomato Stew 116

Chicken Wings and Scallions and Tomato Sauce 72

Chicken with Artichokes and Bacon 71

Chicken Yogurt Salsa 70

Chili Aioli 132

Chili Con Carne (Chili with Meat) 118

Chili Endives Platter 124

Chili Lime Chicken 66

Chili-Garlic Salmon 50

Chili-Lime Shrimps 58

Chimichurri Sauce 131

Chinese Mustard Greens 148

Chinese Steamed Chicken 67

Chipotle-Style Cilantro Rice 137

Chocolate Cake 41

Chocolate Chia Pudding 37

Chocolate Mug Cake 40

Chocolate Oatmeal 25

Chunky Warm Salsa 120

Cheddar Creamy Haddock 55

Cherry Pie 43

Chestnut Mushrooms 149

Cheesy Bacon Quiche 30

Cheesy Broccoli Appetizer Salad 126

Cheesy Broccoli Soup 108

Cheesy Cauliflower Bowls 26

Cheesy Chicken Tenders 72

Cheesy Egg and Bacon Muffins 33

Cheesy Grits with Half-and-Half 142

Cheesy Jalapeño Chicken 69

Cheesy Shrimp and Tomatoes 124

Cheesy Veal Steaks 94

Cilantro Turkey with Pomegranate Glaze 74

Cinnamon Butter Bites 39

Classic Lemon Chicken 64

Cocoa and Milk Pudding 38

Cocoa and Walnuts Sweet Cream 48

Coconut and Avocado Pudding 38

Coconut Boosters 40

Coconut Cabbage 82

Coconut Cauliflower Rice 79

Coconut Cream and Cinnamon Pudding 38

Coconut Curry Cod 52

Coconut Milk Rice 80

Coconut Pancake 42

Coconut Pork 96

Coconut Pudding 37

Coconut Quinoa 139

Coconut Seafood Soup 108

Cod Meal 53

Cod with Orange Sauce 51

Collard Greens and Peas 148

Confetti Basmati Rice 136

Copycat Cilantro Lime Rice 137

Corn on Cob 76

Corned Beef 91

Couscous with Spinach and Tomato 138

Couscous with Vegetables 85

Crab Spread 122

Cranberry Beans Salad 34

Crispy Chicken Wings 68

Crispy Chicken with Herbs 72

Crunchy Brussels Sprouts Salad 126

Cream and Cinnamon Puddings 37

Cream Cheese Pudding 39

Cream Turkey Dinner 74

Creamy Avocado Spread 122

Creamy Broccoli Appetizer 121

Creamy Broccoli Chicken Bone Soup 109

Creamy Chicken with Mushrooms 67

Creamy Cheese Sauce 131

Creamy Corn Kernels with Cottage Cheese 141

Creamy Endives Appetizer Salad 126

Creamy Fig Millet 141

Creamy Polenta 138

Creamy Pork Pasta 97

Creamy Shrimp Pasta 57

Creamy Spinach 147

Creamy Tomatoes and Quinoa 32

Cumin Dip 120

Celeriac and Bacon Mix 35

D

Dates and Ricotta Cake 41

Dump Cake 88

Delicious and Simple Octopus 60

Delicious Berry Cobbler 45

Delicious Green Beans and Blue Cheese 147

Delicious Shiitake Mushrooms Mix 150

E

Easy Asian Chicken 65

Easy Chinese Pork 97

Easy Lemon Pie 43

Easy Mahi Mahi with Enchilada Sauce 56

Easy Plum Jam 47

Easy Sweet Soufflé 42

Egg Drop Soup with Shredded Chicken 109

Eggplant and Cashews Mix 150

Eggplant and Chicken Sauté 69

Eggplant Lasagna 97

Eggplant, Zucchini, And Tomatoes 83

Eggs and Bacon Breakfast Risotto 29

Eggs En Cocotte 30

Espresso Oatmeal 25

F

Fast Shrimp Scampi 60

Filipino Chicken Adobo 71

Fish and Carrot Balls 124

Fish Soup 109

Flavored Parmesan Mushrooms 150

Flavored Pears 46

Flounder with Dill and Capers 52

Fried Rice with Sausage and Egg 105

Fruit Yogurt 36

French Eggs 29

Fennel Chicken 71

G

Garlic Baby Potatoes 86

Garlic Eggplants with Tomato Sauce 35

Garlic Green Beans 148

Garlic Prime Rib 91

Garlicky Beef 92

Garlicky Chicken 64

Garlicky Greek Chicken 63

Garlicky Pork Tenderloin 97

Ginger and Peach Marmalade 47

Ginger Chicken Congee 69

Ginger Cookies Cheesecake 42

Ginger Halibut Soup 109

Ginger Short Ribs 92

Gingered Beef Tenderloin 92

Glazed Fruits 46

Goat Cheese Mushrooms 127

Graceful Vegetarian Recipe 88

Grated Carrot Appetizer Salad 126

Greek Meatballs 125

Greek Style Beans 85

Greek Veggie Soup 110

Green Beans and Cranberries Side Dish 144

Green Beans Appetizer Salad 126

Green Beans Fries 151

Green Cabbage and Tomatoes Side Dish 144

Green Olive Pâté 125

Green Tea Rice Risotto 135

H

Halibut and Broccoli Casserole 53

Halibut En Papillote 54

Halibut with Pesto 53

Ham and Cheese Dip 120

Ham and Spinach Frittata 29

Haricots Verts Side Salad 145

Hollandaise Sauce 131

Honey Polenta with Toasted Pine Nuts 138

Hummus 128

Herbed Sirloin Tip Roast 92

I

Indian Roasted Pork 98

Instant Pot Artichokes 84

Instant Pot Baby Bok Choy 84

Instant Pot Boiled Mussels 61

Instant Pot Curried Salmon 50

Instant Pot Emergency Broccoli Chicken 64

Instant Pot Lemon Shrimps 59

Instant Pot Mushrooms 81

Instant Pot Pesto Chicken 64

Instant Pot Rib 98

Instant Pot Rib Roast 93

Instant Pot Steamed Asparagus 81
Instant Pot Veggie Stew 83
Instant Ratatouille 87
Israeli Couscous 138
Italian Pork Cutlets 98
Italian Salmon with Lemon Juice 52
Italian Vegetable Medley 86

K

Kale and Carrots Salad 127
Kale and Sweet Potatoes with Tofu 87
Kale and Veal Stew 116
Kale and Wild Rice Appetizer Salad 127
Kale Sauté 147
Khichdi Dal 137
Kidney Bean Stew 116
Kidney Beans and Corn Side Dish 144
Keto Almond Bread 39
Keto Brownies 40
Keto Gravy 132
Ketogenic Vanilla Jell-O 42

L

Low Carb Chicken Noodle Soup 111
Low Carb Ham and Bean Soup 111
Leftover Chicken Soup 110
Lemon and Maple Syrup Pudding 37
Lemon and Orange Jam 47
Lemon Artichokes 87
Lemon Beef Meal 93
Lemon Chicken Soup 110

Lemon Cookies 44
Lemon Garlic Chicken 70
Lemon Pepper Salmon 50
Lemon Pepper Salmon 52
Lemon White Fish 55
Lemon-Butter Grouper 56
Lemony Endives Appetizer 122
Lemony Fennel Chicken 67
Lemony Salmon 49
Lettuce Wrapped Tofu 128
Leek and Salmon Soup 110

M

Mango Tofu Curry 88
Maple Brussels Sprouts with Orange Juice 128
Millet and Oats Porridge 28
Mini Frittata 29
Minty Carrots 143
Minty Kale Salad with Pineapple 127
Minestrone 111
Mixed Rice Meal 135
Mixed Veggies 147
Multigrain Rice 136
Mushroom and Beef Meal 93
Mushroom Bacon Skewers 129
Mushroom Chicken Soup 111
Mushroom Rice Meal 79
Mushroom Spinach Casserole 79
Mussels with White Wine and Shallots 61
Mustard Pork and Mushrooms 99

Mediterranean Couscous Salad 77
Mexican Chili Pork 98
Mexican Corn on the Cob 129
Mexican Pulled Pork 99
Mexican Rice 135
Mexican Shredded Chicken 68

N

Nut-Free Keto Fudge 42

O

Onion Penne Pasta 78
Onion Soup with Pork Stock 112
Orange-Butter Sea Bass 57

P

Paprika Chicken with Tomatoes 71
Paprika Pork Loin Roast 99
Parmesan Risotto 134
Parmesan Zucchini Fries 151
Pinto Bean Dip 121
Pine Nut Pork 100
Pineapple and Peas Breakfast Curry 34
Pineapple Pudding 38
Poached Egg Chicken Bone Soup 112
Poached Pears 46
Pomegranate Porridge 28
Pomegranate-Glazed Turkey with Cranberries 73
Pork and Sweet Potato 100
Pork Chops and Peas 100
Pork Chops with Onions 100
Pork Coconut Curry 101

Pork Medallions and Mushrooms 101
Pork Potato Lunch 101
Pork Tenderloin with Celery 101
Pork Vindaloo (Curry Pork) 102
Pork with Coconut Meat 102
Pork with Jasmine Rice 102
Pork with Paprika and Mushrooms 102
Pork with Turnip 103
Potato and Spinach Hash 27
Potato Mash 88
Potato Soup 112
Prosciutto Wrapped Asparagus 129
Pumpkin and Apple Butter 33
Pumpkin Soup 112
Pumpkin Spice Oatmeal 26
Puréed Chili Carrots 87
Pure Basmati Rice Meal 79
Peach and Cinnamon Compote 47
Peaches and Steel-Cut Oats 139
Peaches Oatmeal 26
Peanut Butter Cups 43
Pear and Pork Butt 99
Pearl Barley Porridge 28
Pearl Onions Side Dish 143

Q

Quick Salmon 51
Quinoa and Veggies 85
Quinoa Pilaf 139
Quinoa Risotto 134

Quinoa with Cranberry and Almond 140

Quinoa with Vegetables 140

R

Radishes Side Salad 145

Raisin Butter Rice 136

Ranch Dip 133

Rhubarb and Strawberries Mix 45

Ritzy Corn, Lentil, and Brown Rice Stew 142

Roasted Brussels Sprouts 76

Rosemary Lamb 95

Red Curry Halibut 54

Red Onions and Apples Mix 150

Refried Pinto Beans 140

S

Salmon Head Soup 114

Salmon Meatballs Soup 113

Salmon Stew 117

Salmon Tandoori 49

Salmon with Basil Pesto 49

Salsa Chicken 63

Sardine and Plum Tomato Curry 56

Satay Sauce 131

Sausage and Peppers 105

Sautéed Brussels Sprouts And Pecans 82

Sautéed Beef and Green Beans 93

Sautéed Turkey with Cauliflower Purée 74

Savory Salmon with Dill 49

Scallion and Mayo Spread 123

Shrimp Boil 59

Shrimp Green Curry 58

Shrimp Scampi 59

Shrimps with Mango Basil 59

Simple Banana Cake 41

Simple Buttery Potatoes 151

Simple Cake Bars 44

Simple Chicken and Kale Soup 114

Simple Corn Side Dish 143

Simple Curried Shrimps 59

Simple Egg Spread 123

Simple Italian Flavor Cannellini Beans 141

Simple Lime Turkey Wings 73

Simple Pinto Beans with Spices 141

Simple Pumpkin and Yogurt Cake 41

Simple Ricotta Mousse 44

Simple Red Pepper Hummus 128

Simple Shrimp 58

Simple Spinach Side Dish 143

Simple Steamed Salmon Fillets 49

Slow-Cooked Cabbage and Chuck Roast Stew 117

Smoky Paprika Chicken 66

Smokey and Spicy Pork Roast 103

Sole Fillets with Pickle-Mayo Sauce 57

Southern Peanuts 129

Spicy Prawns 60

Spicy Pulled Pork 103

Spicy Thousand Island Dressing 132

Spiced Chicken Drumsticks 66

Special Cookies 44

Special Pancake 32

Special Ranch Spread 123

Squash Porridge with Apples 29

Strawberry and Chia Marmalade 47

Strawberry and Orange Juice Compote 31

Strawberry and Rolled Oats 139

Strawberry Oatmeal 25

Strawberry Quinoa 32

Stuffed Peppers 86

Stuffed Strawberries 46

Stuffed Sweet Potatoes 86

Steamed Asparagus with Mustard Dip 121

Steamed Chili-Rubbed Tilapia 53

Steamed Cod with Ginger and Scallions 54

Steamed Crab Legs 62

Steamed Greek Snapper 51

Steamed Herbed Red Snapper 50

Steamed Lemon Artichokes 76

Steamed Lemon Mustard Salmon 51

Steamed Paprika Broccoli 81

Steamed Tilapia 55

Summer Beet Salad 77

Sunday Pork Roast 104

Super Beef Chili 93

Super Stew 104

Super Thick Cashew and Almond Milk Yogurt 36

Swiss Chard and Leek Soup 113

Swiss Chard Salad 34

Sweet and Sour Side Salad 146

Sweet Apricot Beef 94

Sweet Potato Beef 94

Sweet Potato Hash 28

Sweet Pearl Onion Mix 149

Szechuan Shrimps 58

Sea Bass Risotto with Leeks 57

Sea Scallops with Champagne Butter Sauce 60

Sesame Bok Choy 84

Sesame Chicken 68

T

Tangy Spinach Pasta 78

Tapioca Pudding 37

Tasty Blackberry Pie 43

Tasty Carrots and Walnuts Salad 146

Tasty Carrots Mix 149

Tasty Maple Acorn Squash Dish 144

Tasty Mushrooms and Rosemary 150

Tasty Spinach and Salami 148

Tasty Vidalia Onions Mix 151

Thai Coconut Shrimp Soup 113

Thai Fish Curry 52

Thai Peanut Chicken 67

Thai Tom Saap Pork Ribs Soup 113

Thyme Chicken with Brussels Sprouts 70

Thyme Duck and Chives 74

Thyme-Sesame Crusted Halibut 54

Tofu and Sweet Potato Mix 33

Tomato and Tofu Bake 87

Tomato Chili Pork 104

Tomato Mussels 61

Tomato Onion Rice 80

Tomatoes and Burrata Side Salad 146

Tomatoes and Corn Side Salad 146

Tomatoes Side Salad 145

Tuna Salad with Lettuce 53

Turkey Breast and Avocado Breakfast 35

Turkey Rice Bowl 75

Turkey with Ginger and Turmeric Soup 113

Turmeric Chicken Soup 114

Teriyaki Scallops 60

V

Veal and Buckwheat Groat Stew 117

Vegan Rice Pudding 134

Veggie Quiche 30

Veggie Stew 117

Vegetable and Lentil Soup 114

Vegetarian Mac and Cheese 84

Vegetarian Smothered Cajun Greens 82

W

Watercress Appetizer Salad 127

White Bean and Kale Soup 115

White Bean and Swiss Chard Stew 118

White Chocolate Mousse 44

Whole Roasted Chicken with Lemon and Rosemary 65

Wheat Berries 139

Wild Alaskan Cod with Cherry Tomatoes 55

Winter Cherry Mix 45

Western Omelet 30

Y

Yogurt Fish Patties 55

Z

Zucchini and Bell Pepper Stir Fry 83

Zucchini and Tomato 88

Zucchini and Tomato Melange 83

Zucchini Bulgur Meal 77

Zucchini Spread 123

Zucchini Toast 27